# SELECT
# MODERN GOVERNMENTS

# SELECT MODERN GOVERNMENTS

*By*

**Prof. Hari Hara Das**

**ANMOL PUBLICATIONS PVT. LTD.**
**NEW DELHI - 110 002 (INDIA)**

**ANMOL PUBLICATIONS PVT. LTD.**
4374/4B, Ansari Road, Daryaganj
New Delhi - 110 002

*Select Modern Governments*

First Edition, 2000

ISBN 81-261-0699-9



PRINTED IN INDIA

Published by J.L. Kumar for Anmol Publications Pvt. Ltd., New Delhi - 110 002 and Printed at Mehra Offset Press, Delhi.

# Contents

# Preface

In the modern times it is impossible to think of a state without a constitution of some kind. Referring to the fundamental necessities of the constitution in the modern state, Jellinek rightly observed: "A state without a constitution would not be a state but a regime of anarchy."

In every state the power-relationship between the ruler and the ruled, determines the nature of the government. Prior to the development of the democratic system, very limited number of people took part in governmental activities. But the development of democratic governments has made mass participation a political imperative.

Alexander Pope observed that, "For forms of government let fools contest whatever is best administrated is best." Despite an element of trust in this observation, the effectiveness or the efficiency of the government is not the prime consideration at the present time. The legitimacy of the government is the prime consideration because people do not want to be governed by the transitory whims of men, however efficient or effective they may be. They want to be governed by known and definite laws. It is the constitution that determines the nature of government and lays down the fundamental principles of law according to which the state is to be governed.

I have great pleasure in offering this book entitled, "Select Modern Governments," to the students both at the graduate and post-graduate level of studies and to those who are preparing for the various competitive examinations. In this volume, a detailed analysis of the government and politics of five different political systems viz., Great Britain, U.S.A., Switzerland, the People Republic of China and Japan has been made. While Great Britain, U.S.A., and Switzerland are Western Countries, China and Japan are the Asian Giants.

Each political system discussed in this book is a unique model by itself and makes an interesting and instructive study. An effort has been made to present a critical and comparative assessment of the various systems with a view to develop the right perspective for understanding the actual working of the various constitutional systems.

The British Constitution is considered to be the "mother of all constitutions" and the British Parliament is the fountain spirit behind the working of responsible democratic governments. The principles of public accountability, Parliamentary Sovereignty, Rule of Law, Bicameralism and the supremacy of the popular will as manifested through regular elections have symbolised the British Political System. Similarly the American Political System has made significant contributions to the theory of government by developing the concepts of federalism, Judicial independence and supremacy of the Fundamental Rights of the individual. It presents the presidential system of democracy in contrast to the parliamentary system of democracy obtaining in Great Britain.

The Chinese Communist system follows the erstwhile Soviet Communist model to a very great extent, but at the same time it has its own peculiarities and special features. It is interesting to note that even the Communist Systems, which are based on the principles of one party dictatorship and centralisation of power, try to work under the garb of popular government and style themselves as "perfect democracies".

This volume also includes the Swiss Political System, which presents a harmonious blending of the parliamentary and the presidential system of government. It is famous for its institutions of "Direct Democracy."

The Japanese Constitution has derived basic principles of governance from the British, American and many other democratic constitutions. The constitution has vested sovereignty with the people of Japan. It has made a great departure from the Meiji Constitution which was inspired by the German and Prussian Constitutions. It has accepted the British Parliamentary model and provides for Limited Monarchy. The new constitution is based upon the principle of renunciation of war and the use of threat or intimidation for the settlement of its disputes with other states.

I would be immensely happy if this book could meet the academic and intellectual requirements of the students, teachers and casual readers.

**–Dr. Hari Hara Das**

# Introduction

## Constitutions and Constitutionalism

In every state there is the existence of a certain power-relationship between the ruler and the ruled. This power-relationship determines the nature of the government. Before the spread of democratic ideas and political consciousness among the people, a limited number of persons took part in political activities. But now-a-days a large number of persons in every country take part in public activities. The effectiveness or the efficiency of the government is not the chief consideration in the present time. The manner in which the government of the state is conducted is the primary consideration because peple do not want to be governed by the transitory whims of men, but by definite laws. The constitution, which determines the nature of the state and the government, therefore, is highly essential for every state. Thus, the constitution is a document or a number of documents, which embody the fundamental principles for the governance of the country. The constitutions bind both the ruler and the ruled and facilitate a proper adjustment of the power relationship between the two parties.

Referring to the necessity of the constitution in a modern state, Jellinek rightly observes, "A state without a constitution would not be a state but a regime of anarchy." The importance of the constitution as a fundamental document was realized during the American war of Independence of 1776, becuase it could transform a number of Independent States into one federal polity. This type of constitutional arrangement has achieved great popularity because it has successfully forged unity among several independent states by making them the constituent units of a federation. Constitutionalism and democracy are now accepted as one and inseparable concepts. In the 19th century the idea that every state should have a constitution of its own and it should have the mandate of the people became firmly rooted. Schulze, has rightly said that, "every community entitled to the name of the state must have a constitution, i.e., a collection of norms by which the legal relation between the government and its subject is determined and in accordance with which the power of the state exercised. A state without a constitution is unthinkable.

A constitution is expected to serve the following purposes:

(i) It incorporates fundamental laws by which the powers of the government are restricted.

(ii) It safeguards the fundamental rights of the individual from governmental encroachment.

(iii) It preserves the political institutions of the country against the whims and caprices of the ruling parties.

## Definitions of Constitution

As constitution is variously defined by different writers, we must examine some of these definitions. James Bryce says, "The constitution of a state or nation consists of those of its rules or laws which determine the form of its government and the respective rights and duties of it towards its citizens and of the citizens towards the government."

Judge Cooley defines constitution as "the fundamental law of state, containing the principles upon which government is founded regulating the division of the sovereign powers and directing to what persons each of these power is to be confined and the manner in which it is to be exercised."

In the words of James Mc Intosh: constitution is, "The body of those written or unwritten fundamental laws which regulate the most important rights of the higher magistrates and the most essential privileges of the subjects.'

Dr. Gilchirst states: "the constitution of a state is that body or rules and laws written or unwritten which determines the organisation of government and the general principles on which these powers are to be exercised."

According to Borgland, "A constitution is the fundamental law according to which the government of a state is organized and agreeably to which the relations of individual or moral persons of the community are determined. It may be a written instrument, a precise text or series of texts enacted at a given time by a sovereign power; or it may be the more or less definite result of a series of legislative acts, ordinances, judicial decisions, precedents and customs of diverse origin and of unequal value and importance."

Finer defines constitution as the "system of fundamental political institutions of a country."

If we analyse the definitions, the modern constitutions reveal the following characteristics:

(a) The constitution may be written or enacted or it may be unwritten or evolved.

(b) It defines the powers of the governor and the fundamental privileges of the governed.

(c) It determines the outline and the organisation of the government and prescribes its powers and functions. The mutual relationship between the different branches of government and the general principles basing upon which the powers of the government are to be exercised are also determined by the constitution.

The supremacy of the constitutional laws are more prominent in the countries which have written constitutional laws. They are given a higher status than the ordinary laws and customs in India, U.S.A., and Switzerland. The importance of the constitution is greatly felt in federal than in the unitary countries. In these countries an ordinary law, which contravenes the provisions of the constitution is declared unconstitutional and becomes invalid. A constitution of a country grows in relation to the social, political and economic environment of the country. Thus it has no isolated existence. A constitution of a country should, therefore, change alongwith the change of time, in order to keep pace with the changing socio-economic forces of the country. It is due to this reason that even the most elaborately written constitutions of the world have sufficient elbowroom for the development of necessary conventions. Any constitution, which fails to incorporate these changes, gradually becomes outdated and loses its claim to survive. Such a constitution gives rise to revolution to change either the government or the existing political institutions of the country.

## What a Constitutional Government means?

A constitutional government is also a democratic government. In the modern time, it is impossible to imagine a government without a constitution. A constitutional government is one where the ultimate power lies with the people. The people rule themselves, through deputies periodically elected by them and the government is responsible to the people for its policies and decisions. In the constitutional government the people are ruled not by the whims and caprice of those who possess political power but by known and definite laws. The people enjoy certain essential privileges. They are guaranteed certain fundamental rights, which are incorporated in the constitution itself. A constitutional government ensures public control over the conduct of administration and the actions of the government officials. A constitutional government is therefore, a government of laws.

**Classification of Constitutions**

Constitutions have been classified by some writers into cumulative or evolved and conventional or enacted. An evolved constitution is the product of history and its origin can be traced to custom, conventions and usages. Its roots are in the past. It takes shape in the course of history due to the action and interaction of political, economic and social forces in the country. On the other hand an enacted constitution is the product of a deliberate and conscious effort and is man-made. It is drafted at a particular period of time and is the result of either the deliberation of a Constituent Assembly or is promulgated by a King. The principles of a written or enacted constitution are incorporated either in one or a number of documents. While the British constitution is an evolved constitution the constitutions of U.S.A. and India are enacted.

**Written and Unwritten Constitutions**

Constitutions have also been classified as written and unwritten.

A written constitution is one is which most of the provisions are written down in one or several documents. In such a constitution all the important provisions regarding the organisation of government, and the fundamental relationship between the rules and the ruled, the nature and scope of activity of the government, the broad principles on the basis of which the government has to exercise its powers, the relationship between the different organs of the government and the general nature of its functions are laid down. A written constitution may be framed by a Constituent Assembly consisting of the people's representatives or it may be enacted by the legislature of an Imperial Power for regulating the administration of a colony under its possession. For instance, the Government of India Act, 1935, was made by the British Parliament for the governance of India. The present Indian constitution has been framed by the Constituent Assembly, which consisted of the representatives of the Indian People. A King may also promulgate a written constitution and make it binding upon himself and his successors to govern according to the provisions of the constitution.

On the other hand an unwritten constitution is one which is mostly based upon customs and conventions and is the product of history. No conscious or deliberate effort is made to frame or draft such a constitution at any particular period of time. In the course of centuries it gradually accumulates new customs and precedents. It also banks upon judicial interpretations and decisions, which greatly help to shape the constitution. An unwritten constitution, therefore, does not present a systematic or a coherent document. But at the same time it has to be admitted that the unwritten constitution is totally unwritten and even the best example of an unwritten constitution, i.e., the constitution of Great Britain contains certain written features. Thus in an unwritten constitution most of the fundamental laws of the country are in the form of customs, usages and judicial decisions. It is, therefore, the result of slow and steady historical evolution, which has been influenced by the political and social forces working in the country or which have worked at different times.

A country, which has got an unwritten constitution, the constitutional laws do not have any sanctity. They are not considered superior to the ordinary laws and can be amended by the legislature in the same ordinary process in which laws are amended. The law courts have no right to declare a law passed by the legislature as invalid on the ground of its contradiction with the provisions of the constitution. The legislature is the only authority to make and unmake the constitution.

### Criticism

There is no constitution in the world which is either wholly written or wholly unwritten. Therefore, the classification of the constitutions into written and unwritten is unscientific, illusory and inaccurate. The constitution of a country cannot remain a static document. It must have to change with the changing time in order to cope with the changed economic, social and political forces. If it fails to be dynamic in character then it would become an unnecessary anachonism. In this context Woodrow Wilson has rightly observed that, "Living political institutions must be Darwinian in structure and practice". The difference between written and unwritten constitution is one of degree rather than of kind. It only indicates that while some constitutions are predominantly written others are mainly unwritten. England the most important example of an unwritten constitution has many written documents, such as, the Magna Carta, of 1215; Petition of Rights, 1628; the Bill of Rights, 1689; the Act of Settlement, 1701; the Act of Union with Scotland, 1707; and the Reforms Act of, 1832, 1867 and 1884. These Charters, Petitions or statutes also form parts of the British Constitution. Again, most of the customs, conventions and usages have also been reduced to written form for the purpose of clarity and definiteness.

It is also impossible to find a wholly written constitution. A written constitution, which is framed at a particular period of time, would become static and outdated if it does not provide for the growth of customs and conventions. This would make the practice of such a constitution difficult, if not impossible. It is highly impossible to embody all the principles of the constitutional law in a documentary form. The American constitution, which is mostly written, also contains many usages, customs and conventions. For instance the constitution provided for the indirect election of the American President, but in actual practice after the development of political parties it has virtually become direct. The liberal interpretation of the American constitution by the Supreme Court has also greatly changed the tone of the constitution.

The above analysis, therefore, points out that there are written features in unwritten constitutions and unwritten features in written constitutions.

## Rigid and Flexible Constitutions

From the above analysis of the written and unwritten constitutions it is evident that the difference between the two is really one of degree rather than of kind. The classification of constitutions into written and unwritten, therefore, has been rejected as unscientific and unsatisfactory. Lord Bryce in his book–Studies in History and Jurisprudence has given a more appropriate classification of the constitutions. He has classified the constitution into rigid and flexible. The process of amendment determines whether a constitution is rigid or flexible. The process followed to amend the rigid constitution is difficult and cumbrous. On the other hand a flexible constitution can be very easily amended. The basis of this division also rests upon the relation, which the constitution has got with the ordinary laws.

If there is no difference between the ordinary law and the constitutional law and the constitutional law can be amended, repealed or altered in the same way as the ordinary laws, the constitution is said to be flexible. It matters very little whether the constitution is largely grounded in customs and conventions. If the ordinary laws and the constitutional laws are on parity with each other and enjoy equal status, the alteration can be made easily. The British constitution is the best example of an elastic or flexible constitution. Here Parliament makes statutory and constitutional laws according to the same rules of procedure. Laws passed by the British Parliament cannot be challenged or vetoed by any other authority. In England the ordinary laws and the constitutional laws stand at a footing of equality.

A rigid constitution is the product of the deliberations of the people, specially elected for the purpose of making a constitution. The constitutional laws enjoy a higher status than the ordinary laws of the country. The constitutional laws and the ordinary laws owe their origin to two different sources. The legislature, which makes the ordinary laws is not competent either to make the constitution or to amend or alter its provisions. A special procedure, which is different, and comparatively difficult, from the one followed in the making of ordinary laws, is followed for amending the constitutional laws. The legislature also has no power to pass laws repugnant to the constitution. In case any such laws are passed by the legislature, the judiciary, which is the guardian of the constitution shall declare it illegal or unconstitutional. The constitution can only be amended or altered according to the procedure prescribed by the constitution. A rigid constitution defines and delimits the powers of the legislature. But it is not reasonable to presume that all the rigid constitutions are either equally rigid or follow the same difficult procedure for their amendment. The American Constitution is the best example of a rigid constitution where as the Indian constitution is the example of a modified rigidity.

The framers of the rigid constitution are always conscious of the fact that the constitution has to be dynamic in character in order to cope with the changing time and circumstances. Therefore they provide for the procedure of amendment so that the constitution can adjust to the needs of the people and the changed economic, social and political forces. But the method of amendment so provided has been deliberately made difficult so that the amendment of the constitution may not become subject to the vagaries of the majority party in the legislature. In this connection the instance of the amendment procedure of the constitution of U.S.A. may be cited. The American Congress alone is not competent to amend or alter the constitution. A proposal for amendment must be passed by both the Houses of Congress by two-third votes and must be ratified by at least three-fourth of the state legislatures. On the other hand, ordinary laws can be passed by both the Houses of the Congress by a simple majority.

## Merits of Written and Rigid Constitution

1. Rigid constitutions are generally written in nature. They are in the written form and the salient principles of the constitution are reduced to writing. Therefore, a rigid constitution is clear and it avoids ambiguity.
2. As it is the product of the deliberations of a Constituent Assembly, consisting of many constitutional experts, it is bound to incorporate many good provisions. While drafting the Indian Constitution the members of the Constituent Assemby carefully studied the different world constitutions and incorporated many provisions of the British, American, Irish, Canadian and the Weimar Constitution of Germany, in our constitution. All possible attempts were made to adopt a suitable constitution for the good of the country.
3. It is argued that the rights of the citizen are better protected under the written and rigid constitution than under a flexible and unwritten constitution. This is the reason that in democratic countries the people insist for the incorporation of their fundamental rights in the constitution. The American and the Indian Constitution have guaranteed a number of fundamental rights to the citizens of their respective states.
4. Permanence and stability are the two great merits of the rigid constitution. Its rigidity protects it against too much mutability. It is not subject to the dangers of public passion and the vagaries of party majority in the legislature. It, therefore, does not become a plaything in the hands of politicians and lends stability to political institutions and ensures continuity of administrative policy.
5. The merit of certainty is there in a written constitution and in case there is any doubt reference can be made to the provisions of the constitution, which are very clear. No authority of government can act arbitrarily. The acts of the government and the public servants must be explained in terms of law, otherwise they are held unconstitutional.
6. There is also an element of conservatism in the rigid constitution and this safeguards it from becoming a victim to public passion.

The element of conservation also helps in safeguarding the fundamental rights guaranteed to the citizens. Even though, there is the provision of amendment, such an amendment can be declared as unconstitutional or illegal by the supreme judiciary of the country because judges are mostly conservative and they go by the letter of the law. It is, therefore, rightly said that constitution is what the judges make it.

**Demerits of Written and Rigid Constitution**

1. The greatest weakness of the rigid constitution lies in its strength. As it cannot be easily amended, it becomes unsuitable to the changing needs and circumstances. It is like an outdated and old-fashioned coat, which has lost its utility. The social, economic and political conditions of a country change very rapidly but a rigid constitution fails to keep pace with the change of time and circumstances. It is unsuitable to meet with emergencies. In the absence of a relatively easy method of amendment, it becomes outmoded and loses its validity.
2. Since amendments are not possible in the usual way, people take recourse to revolution in order to bring significant changes in the constitution.
3. The judges are guided by the conservative elements in the constitution and they ignore the social and political ideals while interpreting the constitution.
4. A rigid constitution will be most unsuitable for an advancing or a developing nation because it cannot adjust itself to the ever growing needs of the people.
5. Since in an elaborately written and rigid constitution deliberate efforts are made to compress all the political principles into one constitutional document, there is no scope for the development of customs and conventions. This stands as a hindrance on the way of proper adjustments.
6. A written and rigid constitution is conservative and narrow in its outlook. It is opposed to progress. In the U.S.A. either 33 Senators or 14 small states can defeat an amendment, however urgent and useful it may be. The American Supreme Court can also nullify an amendment passed by the American Congress and ratified by the required number of States by a majority of one. Out of the nine judges of the American Supreme Court if four are in favour and five are opposed to the constitutional

amendment, it is rejected. Thus the judges assume the role of super legislators.

## Merits of Unwritten and Flexible Constitution

1. The elasticity of the flexible constitution makes it highly adaptable to the changing social, economic and political conditions and the needs of the country. No special procedure is required to amend the constitutional laws.
2. The flexible character of the constitution easily incorporates new provisions and saves the country from the possibilities of a revolution. It can be easily changed to meet any kind of emergency.
3. It is highly suitable to an advancing country because it can adjust to the changing and growing needs of the people.
4. A flexible constitution is extremely responsive to the needs and requirements of the people. It is dynamic and progressive. Judge Cooley has said that, "of all the constitutions which may come into existence for the government of the people, the most excellent is obviously that which is the natural outgrowth of the national life, and which, having grown and expanded as the nation has matured, is likely at any particular time to express the prevailing sentiment regarding government and the accepted principle of civil and political liberty".
5. It also "provides an excellent mirror of the national mind", for it easily incorporates the significant changes. It represents the historical continuity and therefore, past runs in the present and present goes into the future.

## Demerits of Unwritten and Flexible Constitutions

1. The unwritten and the flexible constitution lacks clarity and precision. It is scattered in several documents and is mostly grounded in customs and conventions. It is because of this indefinite and abstract nature it gives rise to ambiguities.
2. A flexible constitution is unstable and lacks permanence. A flexible constitution says Bryce, is "in a state of perpetual flux, like the river of Heraclitus into which a man cannot step twice".
3. A country, in which vigilant public opinion and political consciousness are absent, the flexible constitution will be most unstable. Esmein and Judge Jameson are of the view that unwritten constitution is "suitable to a people who have a strong sense of tradition and a profoundly conservative spirit".

4. Its flexibility makes it an easy prey to the whims and fancies of individuals and political parties. It is frequently changed to suit either the individual or the party interest.
5. It is maintained that a flexible constitution has affinity with an aristocratic form of government and is unsuitable to democracy.
6. It facilitates radical and abrupt changes and may choke mature judgement based upon experience. A radial opinion, which is the product of popular passion, is very often devoid of reason. This emotion plays a predominant role in the flexible constitution. Therefore, it is not suited to a country where the people do not have a high degree of political responsibility, intelligence, political consciousness and training.

Both these types of constitutions have their merits and demerits. The suitability or otherwise of a particular constitution depends upon the people for which it is meant. Modern tendency, however, is towards a primarily written and comparatively rigid constitution.

**Causes for the Growth of Constitutions**

A good constitution must feel the pulse of the people and must be responsive to their needs. It must be dynamic and progressive and change with the change of time. It should have the capacity to incorporate the fundamental political principles, which are essential for the governance of the country. Thus a constitution should not remain static and should have sufficient scope for its development in the course of time. The authors of a constitution while drafting it at a particular time are unable to foresee the future and in the absence of adaptability the constitution will become outdated. It will lose its impact upon the people. In the long run there is every possibility of such a constitution being over thrown by revolution. In view of this, we must study the different factors, which are responsible for the growth of constitution.

Firstly, customs and usages play a great role in the development of the constitution. They keep it in time with the changing time and circumstances. Secondly, judicial decision and interpretations also help in clarifying the ambiguities of a constitution and in giving it a new shape. Lastly, there are the formal amendments, in accordance with the procedure prescribed in the constitution itself, which increase the bulk of the constitution.

The example of the U.S.A. constitution may be cited to elucidate the role played by the different factors in the development of the constitution. The American constitution does not make any reference to some of the most important political institutions like the cabinet and the political parties. It did not provide, till very recently, that the President is to seek election for only two terms. This convention was established by the first President–George Washington. This convention was only violated by Franklin Roosevelt, who offered himself for the third term and even for the fourth term. Similarly the constitution of U.S.A. provides for an indirect election of the President, but it has become direct after the development of political parties. The powers of the American Speaker and the practice of weekly cabinet meeting are also the products of usages. The constitution is also silent about the power of dismissal, although all appointments are made by the President with the consent of the Senate. But the Supreme Court decides that the power of dismissal rests exclusively with the President. The liberal interpretation of the American constitution by the Supreme Court has considerably enhanced the powers of the Federal-Government. Lastly, the bulk of the American constitution has also been increased by the formal amendments. The Indian constitution has also been amended several times to enable it to cope with the demands of the people.

### Constitutional Amendments

The method of amendment of a constitution depends upon its nature. The provisions of a flexible constitution can be easily amended in the same ordinary procedure, required for the making of the laws. In England, the Parliament is competent to change the constitution by the ordinary legislative procedure. Therefore, in the case of an amendment to flexible constitution, no special or difficult procedure other than the ordinary legislative procedure is required. But in case of rigid constitutions a special and difficult procedure is adopted for changing the constitution.

Firstly, the whole body of citizens of a country may be required to take part in approving an amendment to the constitution. The procedure is knows as referendum as it is followed in Switzerland and Australia. In Switzerland, an amendment to the constitution must be approved by a majority of citizens taking part in the voting and also majority of cantons.

Secondly, in federal countries proposals of amendment in order to be valid require the ratification of the component units of the federation. In the U.S.A. a proposal for constitutional amendment, after it is passed by the two-third majority in both the Houses of the Congress has to be ratified by three-fourths of the state legislatures. In India some of the provisions of the constitution in order to be amended require to be ratified by at least half of the state legislatures. In Switzerland and Australia also the consent of the majority of units is required in addition to the consent of the majority of the electrorate, for the validity of a constitutional amendment.

Thirdly, constitutional amendments may be made by a different organ, specially for the purpose. This method is followed in the U.S.A. A convention may be called at the request of two-third of members of each House of the Congress or by two-third of the state legislatures. An amendment proposed by such Conventions must be ratified by three-fourth of state legislatures for its incorporation in the constitution.

Lastly, in a specially prescribed method, the legislature of the country can also bring an amendment to the constitutional laws. The New constitution of India provides that ordinarily an amendment to the constitution shall require two-third majority of members present and voting supported by the absolute majority of the total membership of each House. It becomes valid after the assent of the President. But an amendment effecting matters like, the election of the President, executive power of a state, or the parliament's power to constitute a High Court etc, will require ratification by the legislatures of atleast half the number of state in addition to the provision mentioned above. Certain other provisions such as reorganisation of state boundaries, changing names of states and abolition of second chambers in the states can be amended by the Indian parliament by two-third majority of members present and voting in each House.

## Contents of a Constitution

We have discussed about the nature and the classification of constitutions. Now the question arises as to what is the content of a constitution? The constitution is a body of fundamental rules, which determines the power-relationship between the government and the governed. It is expected therefore, to reconcile the liberty of the individual with the authority of the government. The constitution should check either the excess of governmental authority which head the despotism as the excess of individual liberty, which would result in anarchy. The problem, therefore, is the proper balancing of liberty and authority in such a way that the excess of either of the two is avoided. A constitution, must contain the following provisions:

1. The organisation, nature and functions of government must be determined by the constitution. It also decides the limits of governmental power and the general principles on which the powers of the government are to be exercised. It contains, therefore, a negative aspect and a positive aspect. Thus it should be prescribed as to what functions the government should perform and also prohibit the government from doing certain other things.
2. The constitution should guarantee a charter of fundamental rights to the citizen. This will act as a source of liberty for the citizens. They will be able to know their position in relation to the government as well as in relation to the other citizens in the society. The total integrated development of the individual's personality is possible only when such essential rights are guaranteed to him.
3. The constitution should prescribe the mutual relationship between the different organs of the government. The board principles to regulate the functions of the governmental organs must be determined by the constitution.
4. Every constitution must contain the procedure of its amendment. It should also specify the name of the authority that is competent to affect amendment to the constitution.
5. The constitution should contain a set of fundamental rules and principles for the appointment of public officials to different offices. Many constitutions have made provisions for the Public Service or the Civil Service Commission for the recruitment of public officials on the basis of merit. This may reasonably avoid corruption, favoritism, nepotism and such other vices usually associated with arbitrary appointments. This would also secure the efficiency of the civil service.

## Essential Requisites of a Good Constitution

The goodness of a constitution is relative. A constitution, which is suited to the requirements of one country, might not be suited to the requirements of another country. It is, therefore, difficult to find universality in a particular constitution. Whether a particular constitution is good or bad will depend upon the acceptability of the people and the adaptability of the constitution to the social and political conditions of the country. However, inspite of its relative character, there are certain principles which must be present in a constitution in order to make it an ideal one.

In the first place, a constitution must be definite and precise and all attempts must be made to avoid ambiguity, because ambiguity leads to conflicting interpretations. In this respect a written constitution is more satisfactory than an unwritten one.

Secondly, a good constitution must be comprehensive and it must cover the whole of governmental organisation. It must lay down in clear terms the principles for the exercise of political power. At the same time a good constitution must avoid unnecessary details because they often lead to disputes. A constitution, which deals with unnecessary details soon, becomes outgrown.

Thirdly, the constitution should not be too rigid or too flexible. The extremities of both should be avoided and the balance between rigidity and flexibility should be properly maintained in order to make it an ideal one. Incorporation of necessary changes should not be obstructed by its rigidity. It should not be too much flexible either, because in that case it will become a victim to temporary party whims.

Fourthly, an ideal constitution must provide for an impartial and independent judiciary to decide the disputes and to interpret the constitution. The judiciary should act as the guardian of fundamental rights. A rigid and written constitution generally makes the judiciary the guardian of itself. If the ordinary legislation passed by the legislature is repugnant to the constitution, it is declared as unconstitutional or ultra vires.

Fifthly, an ideal constitution should provide for a charter of fundamental rights for the citizens of the state. These rights are essential for safeguarding the liberty of the citizens and for the development of their total personality. These rights determine the position of an individual in relation to the state and in relation to the other citizens. Any encroachment of these rights by the state should be resisted. However, these rights are not absolute rights. The state reserves the power to curtail these rights during emergency.

Lastly, the constitution of a country should not be an imported one. Moreover, no constitution should be imposed on the people of the country. It must have the support of the people and their willingness to implement its provisions. A constitution must develop in relation to the social, economic and political conditions of the country. It will not be acceptable to the people, if it is imposed upon them against their wishes. President Woodrow Wilson has observed that the constitution must of necessity be a vehicle of life and that its substance is the support and habit of the nation.

In the first place, a constitution must be definite and precise and all attempts must be made to avoid ambiguity, because ambiguity leads to conflicting interpretations. In this respect a written constitution is more satisfactory than an unwritten one.

Secondly, a good constitution must be comprehensive and it must cover the whole of governmental organisation. It must lay down in clear terms the principles for the exercise of political power. At the same time a good constitution must avoid unnecessary details because they often lead to disputes. A constitution, which deals with unnecessary details soon, becomes outgrown.

Thirdly, the constitution should not be too rigid or too flexible. The extremities of both should be avoided and the balance between rigidity and flexibility should be properly maintained in order to make it an ideal one. Incorporation of necessary changes should not be obstructed by its rigidity. It should not be too much flexible either, because in that case it will become a victim to temporary party whims.

Fourthly, an ideal constitution must provide for an impartial and independent judiciary to decide the disputes and to interpret the constitution. The judiciary should act as the guardian of fundamental rights. A rigid and written constitution generally makes the judiciary the guardian of itself. If the ordinary legislation passed by the legislature is repugnant to the constitution, it is declared as unconstitutional or ultra vires.

Fifthly, an ideal constitution should provide for a charter of fundamental rights for the citizens of the state. These rights are essential for safeguarding the liberty of the citizens and for the development of their total personality. These rights determine the position of an individual in relation to the state and in relation to the other citizens. Any encroachment of these rights by the state should be resisted. However, these rights are not absolute rights. The state reserves the power to curtail these rights during emergency.

Lastly, the constitution of a country should not be an imported one. Moreover, no constitution should be imposed on the people of the country. It must have the support of the people and their willingness to implement its provisions. A constitution must develop in relation to the social, economic and political conditions of the country. It will not be acceptable to the people, if it is imposed upon them against their wishes. President Woodrow Wilson has observed that the constitution must of necessity be a vehicle of life and that its substance is the support and habit of the nation.

# The British Constitution

# 1

# The British Constitution

## Development of the British Constitution

Great Britain consists of England, Wales, Scotland, Northern Ireland, Island of Man and the Channel and is situated on the north-west corner of Europe with a total area of 93,371 sq. miles. The English channel which is about twenty three miles in breadth, separates Great Britain from Europe and in the 17th and 18th centuries it saved the British people from external invasions. As a result of this sense of security the British people could freely develop and consolidate their political institutions, without any interference from external forces. Britain remained unaffected by the revolutionary and counter revolutionary currents and cross currents which overtook the other European countries from time to time. Thus the English channel which gave the British people a sense of security and protection, imparted to them an insular outlook that promoted conservatism and commitment to traditions and customs. The British people always preferred evolution to revolution and did not like to change merely for the sake of it. This is evident from the fact that even to-day most of the institutions and constitutional practices, which might appear otherwise anachromistic, have been retained in Great Britain. It occupies a central position in the whole world and as such, particularly after the discovery of North America, it became the centre of world commerce and trade. The need for promoting and safeguarding its commercial interest led England to build a powerful naval force, which ultimately resulted in its empire-building activities.

Different people and races came to England and conquered it and the most important among them were Celts, Romans, Anglo-Saxons, Jutes, Danes and Norwans. But fortunately for Great Britain, the people of these diverse races lost their independent identity and got assimilated as a result of which there was the development of a homogeneous culture, language and history.

There is also religious diversity in England. Majority of the people are protestants by religion, but the catholics are also there in a sizeable number. The Protestants are also divided into several sections like the Church of England, the Methodists, the Baptists and the Presbyterians. In England majority of the people belong to the Church of England, where as in Scotland, the Presbyterian Church has the allegiance of the bulk of its population.

Great Britain is a highly industrialised country and the factory workers constitute 54. p.c. of its total population. About 6 p.c. of the total population depends upon agriculture. There is a large and influential middle class consisting of business-men, shop-keepers and people belonging to other professions. The ascendance of the Liberal party in the British political scene in the 19th century was due to the dominant role of the middle class. The importance of the middle class was, however, reduced due to the development of largescale industries which gave rise to unprecedented accumulation of wealth and monopoly capitalism. The society was divided largely into two classes–the Capitalist and the Workers. The upper middle class joined with the capitalists and accepted the Conservative party as its representative. On the otherhand the Labour Party became the representative of the large number of factory workers, white collar labourers and the shopkeepers.

Although Great Britain has rich coal and iron reserves, she has to depend on other countries for rubber, oil, timber and many other mineral resources. The necessity of finding raw materials for her industry and the market for the factory products forced Great Britain to engage itself in empire-building activities and it become one of the gigantic imperial powers where the "sun did never set". But the emergence of United States, Gemany and Japan as major powers, between the two World Wars, greatly reduced British dominance as an imperial and industrial power.

Over the years, Great Britain continued to be the place where many constitutional experiments were conducted. It is the classic example of a parliamentary democracy and constitutional practices like Bicameralism, unitary form of Government, flexibility of constitution and Rule of Law took their birth in this country. It is not possible to have a proper understanding of the political systems of the world without studying the British constitution. Most of the British constitutional practices have their indelible impact on the constitutional systems of various countries of the world. The Indian constitution is also greatly indebted to the British political system for most of its features, which have been adopted in toto from the British model. Due to this all-pervading impact of the British constitution, it has been rightly described as the 'Mother Constitution'.

## Brief Survey of the Evolution of the British Constitution

In Great Britain a Constituent Assembly of the type noticed in other countries, was never convened to draft a constitution for the country. There was a slow but steady evolution of the constitution and the constitutional history of the British people goes back to 1300 years or so. The development of the Constitution has kept with the rise in the political consciousness of the people and this may be considered as the most remarkable aspect of the British constitution.

The constitution has evolved through the ages and has resulted in the peaceful transformation of absolute Monarchy into Constitutional Monarchy.

It is not possible to give the detailed history of the development of the British constitution over a period of several centuries, but the landmarks in the constitutional evolution of Great Britain can be analysed under the following heads:

### The Anglo-Saxon period:

The institution of Kingship developed during this period in the 7th and 8th century A.D. The office of the King was partly heraditary and partly elective.

The king occasionally called the Advisory Council called– 'Witenagemot' or the 'Council of Wise Men'. It was all powerful for sometime, but power of the Witenagemot was gradually passed into the hands of the king.

### Establishment of Local Self Government:

It was another noteworthy development during the Anglo-Saxon period. The whole country was divided into Shires and Shires were divided into Hundreds and Hundreds into villages and towns. Each Shire had a Shire-moot and each Hundred had a local council. Justice was administered by heads of Shire-moots and Bishops. From the stand-point of constitutional development, the establishment of Local Self Government may be considered as a significant achievement.

The rule of Alfred the Great (871-901 A. D.) also provided a new dimension to constitutional development during this period. He organised the Army and Navy and also organised a system of education. He enacted and enforced a code of law.

### The Norman Period

The Normans established their authority in England in 1066 AD. William the Conqueror (1066 AD) introduced feuda system to improve the tone of administration. Each unit was placed under a Baron who maintained an army to help the king when needed. He abolished the 'Witenagemot' and established in its place the 'Magnum Concilium'. This council met thrice in a year and was to collect the royal revenue and maintain the accounts. He also established the 'Curia Regis' or the Permanent Council. The Privy Council of England emerged out of the Curia Regis and in the 17th and 18th centuries, the Council of Ministers developed from the Privy Council. It is needless to say that the present Cabinet of Great Britain developed out of the Council of Ministers.

Another important Norman ruler, Henry II, firmly established governmental authority by introducing the system of travelling Judges. This practice helped the growth of common law in England. Thus for the first time the concept of a system of law common to all people had remarkable impact on the administration of Justice. But the feudal system depended on personal factor and it succeeded when the king was strong, wise and judicious. Under a weak and despotic king the system failed to work properly.

King John (1196 to 1215 A.D.) was cruel and arbitrary. He was the most wicked and tyrnnical ruler of all the kings of the Norman period. He imprisoned all the Barons who opposed his oppressive methods. Due to this there was a revolt of the Barons of the high order and he was forced to agree to a charter of demands called the Magna Carta in 1215 A.D. This was the first epoch-making charter of liberty. As per the provisions of the Magna Carta, the King could tax only with the consent of the Council consisting of Barons of high rank, title-holders of Shires and Sheriffs. The Magna Carta did not give any right to the common people. It only gave some powers to the Barons of high order and the rich aristocratic classes to control the powers of the king. But this could be accepted as a great charter of liberty as it was a significant development in the direction of limited monarchy.

The Magnum Concilium, created during the Norman period

may be rightly called the mother of the British Parliament, though initially it was only an assembly of great nobles and Clergymen. Henry III quarrelled with the Barons in 1258 and paved the way for the growth of the present parliamentary set-up in England. The Barons met at Oxford and constituted a committee of 15 members to check the autocratic powers of the king. The king surrendered for some time but then tried to defy the committee and assert his own powers. The Barons revolted under the leadership of Simon De Montford and the king was defeated. Simon invited the representatives of the lessor gentry to the parliament for winning popular support for levying new taxes. Thus two knights from each Shire and two Burgesses from each town were invited to the parliament.

Another step was taken by Edward I in the direction of the development of Parliamentary Government in England. He summoned the first Model Parliament in 1295 A.D. which has 572 representatives– 172 from Shires and Boroughs and 400 from among Barons, Clergymen, Bishops and so on. This might be called as the first 'Peoples' Parliament'. The number of representatives in this parliament was large. As the Burgesses were called alongwith the knights, Clergymen and Barons, the difference between the higher and lesser gentry began to give way.

Parliament began to meet in three groups in the beginning: Nobility, Clergy and Commons. By the end of the 14th century, there emerged the Bicameral parliament in England. The House of Lords consisting of the Barons, Bishops and the people of high rank in society, came to be regarded as the first House. The House of Commons consisted of Knights, traders and merchants. The composition of the British parliament and its emergence in the present form was the result of chance and socio-economic complexes of the time.

Edward I conceded to the following demands of the Parliament:

(i) The king must not levy new taxes without the permission of the parliament.
(ii) Parliament shall have the right to appoint Commissioners to audit the accounts.
(iii) The Kings Ministers shall be appointed by the Parliament.
(iv) Ministers shall resign before the beginning of a new session and shall answer all charges against them.

But despite all these powers, parliament's authority was more theoretical than real because the king had the final power either to summon or dissolve the Parliament. Kings did not summon the

Parliament if they found it non-cooperative and dissolved it when it became unrully.

**Plantagenet and Lancasterian Dynasties**

There was ascendency of the Parliament during the period of the Plantagenet dynasty (1154 A. D. to 1399 A.D). The plantagenet parliament became very powerful and King Edward II was dethroned by it in 1327 A.D. Richard II also bowed before the Parliament. Ultimately King Henry of the Lancaster dynasty was seated on the throne of England by the Parliament. During this period a number of important constitutional changes were made with a view to establish the supremacy of the Parliament. Henry IV came to power with the help of the Parliament and some significant developments took place during his regime which also helped the growth of parliamentary government. During his time the word Privy Council was used for the team of Ministers. In 1901 A.D. the Parliament demanded that the king should hear petitions consisting demands of the people and should promise to redress them before new taxes were approved by it. The House of Commons also got the exclusive power of introducing Financial Bills in 1407.

But due to the Wars of Roses, Parliament could not consolidate its powers and the necessity of a strong ruler was felt to provide peace and order to the country. Due to this the Tudor rulers were able to exercise arbitrary power and for some time again the power of the Parliament was superceded by the Monarch.

**Tudor Period (1485-1603 A.D.)**

Tudor despotism was tolerated by the British people as they wanted to solve the problems of anarchy and confusion. In a way it may be presumed that Tudor despotism was based on popular consent. The Tudor Kings had collected sufficient money by various methods and did not have to depend on the support of the parliament for new taxation. Thus they could manage without parliaments. During this period, the parliament was, therefore, relegated to the background.

**The Stuart Period (1603-1714 A.D.)**

The Tudor kings were able to provide England with the much needed political stability and order and towards the end of this period the British people again started asserting their own rights. This resulted in a series of wars between the people and the Stuart kings who came after the Tudor dynasty. Foundations of parliamentary democracy in England were laid during this period.

The famous Petition of Rights was forced upon King Charles I in 1728 which laid down the following conditions :

(i) The king could not levy new taxes without the approval of the parliament;
(ii) No loans could be raised by the King without the prior approval of the parliament;
(iii) No arbitrary imprisonment could be made by the king without assigning definite cause; and
(iv) No Martial law was to be enforced by the king during peace time.

Another important achievement of this period was the passing of the Habeas Corpus Act of 1679. According to this Act, no one arrested could be detained without trial and a court order justifying his detention.

William and Mary conjointly became the rulers of England with the help of the parliament after the Glorious Revolution of 1688. They had to agree to the condition laid down by the Parliament in the Bill of Rights, 1689, at the time of their accession to the throne.

The following provisions were incorporated in the Bill of Rights of 1689:

(i) The King could not levy new taxes without the approval of the Parliament;
(ii) Parliament must be summoned atleast once every year;
(iii) No army should be maintained without the prior sanction of the parliament;
(iv) King should not establish new courts to prejudice justice in his favour; and
(v) The freedom of speech of the peoples' representatives should not be curtailed.

During this period the parliament also passed the Act of Settlement of 1701 to decide upon the question of succession and the connected problems as Queen Anne had no issue. According to this Act Queen Anne was to be succeeded by the sons of Sophia, the grand daughter of James I. It also provided that the king could not declare war or enter into peace without prior approval of the Parliament.

Another interesting matter was the development of the party system over the discussion on the Exclusion Bill. King Charles II had no children and there was the probability of his being succeeded to the throne by his brother James II. Parliament did not want him to succeed as he was a staunch Catholic and hence the Exclusion Bill was passed to deprive James II from succeeding to the throne of England. The Bill proved to be highly controversial and the parliament was divided into 'Whigs' and 'Tories'. The Whigs supported the Exclusion Bill, but the Tories were opposed to it. To controversy subsided after some time but the Whigs and Tories remained as two rival political parties in the British parliament and they contributed to the growth of modern party system of England. The origin of bi-party system in England may be traced to this incident.

King William selected his Ministers from the Whig party which was responsible for making him the King of England and incidentally the Whigs were in majority in the Parliament. This gave rise to the practice that the Ministry would belong to the majority party in the Parliament. The team of Ministers appointed by King William was called by him as the "Junta" and the future Cabinet Government of England was taking shape during the years 1693-96.

The Parliament passed the Mutiny Act in 1689. The practice of maintaining a standing army was abolished. This was responsible to curtail the despotic powers of the king who very often used the army against the parliament and political dissenters. By the Mutiny Act soldiers were admitted to the Army only for one year and the king was bound to call the Parliament to approve, the continuance of the Army.

The Parliament also passed the Triennial Act of 1694, by which the tenure of the Parliament was fixed at three years. Soon it was replaced by the Septennial Act which enhanced the tenure to seven years. Thus the Parliament got the power to fix its own tenure free from the intervention of the Monarch.

Union between Scotland and England was brought by the Act of Union of 1707. House of Lords and the House of Commons were to have 16 and 45 members respectively from Scotland.

With the accession of the Hanoverian dynasty many of the powers of the parliament were consolidated. The ascendency of the Parliament became an undisputed factor in the political history of Great Britain.

### The Final Phase

George I was the creation of the parliament as he became the king of England due to the provisions of the Act of Settlement, 1701. He was guided by a sense of gratitude towards the parliament and could never think in terms of challenging its powers. Moreover, the first two Hanoverian Kings, George I and George II did not know English and hence did not take much interest in the meetings of the cabinet. They invariably remained absent from the meetings and allowed the seniormost member to preside over the meetings. This led unconsciously to the development of the office of the Prime Minister and the practice of excluding the Monarch from Cabinet meetings. The practice that the Prime Minister should preside over the meetings of the cabinet continues till today and it is one of the most fundamental principles of parliamentary government.

Despite the increase in the powers of the parliament, it was inherently weak because it represented only a very small section of the people. There was a demand both inside and outside the parliament for extension of parliamentary franchise, which became a reality in the 19th century. Limited franchise was granted to the representatives of the middle class by the Reform Act of 1832. The number of peoples representatives in the local bodies was increased by the Municipal Corporations Act of 1832. Craftsmen and town labourers also got the right to vote, through the extension of franchise by the Reform Act of 1867. The Reform Act of 1884 granted the right to vote even to the farm labourers. There was further democratisation of the political process by the Local Government Act of 1888, which provided for County Councils, to be elected by the people. In this context mention may also be made to the Local Government Act of 1894 which provided for the division of administrative countries into urban and rural districts. These districts were to have their own elected councils.

The Parliament Act of 1911 was a significant landmark in the constitutional history of Great Britain as it granted exclusive supremacy to the House of Commons over Money Bills. The House of Lords was reduced to the position of a secondary chamber by the grant of only suspensive veto for two years in respect of ordinary bills, in place of the absolute veto, which it previously enjoyed. The dispute for supremacy between the House of Lords and the House of Commons was settled for all times to come.

There was further extension of franchise for women over thirty years of age by the Act of 1918 and this Act was followed by the Equal Franchise Act of 1928, which accepted the principle of universal Adult Franchise and all men and women over 21 years of age got the right to vote.

The Statute of Westminster of 1931 was another significant

constitutional landmark of the period. By this Act the relationship between the king and the Dominions was determined and this Act also had a major contribution in the evolution of the Commonwealth of Nation's which continues till to-day.

It may be said that the long drawn out process of democratisation was completed by the passage of the Parliamentary Act of 1949 which further curtailed the power of the House of Lords to veto an ordinary bill from two years to one year.

From the foregoing survey of constitutional development in Great Britain it is evident that the most important feature of this long drawn out process of evolution over nearly 1300 hundred years, has been the slow but steady transfer of power from the hands of the Monarch into the hands of the Parliament in a peaceful and more or less silent manner.

# 2

# Important Features of the British Constitution

There is no constitution in England which may be said to have been neatly planned, drafted and adopted by a constituent Assembly, as it has been the case with most of the countries. Over hundreds of years, the process of constitutional evolution has gone through unchecked and unhindered despite resistance from several kings and at present the democratic authority of Britain is based on three major assumptions which have been generally accepted by the people. These basic principles are: (i) that political authority is derived from the people and their consent; (ii) that sovereignty of the parliament is legally unlimited; and (iii) that political authority should serve the general good of the people.

## Evolutionary Nature of the Constitution

The British were never in favour of any revolution and while being highly assertive about their rights, they allowed the slow historical and evolutionary process to give shape to their constitution. In the words of Boutmy, "the English have left the different parts of their constitution just where the wave of history had deposited them; they have not attempted to bring them together to classify or complete them, or to make a consistent or coherent whole". Due to the absence of a coherent and cogent constitutional document some writers and constitutional experts have doubted the existance of the British constitution. Alexis de Toequeville, a French thinker said: "If by the term constitution, we mean a formal and precise code of laws, which has been deliberately drafted, and which can be changed only in accordance with a prescribed procedure, then, of course, England has no constitution". It may however, be admitted that Tocqueville was a great admirer of the British constitution. Thomas Paine of America was also of the view that in strict sense of the term in Britain there was no constitution. He was of the view that "a constitution to be real must be produced in a written form and as England cannot produce it, it has no constitution". But such views expressed by some writers are due to the fact that they are oblivious of the fundamental constitutional documents which hve gone into the making of the British constitution. The Magna Charta, the Petition of Rights, the Bill of Rights, the latter two being the enlarged editions of the former, constituted the basic source of the British constitution and the several Parliamentary Acts which perfected the democratic process, also contributed to the growth of the constitution. The whole process has been compared with "a river whose moving surface glides away at one's feet, meandering in and out in endless curbs, now seeming to disapper in a whirl pool, now almost lost to sight in the verdure".

Munro in his book, 'The Governments of Europe', writes that the British Constitution "is the result of a process in which charters, statutes, decisions, precedents, usages and traditions have piled themselves one upon the other from age to age. Or, to use another metaphor, it is a rambling structure, to which successive owners have added wings and gabbles, porches and pillars, thus modifying it to suit their immediate wants or the fashion of the time".

## The Unwritten Constitution

Although the British Constitution was not adopted or enacted by any Constituent Assembly as in the case of some other constitutions and is regarded as a basically unwritten constitution, it can be easily noticed that a large part of the constitution is in writing in the form of charters and statutes etc. In addition to the Petition of Rights, 1628; the Bill of Rights, 1689; the Act of Settlement, 1701; there are many other Acts like the Act of Union with Scotland, 1707; the Reform Acts of 1832, 1867 and 1884, the Parliament Acts of 1911, and 1949; the Irish Treaty, 1921; the Franchise Acts of 1918 and 1928, the Statute of Westminister, 1931 which have significantly contributed to the growth and development of the British constitution. Mention may also be made of the judicial decisions interpreting the charters and statues, conventions and customs, usages and the common law, which have played their role in the development of the constitution. In this context the definition of Munro seems to be most befitting. "It is a complex amalgam of institutions, principles and practices; it is a composite of charters and statutes, of judicial decisions, of common law, of precedents, usages and traditions. It is not one document, but thousands of them. It is not derived from one source, but from several. It is not a completed thing, but a process of growth. It is a child of wisdom and chance, whose course has been sometimes guided by accident and sometimes by high design".

## Cromwell's Constitutional Experiment

In the long history of its constitutional experiments, certain revolutionary changes were adopted during the regime of Cromwell. He abolished Kingship in Great Britain, and issued the Instrument of Government in 1653. This document contained the powers and functions of the executive and legislative branches of the Government. He abolished the House of Lords and established a Republic or a British Commonwealth with a single legislative chamber. But this arrangement could not continue for a longer period and immediately after the death of Cromwell, the written constitution proclaimed by him and the republican form of Government were given an unceremonious sendoff and the parliament decided to return to old form of government based on ancient and fundamental laws. Monarchy and bicameralism were again restored.

It can be safely aruged that it is wrong to hold the view that "In England the constitution–there is no such thing", merely because of the fact that it is largely in the form of urwritten conventions. It is not necessary that a constitution should be always written. A constitution consists of certain rules which must determine the structure and regulate the conduct of the government of a country. There is no hard and fast rules whether the constitution should be written or unwritten. To say that in England there is no constitution because all its principles are not written would be a travesty of the truth and would be far away from the true understanding of the nature of constitution. England has got the best democratic constitution of the world, which may be called the product of history. The British constitution has acquired its modern form through a process of evolution, to which many factors have made their contribution.

## The Constitutional Landmarks

In this connection reference has already been made to constitutional landmark and the statutes. In the opinion of Ogg, the constitutional landmarks are those agreements between the people and the king during the periods of national crises, when the kings who were trying to misuse their power, had to surrender before the people demanding more rights. These significant agreements defined the powers of the king and gradually curtailed his powers while granting more and more rights to the people. In the words of Laski, "Monarchy has been sold to democracy as a symbol of itself" and this has been largely materialised through these constitutional landmarks like the Magna Charta, the Bill of Rights and the petition of Rights.

### The Role of the Parliamentary Statutes

The British parliament passed statutes from time to time to assert its own rights and privileges and the liberties of the people as well as to define and restrict the powers of the Monarch. Laws were also passed to reduce the importance of the House of Lords and to extend the franchise to a larger section of the people. All these Acts have formed parts of the British constitution and have helped the process of its transformation from absolute Monarchy to Parliamentary democracy. It is due to its long history the British Parliament is said to be the mother of all parliaments and the constitution of Great Britain is the oldest among the existing constitutions of the world.

### Judicial Interpretations and Legal Commentaries

Judicial interpretations and legal commentaries have also contributed to the growth and development of the British constitution and have formed a significant part of the constitution. The rights and liberties of the British people have become a part and parcel of the constitution as a result of judicial decisions and interpretations of the constitutional law. Treatises and legal commentaries written by distinguished jurists and lawyers defining and criticising the scope of constitutional provisions have inspired the Parliament to incorporate some of the suggested provisions or to amend or repeal the undesirable provisions existing in the constitution. Among such writers and legal commentators reference may be made to the names of Blackstone, Coke and Dicey. Everybody must be aware of the classic analysis of the concepts like Rule of Law and conventions of the constitution made by Dicey.

### The Common Law

Certain principles and rules were enunciated by the judges while deciding the cases which were brought before them. In the course of time these principles and rules have acquired the status of law. These rules and principles have not been either accepted or codified by the parliament but this has in no way reduced their legal sanctity. These rules and principles are followed very strictly by courts of law and on the event of their violation the lawbreaker can be punished as in the case of violation of other fundamental principles of law. Ogg is of the opinion that Common law consists of "a vast body of legal precepts and usages which through the centuries have acquired binding and almost immutable character". Some of the fundamental principles of the British Constitution are provided by the Common Laws and the most important of them all is right of the people to trial by the jury.

### The Flexible Constitution

A flexible constitution is one which provides for the same principle of amendment both for the ordinary laws and the constitutional laws of the country. The British constitution has acquired its organic character from its flexibility. In England there is no difference between the ordinary and the constitutional laws. The British parliament is competent to change any constitutional law through the same procedure by which it can be change an ordinary law of the country. In the U.S.A., India and many other countries for the amendment of the constitutional provisions certain special procedures have been specified in the respective constitutions. The procedure of amendment of constitutional law is difficult and cumbersome. An additional factor of the flexibility of the British Constitution is that it can be changed even without formal amendment, with the help of conventions.

### A Unitary System

The British Constitution provides for a unitary form of government as opposed to the federal system. Under this constitution the Central government enjoys exclusive supremacy and the administration is centralised. Although there may be regional and local governments and they may be granted some limited powers, they are subordinate to the central government which can at any moment withdraw the powers delegated to these bodies. In England there is one supreme central government which supervises and controls all the works of administration and the local governments are only its subordinate agencies.

### The Supremacy of Parliament

The parliament in England is all-powerful and it is the sovereign law-making, law-amending and law-reprealing body. Due to its omnipotence the parliament can change any charter or statute; can set aside any judicial decision; can terminate any usage or custom and reject any rule of the common law. In Great Britain there is no difference between the constituent authority and the law-making authority of the parliament. Supremace of the British parliament is a reality and it cannot be legally challenged by any authority. It is the most powerful legislative body in the whole world. The British parliament reserves the right of changing the rules of succession to the British throne as it was done by the Act of Settlement in 1701. Bagehot has rightly pointed out that, "Parliament could abolish trial by jury, pass bills of attainder, confiscate private property without compensation, take the suffrage away from all but tax-payers, and even turn England into a republic". This statement of Bagehot highlights the unlimited and supreme powers of the British parliament. It may however, be pointed out that despite its supremacy and legal competence, the British parliament does not do things which the electorate would not like. Laws passed by the British parliament are final and they cannot be declared as unconstitutional or ultravires by the British courts as is the case in the United States of America and India.

### Constitutional Monarchy

The continuance of Kingship is the product of England's monarchical heritage which can be traced to centuries back. Although in theory there is absolute monarchy in England and the King has all the executive, legislative and judicial authority, but in practice, he takes no direct part in the administration of the country. The king reigns but does not rule. The president of U.S.A. rules but does not reign and the Indian President neither rules nor reigns. The British Prime Minister and his cabinet are the real executive rulers. The king is the nominal head. But the British people hold the institution of Monarchy with great love and esteem and although several attempts were made to abolish Monarchy, it was again restored in due deference to the wishes of the people. Analysing this position Ogg has observed that, "The Government of the United Kingdom is in ultimate theory an absolute monarchy, in form, a constitutional limited monarchy, and in actual character a democratic republic".

### Parliamentary Government

England is the example pre-excellence of a parliamentary government. These are three prerequisities of a parliamentary government: (i) dual executive, (ii) close relationship between the executive and the legislature, and (iii) uncertainty of the tenure of the executive. All these three features are present in the British constitution.

The King is the nominal head of the executive and acts as the depository of power when the government is out of office and the constitution of the real executive is being sought at the polls. The party which gets majority in the House of Commons forms the government and the Prime Minister and the Cabinet constitute the real executive of Great Britain. All the executive powers in reality are exercised by them. It may therefore, be said that the parliamentary government in England wears a crown.

The second feature of the parliamentary government refers to the close relationship between the executive and the legislature. The real executive in England is a committee of the parliament taken from it and responsible to it. This means that the executive is also a part and parcel of the legislature and has no right to continue in office the moment it loses the confidence of the legislature. There is also close functional collaboration between the executive and the legislature which means that the executive participates in legislation but the legislature has the ultimate power to supervise and control the executive. In England the cabinet is a committee of the parliament and its members are largely chosen from among the members of the majority party in the parliament. The members of the cabinet are answerable to the parliament in general and to the House of Commons in particular and if their work is not satisfactory they can be drivenout of office at any time. Thus parliamentary government provides for an element of concentration of powers as opposed to separation of powers as practised in the Presidential system of U.S.A. In the words of Ramsay Muir, "if separation of the powers is the essential principle of the American Constitution, concentration of responsibility is the essential principle of the British Constitution".

The third prerequisite of the parliamentary government is the uncertainty of the tenure of the executive as opposed to the fixed tenure of the presidential executive. In England the life of the Cabinet is uncertain and eventhough it is elected for a period of five years, it can be removed from office before the completion of the term by a vote of noconfidence. From the foregoing analysis it is evident that parliamentary democracy exists in England in all its classic features.

## The Element of Unreality

There is an element of unreality in the British Constitution which should be taken note of, inorder to have a proper understanding of the constitution and its working. There is a wide gap between theory and practice. The unique things about the British constitution is that, "nothing is what it seems to be, or seems to be what it is". Even now the Crown is regarded as the source of all authority and everything is done in the name of the Crown. The Prime Minister and other Ministers are appointed by the Crown and they hold office at the pleasure of the Crown and all officers of the government are also appointed in its name. Laws passed by the parliament become Acts after the consent of the Crown is given. Everything is called "His Majesty's, such as His Majesty's Courts, His Majesty's Nevy, His Majesty's Forces, His Majesty's Government, His Majesty's Opposition and so on. But in actual practice, the king does not take any part in the governance of the country. In reality, the prerogatives of the Crown have become the privileges of the people and these are now exercised by the Ministers who are accountable to the parliament and through the parliament ultimately accountable to the people. The powers of the people are analysed by Munro in the following words: "No freeman shall be arrested, or imprisoned, or dispossessed of his land, or outlawed, or exiled, or in any other way herassed, no will we impose upon him, nor send him our commands save by the lawful judgement of his peers or by the law of the land". Another element of unreality is that although in theory there is parliamentary supremacy in England, in actual practice, the Cabinet has become so very powerful that, there is a talk about Cabinet dictatorship. Referring to the divergence between theory and practice Munro has rightly observed that, "The unique feature of the British Constitution is to be found in its curious divergence from the actualities of government".

### The Rule of Law

It is one of the most important features of the democratic constitution of Great Britain. Rule of Law implies that there is supremacy of law rather than the supremacy of a man or a group of men in the country. The law should be uniform for all and it should be administered by the ordinary courts of the country. It also provided that irrespective of the social or governmental position, every man should be subjected to the ordinary law of the land and should be brought under the jurisdiction of the ordinary courts. Thus Rule of Law means, "the supremacy or dominance of law, as distinguished from mere arbitrariness, or from some alternative mode, which is not law, of determining or disposing of the rights of individuals". Rule of law means that the state shall not ordinarily impose undesirable obligation on any individual, should not interfere with his property rights, should not abridge or curtail his personal liberty. Any such interference must be done in a legal manner and under legal authority. Thus Rule of Law is at once the source and guardian of the rights and liberties of the people of England. Wade and Phillips put it in the following words: "The exercise of the powers of government shall be conditioned by law and that the subject shall not be exposed to arbitrary will be his own ruler".

The simple meaning of Rule of Law is that no one is superior to law and the whole country is governed by the law. Lord Hewart rightly observed that, "The underlying contrast, the antithesis is between the supremacy of law on the one hand and on the other hand the arbitrary exercise of law less power".

Dicey has made a classic exposition of the principle of Rule of Law. This has got three implications. According to his first interpretation, no one in the country can be punished, imprisoned or deprived of his life and property unless his crime has been proved in an ordinary court of law, in a manner established by the ordinary legal procedure in which he has full opportunity for self-defence. Analysing his concept Dicey said, "That no man is punishable or can be lawfully made to suffer in body or goods except for a distinct breach of law established in the ordinary legal manner before the ordinary courts of the land". Dicey made it categorically clear that. "A man can be punished for breach of law but he can be punished for nothing else".

Regarding the second implication Dicey says that, "The Rule of Law further means that every citizen is subject to the ordinary law of the realm and amenable to the jurisdiction of the ordinary tribunals". The second interpretation of Rule of Law gives emphasis on equality before law. This principle is analysed by Dicey in the following words; "Every official from the Prime Minister down to a constable or a collector of taxes is under the same responsibility for every act done without any legal justification as any other citizen. There are however, some exceptions to this provision:

(i) The king is above law and no suit can be filed against him. It is said that, "The King can do no wrong".
(ii) For acts done beyond their jurisdiction, unknowingly, in the due discharge of their official duty, judges will not be held responsible in their personal capacity.
(iii) For acts done in their official capacity public officers enjoy personal immunity from prosecution.

(iv) If they have not acted maliciously, justices of peace also, will not be held personally responsible for their official deeds.

(v) There are certain special laws which regulate the conduct of people working in some special professions. There is Martial Law for military personnel, Ecclesiastical laws for Clergymen and Regulations laid down by the Medical Council for the conduct of the doctors. These laws exist and operate side-by-side with Rule of Law and neither will be held null and void for the other.

According to Dicey's interpretation the third implication of Rule of Law is that the general principles of the constitution are the result of judicial decisions. The rights and liberties of the British people have emanated as a result of judicial decisions in ordinary cases and subsequently these have become part and parcel of the British constitution. Dicey has put it in these words: "The general principles of the constitution are the result of judicial decisions determining the rights of private persons in particular cases brought before the courts".

Rule of Law protects the individual's right to personal freedom as according to it no one can be arrested except for a definite breach of law, which must be proved in a duly constituted ordinary court of law. There must be open trials of cases and the accused has the right of being represented and defended by a Counsel. It is the accusory which must take the burden to proof the guilt of the accused person and the case it tried in accordance with an extensive body of accepted rules of procedure and laws of evidence. The accused has a right to trial by jury in all serious criminal cases. The judgement is pronounced in the open court and the accused has the right of appeal to a High Court.

Rule of Law also guarantees the Right to freedom of speech and in England every individual citizen is free to write or speak anything, subject to the provision that he will be held responsible before a Court of Law for writings of defamatory or libellous nature.

In accordance with the provisions of Rule of Law, the right of the individual to hold public meetings and exchange his views according to the provisions of the ordinary laws of the country, is upheld. All these liberties are further protected by the fact that all persons are emanable to the same ordinary laws of the land and the same ordinary courts. Thus there is a guarantee against any kind of discrimination. Any citizen can sue any government official for abuse of power, under the ordinary procedure of law and in the same ordinary courts. In England there is neither Administrative Law nor Administrative Courts as in France.

## Rule of Law: An Appraisal

In England where there is no declaration of Fundamental Rights as in U.S.A. or India, the Rule of Law has been able to guarantee rights and liberties to the British people. Another advantage of the principle of Rule of Law is the establishment of a democratic society where all the citizens are treated equal before the eyes of law and nobody is allowed any special privilage.

But at the same time it may be admitted that it is not an unmixed blessing. In certain cases dealing with government officials, some technical points are involved and in all such cases the interest of justice could be better promoted by deciding them under Administrative Law, rather than under the Common Law and Common Tribunals. Since there is provision of payment of compensation by the State under the Administrative Law system, which is not there under the Rule of Law, the aggrieved party has a better chance of being compensated for the wrong done to him, under Administrative Law.

## Rule of Law under Partial Eclipse

The complexity of modern life and the increased socio-economic problems have necessitated new laws and methods to solve the problems. This has resulted in the partial eclipse of the Rule of Law in England. The parliament has passed various Acts like the Factory Acts, the Educations Acts etc. which have given semi-judicial powers to officials and the jurisdiction of ordinary courts of law, becomes proportionately limited. Due to inordinate delay in disposal of cases in the ordinary courts of law, the people in general have shown a distrust of the Court of Law.

The foundation of the Rule of Law has been further weakened by delegated legislation. Orders-in-Council and provisional orders, which do not constitute law in the strict sense of the term, cannot be questioned in the Law Courts.

The parliament has also passed several Acts by which special protection is granted to government official against legal proceedings in ordinary courts of law. The Public Authorities Protection Act of 1893 as amended by the Limitation Act of 1939 and the Crown Proceedings Act of 1947, are some of the Acts which have excluded the jurisdiction of the ordinary courts in cases pertaining to the servants of the Crown. This special privilege of the officials has shattered one of the most fundamental principles of the Rule of Law i.e., equality before law.

But inspite of these challenges to the principle of Rule of Law, it is still being considered as the guardian angel of the rights and liberties of the people. No doubt, in England there is the emergence of Administrative Law, but the judiciary is still an unfailing custodian of the rights and privileges of the people. The British Judiciary has carved out a place of distinction for itself due to its impartiality, independence and integrity. In this connection it is worthwhile to quote Prof. Laski: "Ever since the revolution of 1688 the independence and incorruptibility of the British judges has been beyond dispute in this country. The rights and liberties of the people are also guaranteed by age old traditions and usages, which are more effective than mere legal documents. The judiciary in England guarantees the rights and liberties of the people by acting as the custodian of these usages and traditions. Rights of the people cannot be guaranteed by their mere incorporation in the constitution. The people must have an awareness to protect their rights at any cost and this feeling should be supported by an independent and impartial judicial system.

### The Cabinet

It is an offshoot of the privy council and was not recognised by law till the passage of the Ministers of the Crown Act. It consists of about 20 to 25 members all of whom are formally appointed by the King on the recommendation of the Prime Minister. These Ministers are chosen from among the leading members of the party having a majority in the parliament, especially in the House of Commons. The Cabinet consists of the important Ministers of the Ministry and all members of the Ministry are not members of the Cabinet. All important decisions regarding the policy of the government, rest with the Cabinet, which meets under the Chairmanship of the Prime Minister. The principle of collective responsibility of the Ministry has taken firm roots in Great Britain. The Cabinet is not only supreme in administration but it has also a freehand in legislation and finance. The Prime Minister can dissolve the House of Commons and order for fresh elections. He has also got the power to compel his cabinet colleagues to resign in case of serious differences of opinion or breath of cabinet rules.

### Parliament

It consists of the King, House of Lords and House of Commons. But at present the parliament has come to mean only the House of Commons. The most important fact about the parliament is that it is a sovereign law-making body and can pass any law. But this supremacy of the parliament is limited by cabinet dictatorship, judge-made laws, delegated legislation and the growth of Administrative Law. Law passed by the British parliament also does not extend to the Dominions, after the passage of the Statute of West minister of 1931.

## House of Lords

It consists of 845 members of a mixed body of six groups, comprising of: (i) Hereditary peers, (ii) Elected Peers of Scotland, (iii) Life Peers of Ireland, (iv) Ecclesiastical Peers, (v) Law Lords and (vi) Princes of the Blood Royal. Three members from the quorum, but presence of at least 30 members is required to transact business of the House. Lord Chancellor is the President of the House which holds its sessions simultaneously with the House of Commons.

The functions of the House are mainly legislative, judicial and deliberative. Since the passing of the Parliament Act of 1911, and its subsequent Amendment in 1949, the House has lost effective control over ligislation–ordinary and financial. It now acts as a deliberative body and exercises judicial power both original and appellate, which is done by the nine Law-Lords.

Due to its undemocratic character, the House has lost its former importance and various proposals have been made either to abolish or to reform it. But the House still continues because it renders certain tangible services to the nation. Bicameralism has now become an indispensable part of the British political system.

## House of Commons

It is the lower House consisting of members elected by Universal Adult Suffrage by citizens of 21 years of age, for a term of 5 years. Members receive salary of fixed by the House as well as certain privileges to enable them to maintain their dignity and discharge their legislative functions properly.

The House is the repository of all legislative powers. It controls the executive. It also controls the finance and exercises general supervision over all the affairs of the state. But in the modern times the powers of the House have passed into the hands of the Cabinet, which virtually rules the country.

## Bureaucracy

It refers to the top men of the permanent Civil Service, who advised the Ministers and helped them not only in the day-to-day administration but also in the formulation of policies and laws. The

Minister being a bird of passage has to depend largely on these permanent officials who are experienced men in their departmental work. But the ultimate responsibility lies with the Ministers for their acts of omission and commission and the civil servants remain in the background. Bureaucracy thrives under the choak of Ministerial responsibility in Great Britain. This has resulted in greatly increasing the powers of the bureaucracy.

## Judiciary

There is a highly curtalised system of judicial hierarchy in Great Britain. The courts are based on vertical division between criminal and civil cases. The House of Lords is the highest Court of Appeal in the civil and criminal cases. The Privy Council is the ultimate Court of Appeal in cases which come from the Ecclesiastical Courts.

# 3

# Conventions

The conventions of the British constitution are certain rules and practices of political life which enable the system to operate in an effective manner. Dicey defines these conventions as "those customs, practices, maxims and precepts, which are not enforced or recognised by the Courts, make up a body of laws, but constitutional or political ethics". The conventions of the constitution are considered as the Code of Honour and they act like grease for the smooth working of the complicated governmental machine. In the words of Freeman, "they are a code of precepts for the guidance of public men, which will not be found in any page of either the Statute or the Common Law, but which are in practice, held hardly less sacred than any principle embodied in the Magna Carta or the petition of Rights". Without these conventions Parliamentary democracy cannot function in England. The conventions have become part of the constitution due to their utility. They help in the day-to-day working of the British constitution, some times replacing a law and some times supplementing it. The unwritten maxims which are called conventions by Dicey are referred to as "customs of the constitution" by Anson. J.S. Mill called them as the "unwritten maxims" of the constitution. Dicey says, "Our modern code of constitutional morality secures, though in a round-about way, what is called abroad the sovereignty of the people". Most of the conventions are related to the constitutional theory of the state and hence respected by all. It has been rightly stated about the conventions that, "they consist of habits, traditions, customs and practices which regulate a large proportion of the actual day-to-day activities of even the most important of the public authorities. They clothe the dry bones of the law with flesh, make it work, and keep it abreast of changing social needs and political ideas".

## Law and Conventions

It is pertinent to examine the relation between law and conventions as conventions very often either replace or supplement a particular law. The conventions of to-day may become the laws of tomorrow.

The laws are enacted by the parliament, while the conventions originate by themselves for filling up the gaps in the constitution. However, because of their immense utility and acceptability some conventions may be subsequently passed in the form of laws.

Another difference between the laws and the conventions is that, while the conventions are unwritten maxims, the laws are written. Due to this the laws are definite, but the conventions are indefinite and some times there is a controversy as to whether a convention exists or not.

Yet another difference between the laws and conventions is that the laws are enforceable by the courts of law, but the conventions are not. In the words of Ogg: "The conventions although they may, and frequently do, relate to matters of the utmost importance, (including, to a very large extent, the inter-relations of the different parts of the government) are not thus enforceable". However, this should not lead us to think that the conventions do not have sanction behind them. The conventions are obeyed as rigidly as the laws are obeyed.

## Sanction behind the Conventions

It is strange that eventhough the conventions do not have the police power of the state at their back and call, yet there is no violation. They are meticulously followed as the laws are followed. It may be mentioned here that the utility of the conventions is the greatest factor of sanction behind them. They meet the constitutional requirement of the people which either the existing laws are unable to fulfil or they are opposed to it or silent over it. The conventions have taken their growths to regulate, replace or bridge the gap between existing law and the needs of the people.

Propounding his theory of sanction behind the conventions, Dicey is of the opinion that the laws and the conventions are so closely related that if a convention is broken, a law is also automatically violated. As violation of law is legally forbidden, it also amounts to providing sanctions for the conventions. Some examples are furnished by him to illustrate his view point. The convention that the British Parliament must meet at least one a year, is closely connected with two laws, (a) that the budget should be passd every year, and (b) that the Army Act should be renewed annually. These two laws cannot be violated, hence the convention that the parliament should meet at least once a year is strictly followed. But this view is only partially correct as there are certain conventions is England which are not connected with any law, nonetheless, they are also equally followed like other conventions. There is a convention that when the House of Lords sits as the Court of Appeal, only the nine Law Lords shall take part. Another convention relates to the practice of giving three readings to a Bill, before it is finally passed. These conventions are not boundup with any laws, yet they are respected and till to-day no attempt is ever made to violate these conventions. From this it is evident that although there is sanction behind conventions, it is not the sanction suggested by Dicey.

Laski is of the opinion that the conventions are followed in England, because they are related to the constitutional theory of the time. Almost all the conventions promote the smooth functioning of parliamentary democratic institutions and hence they are followed. Had there been a single convention supporting the monarchical system, it would have been rejected by the people. Laski has given another reason also for the sanction behind the conventions and that is the unanimous support of all the political parties. The Labour and the Conservative Parties have accepted principles of constitutional Monarchy and the capitalistic foundations of their democracy and hence they support all the conventions and have equal respect for them. Laski seems to be more logical in his arguments, but he has ignored the conservative character of the British people which plays a great role in providing sanctions behind the conventions.

It may however, be said that no single factor can be pinpointed as the sanction behind the conventions. Several factors like utility of the conventions, the support of political parties, the conservatism of the British people and the over-whelming support of public opinion, have provided sanctity and unforceability to the conventions.

## Role of Conventions

The conventions play such a vital role in the British constitution that they are considered as flesh of the dry-bones of the body politic. Without these conventions the working of the several institutions of the government and state will be impossible.

### Conventions and Constitutional Growth

The transformation of the British political system from Monarchy to parliamentary democracy, was made possible through the conventions. Conventions helped the process of democratization. The powers of the kings were slowly limited by conventions. Had there been a direct attempt to reduce their powers by laws, they would have certainly resisted the process. But most of the time they were not aware of the process of democratisation through the conventions. For example the first two Georges, did not attend the meetings of the cabinet and due to lack of knowledge in English were indifferent to governmental activities. This led to their gradual exclusion from cabinet meetings and this power was assumed by the Prime Minister. By the time of George III this practice had already assumed the sanctity of a convention and therefore, despite the attempts of the King, it could not be broken or violated.

### Healthy Relationship between the Legal and the Political Sovereign

Most of the British conventions have provided the basis for the development of healthy relationship between the legal and political sovereign i.e., the relationship of the King with the Cabinet and the parliament. The convention that the King should not refuse consent to any Bill passed by the parliament puts an end to all possibility of conflict between the King and the parliament and results in a synthesis between the will of the legal and political sovereign. This reconciliation between the legal and the political sovereign is also evident from the convention that the King should appoint the leader of the majority party as the Prime Minister. By this the King is denied any political role in the selection of the Prime Minister and thus it results in harmonious relationship between the legal and the political sovereign.

### Conventions Promote Healthy Relationship between the Executive and the Legislature

Healthy relationship between the House of Commons and the Cabinet is highly essential for the success of parliamentary government in England. There are many conventions which help to promote cordial relationship between the executive and the legislature. Parliamentary system provides for the accountability of the executive to the legislature and the parliament exercises its control over the executive through several methods. The Council of Ministers, although elected for a period of five years can be driven out of office, much before the completion of that period by a vote of noconfidence. But this might make the parliament too harassing or too refractory in its attitude, which is likely to spoil the smooth working of the government. This can be checked by the power of the Prime Minister, to demand the dissolution of the House of Commons, if it becomes an irresponsible and destructive critic. It may be mentioned here that the Prime Minister's power to demand dissolution, which the King is bound to oblige has developed in the form of a convention. Due to this convention, the parliament's power to driveout the council of Ministers at any time is counterbalanced by the Prime Minister's power to demand dissolution of the House of Commons.

## Conventions help the Evolution of better Government

There are several conventions in England which help to improve the tone of governmental administration. The convention that every Bill should be given three readings before it is finally passed helps to improve the quality of the legislation. Similarly for the proper administration of justice, there has developed a convention that when the House of Lords meets as a Court of Law, only the nine Law Lords shall take part.

From the foregoing analysis it is clear that without the conventions the British constitution would have become paralysed. They may be taken as the life-blood of the British Constitutional system. Unlike America, where the conventions have only helped to regulate the relationship between the President and the Congress, in Great Britain the very evolution of the democratic system of government is based upon the conventions. The convention of the Recess appointment in the Senate's stubborn refusal to confirm appointments made by him. There is the convention of executive agreement with the help of which the American President can avoid a hostile senate and carry on his treaty negotiations with any foreign power or maintain the secrecy about negotiations and international understandings. The convention of Pocket Velo gives the President the power not bound to respect his messages for legislation and demands for financial support for the implementation of his policies. Thus there is remarkable difference between the British and the American conventions.

# 4

# The King and the Crown

There are many vital differences between the King and the Crown. The king as a person does not rule, but now the crown rules Great Britain. The powers of the king have been transferred to the crown in the course of several centuries. The transformation of the British political system from absolute Monarchy to parliamentary democracy with a constitutional limited Monarchy was possible through a slow and gradual process. Before the establishment of parliamentary supremacy in England the king had absolute power and he could do whatever he liked. He could disband the army and navy, begin a war, make a peace, conclude treaties, pardon the offenders and make all his subjects as peers. There was absolutely no legal restraint upon his powers. But during the course of time, the king's prerogatives have become the privileges of the people and are exercised by the cabinet in the name of the Crown. The king can do no wrong as he does not perform any act in his personal discretion. The Cabinet performs all legislative and executive functions and is the real ruler of the country. The king however, possesses important political rights such as (a) the right to be consulted, (b) the right to encourage and (c) the right to warn the cabinet.

The king is a person and the crown is an institution and in the office of the crown all the governmental powers have been institutionalised. The crown is now the supreme executive and policy-making body. It includes the king, cabinet and parliament. The king as an individual is subject to death and decay but the crown as an institution is permanent. The king is an individual, whereas the Crown refers to a collectivity consisting of the king, who is the formal head, the parliament, the Cabinet and the Civil Service. The Crown is an abstract idea implying government and on the other hand the king is a concrete embodiment of governmental powers. While distinguishing the king from the Crown, it may be said that the king as a human being may die, but the Crown as an institution shall survive permanently. Whatever may be the contingency, the powers, functions and prerogatives of the crown cannot be suspended even for a minute. The king may come and may go, but the crown goes on for ever. The Crown to-day embodies the powers of the government in its entirely and the king is just a part of it, exercising the power of the Crown only nominally on the advice of the Ministers. Ogg has rightly defined the Crown as, "The supreme executive and policy-framing agency which means practically a subtile combination of king, Ministers and to a degree Parliament".

After having discussed the differences between the King and the Crown it is worthwhile to point out that these distinctions are only conventional and they are not recognised by law. In the words of Gladstone, "there are many subtile distinctions in the vernacular of the British Government, but none more vital than the distinction between the King and the Crown".

Monarchy is a hereditary institution and before the passage of the Act of Settlement in 1701, the rule of primogeniture was followed. But the Act of Settlement of 1701, established the rules of succession to the British Crown and proclaimed the supremacy of the parliament over the king. Parliament has the right to fix the annual sum to be paid to the king from the national treasury, for the support of the Monarch and the members of the royal family and this sum is known as the Civil List.

In England, although till now everything is named after His Majesty, such as "His Majesty's Government' and 'His Majesty's loyal opposition', and so on, but there has been a metamorphosis in the nature of administration. This has been aptly described by Munro in the following words: "These expressions, however, are merely the survivals of ancient usage; they do not point to the exercise of any personal authority on His Majesty's part. The substance of power has departed, leaving only the shadows behind. Yet the persistence of this fiction of Royal supremacy is not without value. In the public imagination it has a unifying, dignifying and stabilizing influence. Englishmen agree that it exerts a psychological inflence in moderating the bitterness of partisan feeling. For, after all, it is His Majesty's government that is ruling the counntry, not a Conservative government, or a Liberal government or a Labour government. And it is 'His Majesty's loyal opposition' that sits on the other side of the House. It is allegiance to His Majesty that binds all British subjects together". The above discussion makes it evident that the term Crown in the British Constitution stands for government with all its three branches– legistative, executive and judicial.

## Powers of the Crown

It should be made amply clear that when we talk about the powers of the Crown, we actually refer to the powers of the government as an institution, which are formally attributed to the King but in reality are being enjoyed by the parliament, the Cabinet and the Civil Service. The powers of the Crown are gradually increasing with the progress of the time. England has become a welfare state and people need more and more services from the state. With this the responsibility of the state also increases and alongwith it there is an increase in the powers of the state. But even for a moment nobody should think that the increase in the powers of the Crown has anything to do with the powers of the King. The Crown is only symbolic of Kingship. At present the King is just a nominal head of the country and the executive is the Cabinet. Munro describes the Crown "as an artificial and juristic person". Begehot called it as "a convenient working hypothesis". According to Sydney Law the Crown is only a myth. Whatever may be the interpretation given to the term Crown, it is beyond any doubt that it has now come to represent the whole British government in its entirely. The important powers of the Crown are analysed as follows:

## Executive Powers

The Crown is the chief executive head of the state and all executive authority is invested in it and is exercised by its name. The Crown is responsible for the proper implementation of the laws passed by the parliament. The higher executive and administrative officers, with only few exceptions are appointed by the Crown and it enjoys the power to either suspend or dismiss these officials. The Crown exercised control and supervision over the entire personnel of civil administration. The army, navy and airforce are under the sole command of the Crown. The Crown has the power to declare war and conclude peace, without the approval of the parliament, but in practice this is not possible as to fight a war, funds are needed and for that purpose parliamentary sanction is a must. The Crown represents the nation in conducting relations with the foreign countries and is also responsible for the foreign relations of the state. British Ambassadors and High

Commissioners to other countries are appointed by the Crown and it also receives the Ambassadors of other countries accredited to England. According to Munro, "The Crown is also the treaty-making authority, and all international agreements are made in its name. Treaties can be drawn, ratified, and put into operation without parliamentary concurrence, provided, of course, that they do not stipulate for the cession of territory, or the payment of money, or for something else that requires parliamentary action to make them effective". The executive powers of the British Crown are even more extensive than the executive powers of the American President. The Prime Minister and the Cabinet, supported by a stable majority in the parliament can exercise powers, which the American President can never think of exercising. The British Prime Minister and his Cabinet, who constitute the real executive of the country in fact decide every thing such as, execution of laws, appointments to various offices, conducting foreign affairs and signing treaties, declaration of war, conclusion of peace and so on. The British King has nothing to do with the exercise of these powers in his individual capacity although these powers are said to be the powers of the Crown.

**Legislative Powers**

In England there is parliamentary system of government and the Crown's sphere of activity also extends to the legislative field. The Crown has the power to summon and prorogue the parliament and dissolve the House of Commons only, as the House of Lords is a parmanent chamber and cannot be dissolved. Inorder to become an Act a bill needs the consent of the Monarch, which has now become just a formality and has never been refused since the time of Queen Anne. The session of parliament opens with a speech from the Throne, which outlines the general policy and the legislative programmes of the Cabinet. This address is prepared by the Prime Minister and represents the views of the government. The King performs these functions not in his individual capacity, but on the advice of his Prime Minister and the Cabinet.

After the bills are passed by the parliament, they are presented to the King for his assent, as no bill can become law without his assent. King's assent has now become a formality and the King does not read the various measures passed by the parliament. He also does not assume any responsibility for extending his consent to a bill. The entire responsibility is that of his Council of Ministers. His veto power has become obsolete. It is evident from all this that the King lost real authority in the making of laws as in the exercise of executive powers. However, the King has a right to be consulted, the right to encourage and the right to warn the Cabinet and the Prime Minister always keeps the King informed of all the important measures that are decided to be laid before the parliament. On all such matters the King may express his opinion, which may or may not be accepted by the Cabinet. But this would depend on the ability and personality of the King and his relations with the Prime Minister.

It may be mentioned that due to the practice of delegated legislation, the legislative powers of the Crown are on the increase. The parliament is overburdened with work and the bills are passed in broad outlines and their details are to be filled under delegated legislation by the Crown through Orders-in-Council.

## Financial Powers

The Crown also plays a role in the formulation of the budget of the state. No item of demand can be included in the budget without the recommendation of the Crown. The parliament has got the power to cut the demand, but cannot increase it. The Chancellor of the Exchequer, presents the budget in the name of the Crown.

## Judicial Powers

The Crown is called the foundation of justice. The term was very much applicable to the powers of the King when absolute Monarchy was obtaining in England and the King could intervene to set aside the decisions of the Courts at his will. This is no more the case in the present times. The Crown, however, functions as the fountain of justice only in those cases which are brought before the Judicial Committee of the Privy Council. Judges are appointed by the Crown, but they cannot be dismissed by it, except on a resolution passed to that effect by both the Houses of the Parliament. The judges continue in office during good behaviour and the Crown has no control over them or their official actions. In the words of Munro, "the Crown cannot of itself establish any new Court, or change the jurisdiction or procedure of any existing Court, or alter the number of judges or the mode of their appointment or the tenure of their office".

## Fountain of Honour

The British Monarch is considered as the 'Fountain of Honour'. The King rightly deserved this expression in the olden times when he enjoyed absolute powers, when he had the right to create new peers and confer titles at his own discreation. Now the situation has entirely changed and the public honours and titles are conferred by the king on the advice of his Prime Minister or British subjects who excel in any walk of life or make a significant contribution in any field.

**Ecclesiastical Powers**

The Crown is the Head of the Church of England and as such it exercises ecclesiastical powers. In 1534, the Act of Supremacy was passed during the reign of Henry VIII, and the king of England became the Head of the Church of England and the authority of Pope was abolished. This was a revolutionary and unique step taken by England to assert its sovereign authority, due to a personal quarrel between the Pope and King Henry III. Since then the Monarch assumed the power of appointing all the Church officials like the archbishops, bishops etc. Now all these powers are exercised by the Crown. The Church of England Assembly (powers) Act was passed in 1919. According to this Act the National Assembly of the Church of England, which is not a statutory body, can pass measures concerning the Church of England and present them for the royal assent, subject to the condition that a resolution to that effect is passed by both the Houses of Parliament.

**Monarchy: An Assessment**

The foregoing analysis shows that the Crown exercises a vast range of powers, covering legislative, executive and judicial spheres and this constitutes a grave violation of Motesquieu's theory of Separation of Powers. If all these powers which are exercised by the Crown were to be really exercised by the King of England, then he would have become the most powerful dignitary of the world. But Monarchy now has become only a symbolical institution and the king has lost all his powers through the process of democratisation. Now all the decisions are taken by the Ministers and they are submitted to the Monarch for his consent, after they are approved by the parliament. The sanction accorded by the King is just formal and in all such matters, he is to be guided by his Ministers. From this, however, nobody should get the impression that the King is just a non entity, a golden cipher or a rubber stamp. The Kings powers have no doubt been reduced but he still wields great influence. The King holds a hereditary office for life and has the opportunity to witness the rise and fall and success and failure of many cabinets. This helps him to become a store-house of political wisdom. Apart from this, according to Bagehot the King enjoys the triple rights–the right to be informed, the right to encourage and the right to warn the Cabinet, which give his words great weight and influence. No Minister can take lightly any advice given by the Monarch, without sometimes inviting risk for himself and his Ministry.

Another factor which enhances the influence of the King is that his office inspires awe and reverence in the hearts of the British people. The people attach great respect and dignity to the office of the King. The support of the people increases the influence of the King. It is however, to be admitted that in England the extent of the King's influence is a matter of personal equation. If the King is popular and has a dominating personality and his Ministers are comparatively less popular and less prominent then the King's influence will be greater. But on the contrary, if the Prime Minister and the Members of the Cabinet are more popular and eminent in comparison to the King, then his influence will be less.

There is no doubt that Monarchy is an useful institution. Despite its democratisation and transfer of its powers into the hands of the Cabinet, Parliament and Civil Service, it fulfils a basic requirement of parliamentary government i.e., the requirement of a nominal figure-head. In addition to the fact that the British people have great love and respect for this institution, there is also the support of history behind it. There is no doubt that he does not exercise power or wield any authority but the extent of his influence cannot be undermind. The two factors which give weight to the influence of the King are his conservative office and his political neutrality. The King's advice has no political colour as he is above party politics and as such it is purely objective and national in spirit. Although Laski questions the aspect of political neutrality of the King and states that the King is more inclined towards the Conservative Party than the Labour Party, he admits to the authority of the King as being accepted by the common man in England. According to Barker, the political neutrality of the British King is a fact and not a fiction. The faith of the people in the political neutrality of the King makes them to look upon him as the custodian of the national interests. This is also a very strong factor in support of the survival of Monarchy in England. In view of these facts Lowell observes that, "If the Crown is no longer the motive power of the ship of the State, it is the spar upon which the sail is bent and as such it is not only useful but an essential part of the vessel also".

The institution of Monarchy is considered as an essential part of the British political system. In the past it served as an umbrella for British Imperialism and at present, it is looked upon as a golden link joining the member countries of the Commonwealth together. It is argued that if England adopts a republican form of government, with an elected President, the people in the Commonwealth countries might not have that much respect for him as they do have for the non-partisan Queen of royal blood and they may even demand chairmanship of the Commonwealth by rotation.

Monarchy has a deep foundation in the psychology of the British people. Kingship has continued in England through the ages, except for a period of eleven years during the regime of Cromwell, when a republic was established by him. The institution of Monarchy has become symbolic of political stability. It is aptly said that with the King in the Buckingham Palace people will sleep more quietly in their beds. Another factors in support of Monarchy is the conservative character of the British people. They have high esteem for their old institutions and practices and they would not like to change them merely for the sake of change. British people would not like to change an institution unless it is proved that it would be harmful for the country. Kingship is a prized institution and since the democratization of Monarchy the experience of the people with this institution has been particularly a happy one. They therefore, never think in terms of changing the institution.

The psychological bonds of the British people with the institution of Monarchy are further strengthened because the King is the Head of the British Society. He sets the social and moral norms which provide psychological sanctions for the acts of the people. Institutions which get the royal patronage of support, flourish because people give their whole-hearted support to such organisations.

In defence of Monarchy it may be said that Monarchy is not a very expensive institution and more or less the same amount has to be spent for maintaining an elected President. The Civil List is about one percent of the total revenue of England and even an elected President cannot be maintained with a sum less than that.

Many Kings have helped to improve the relations of England with foreign countries. George V had played an important role for the settlement of the Irish question. Friendly relations were established with France due to the efforts of Edward VII, at a time when England had no friend in Europe.

Thus there are several factors which strongly support the

continuation of the institution of Monarchy in England. In the past several proposals were forwarded for the abolition of the House of Lords, reduction of the powers of the House of Commons and also to reform the Cabinet; but none for the abolition of Monarchy from any important source. The retention of Monarchy is accepted even by the Labour Party. Some eight or nine decades ago, the Republican group demanded the abolition of Monarchy, but that constituted a negligible minority.

Munro has rightly stated that, "The British people have come to realize that the monarchy, seated above the turmoil of personal and partisan strife, neutral in politics and with no ambitions to gratify, lending dignity to government but not standing athwart the path of the public will–they have come to recognize that whatever may be the causes of their varied troubles, the monarch is not one of them. If the Crown, as has been well said, 'is no longer the motive power of the ship of the State, it is the spar upon which the sail is bent, and as such it is not only a useful but an essential part of the vessel".

# 5

# The British Cabinet

There is no statutory provision in support of either the creation of the cabinet or its multifarious powers and functions. The British constitution does not provide for a Cabinet and it is the product of historical growth, with powers and functions supported by conventions and long standing customs. With the democratisation of Monarchy, the Cabinet has become immensely powerful and is the real ruler of the country. But inspite of its great importance and indispensable nature, it has come into existence just by chance.

There is only one Act which makes a reference to the Cabinet. In 1937, parliament passed the Minister of the Crown Act, which provided a schedule of salaries for the members of the Cabinet and also provided a salary for the leader of the opposition in the House of Commons. However, this Act does not specify the powers and functions of the Cabinet, which exercises a vast range of powers and functions based on conventions and long-standing customs. It has been rightly said that, "the Cabinet is the most important single piece of mechanism in the whole structure of British government", and further, "while every act of the state is done in the name of the Crown, the real executive head of England is the Cabinet".

All the writers on the British political system have recognised the importance of the Cabinet as an indispensable institution for the working of the parliamentary government. In the words of Bagehot, the Cabinet is "the combining committee, a hyphen which joins, the buckle which fastens the legislative parts of the State with the executive part". According to Gladstone, the Cabinet "is perhaps the most curious formation in the political world of modern times, not for its dignity but for its subtlety, its elasticity and its many-sided diversity of powers". To Lowell, Cabinet is "the key-stone of the political arch", and to Ramsay Muir, it is "the steering wheel of the ship of the State". Sir

John Marriot gives a rather pictorial description, when he defines the Cabinet as "the pivot round which the whole political machinery revolves".

It is a paradox of history that such an important institution like the Cabinet has been the result of slow and gradual development through the course of history and was inspired more by chance than by deliberate planning of high design.

## Origin of the Cabinet

It would be worthwhile to make a brief survey of the origin and development of the cabinet through the course of time. The Curia Regis, was developed during the Norman times, as a small body of people to give advice to the King on matters of administration. The member of the Curia Regis were high officials of the royal household and were appointed by the King in his own discretion. The Curia Regis gave rise to the Privy Council, which became a powerful body during the Tudor and Stuart period. The Privy Council became a very powerful body and its members were responsible only to the King and none else. The parliament had no control over the Privy Council. Parliament, however, had the right to impeach a Privy Councillor, but the King had the power to pardon him and very often the King exercised this power to protect his Privy Councillors from the wrath of the parliament.

Gradually the Privy Council became a very huge body and the number of its committees was also increased. As a result of its unwieldy size, it was difficult for the King to consult the entire Privy Council for advice.This led to the practice of calling only some selected members of the Privy Council to give advice to the King. The Cabinet acquired a formal shape during the reign of Stuart King, Charles II. He appointed a group of advisers, who came to be known as 'Cabel'–a combination formed by taking the first letters from the names of five Ministers who were: Clifford, Arlington, Buckingham, Ashley and Lauderdale.

In course of time the principle of ministerial responsibility was established in the famous case of impeachment of Danby (1679). The Cabinet system took deeproots in the political soil of Great Britain, as in this case it was decided that the Ministers would be responsible for any act done by them in the name of the Crown and they could not take the cover of king's authority to protect themselves from impeachment by the parliament. The growth of Cabinet system was further accelerated by the development of party system in England.

However, even after the removal of Danby through impeachment, Charles II, James II and even Cromwell did not concede to the demand that the parliament had the right to choose the King's advisers and that they should be accountable to the parliament.

The Glorious Revolution of 1688, which marked the definite victory of the parliament over the King, made a significant contribution to the development of the Cabinet system of goverment in England. William and Mary who came to the throne of England after the Glorious Revolution of 1688, were grateful to the parliament for coming to this exalted office and they agreed to the demand made by it, that the King's advisers and Ministers should be responsible to the parliament. But they also appointed their Ministers in their own discretion without consulting the parliament.

The practice of choosing the members of the advisory committee from one political party also developed quite accidentally during the time of William III and became one of the fundamental principles of Cabinet government, namely, political homogenity. In the beginning King William III selected his Ministers from both the parties–Whighs and Tories. It was very soon realised by him that this practice was unworkable as the Ministers chosen from different political parties did not see eye to eye. The Ministry could not work with a spirit of cooperation and co-ordination. As the Whigh party was more akin to King William III, he then started selecting his Ministers only from the Whigh party in 1695 which incidentally had the majority in the parliament at that time. This led to the development of the convention that the leader of the majority party in the House of Commons would be selected as the Prime Minister and he would form the Council of Ministers from among the members of his party. The cabinet based on this principle was formed in 1697, which was popularly known as "Sunderland's Funto". This practice was also followed by Queen Anne.

The Hanoverian period which began in 1714, however, significantly contributed to the growth and development of the Cabinet system of government in England. King George I, who was a Hanoverian by birth, had no knowledge of English and did not take much interest in British politics and administration. He did not preside over the meetings of the Cabinet and allowed one of the senior Ministers, Sir Robert Walpole, to preside over the meetings of the Cabinet. Walpole is thus regarded as the first British Prime Minister in the modern sense. He held this office by virtue of being the leader of the majority party in the parliament. Walpole continued as Prime

Minister for a long period of twenty years both under George I and George II. Prior to the appointment of Walpole as Prime Minister, some Kings appointed their favourites as Chief Minister, but they were not party leaders. In the true sense Robert Walpole was the first Prime Minister of England. He made great contribution to the development of the Cabinet system of government in general and the office of the Prime Minister in particular.

In 1742, Robert Walpole lost the majority support in the parliament and resigned from office and there by established one of the most important features of parliamentary government that the government which loses majority support in the parliament or more specifically in the House of Commons has to resign, irrespective of the confidence of the Monarch. Walpole also started the practice that the Prime Minister has to appoint his team of Ministers and any Minister who does not enjoy his confidence cannot continue in the Council of Ministers. Due to his close personal relations with the Hanover Kings he communicated to them all the decisions of the Cabinet and helped the development of the parliamentary practice that the Prime Minister has to act as a link between the King and the Cabinet. By demanding that all the members of the Whigh party should support the Cabinet Robert Walpole contributed to the development of the principle of party solidarity and thus the Cabinet system and the party system were developing side by side.

It is interesting to note that most of the principles of Cabinet government had taken deep roots in the political soil of England by 1760, when George III came to the throne of England. Unlike his two predecessors, George III was ambitious and he wanted to revive the personal influence of the King, but did not succeed.

Many other important practices of Cabinet government were established during the course of the last two centuries. There was the development of the principle of collective responsibility of the Cabinet. According to this principle the Cabinet is treated as a single unit and all the members either sail or sink together. When the Prime Minister resigns, all the Members of the Cabinet also go out of office. Impeachment of one Minister pertaining to vital lapses may be virtually treated as a vote of noconfidence against the whole Cabinet. The members of the Cabinet are responsible to the King, to the parliament and also to one another. Responsibility to the King is only an euphemistic expression and as long as they enjoy majority support in the House of Commons, it would be presumed that they enjoy the confidence of the king.

## Privy Council and the Cabinet

In the British constitution there are so many terms like the Privy Council, the Ministry, the Cabinet and the government. Even till to-day all the acts of the Crown are declared to be "by and with the consent of the Privy Council". In theory the Cabinet is unknown to law and the Privy Council still controls all governmental action and the administration of the country. To avoid the legal flaw, a Cabinet member is automatically made a Privy Councillor and the decisions of the Cabinet become the decisions of the Privy Council. There are about 350 members in the Privy Council and its roots lay in the Curia Regis of Norman times. It is a historic institution which played the role of adviser to the King. The members of the Privy Council come from different categories such as present as well as past Ministers, eminent political leaders, distinguished scientists, literatures and artists, archbishops, retired judges and other persons who had held high administrative posts under the British Government. On the other hand the Cabinet may be considered as the child of the Privy Council as it originated from it and is a much smaller body consisting of 18 to 20 Ministers only. The Privy Council is a defunct body, but the Cabinet is the active and real political executive of the country. All the Cabinet Ministers are members of the Privy Council, but all the Privy Councillors are not members of the Cabinet. Only on solemn occassions like the coronation ceremony the Privy Council meets as a whole body and on all other occassions the Cabinet performs the works on its behalf. Thus the Privy Council merely plays a ceremonial and formal role in the British political system. The Cabinet, on the contrary, formulates policy and enforces it and runs the day-to-day administration of the country. It is the most vital and dynamic institution of the British parliamentary system of government.

## The Cabinet and the Council of Ministers

The Council of Ministers is a bigger body consisting of about sixty members. Besides the Cabinet Ministers, it also includes all Ministers and Parliamentary Secretaries. All the members of the Council of Ministers are members of either House of the Parliament and are responsible to it for their policies and actions. The Cabinet on the otherhand is a small body which consists of 18 to 20 Ministers who have important port folios like finance, defence and foreign affairs etc. Ministers who are included in the Cabinet are: The Prime Minister, who is the First Lord of the Treasury, the Chancellor of the Exchequer, the Minister of Defence, the Secretary of State for Foreign Office, the Secretary of State for Colonial Office, the Lord President of the Council, the Lord Privy Seal and so on. The Ministers of the Cabinet who have a higher rank than the other Ministers, meet in a collective capacity for the purposes of policy formulation and enforcement. All the other Ministers are in charge of certain departments. They are only concerned with the enforcement of policy and do not take part in policy formulation. However, both the categories of Ministers are appointed by the Prime Minister and they are chosen from among the members of the parliament. They continue in office till they enjoy the confidence of the parliament and work according to the principle of collective responsibility. When the Prime Minister resigns the whole Council of Ministers has to go out of office. Thus the Ministry is a bigger body and the Cabinet is a smaller body within the Ministry. The Members of the Cabinet are Members of the Ministry, but all members of the Ministry are not members of the Cabinet.

### The Formation of the Cabinet

The formation of the Cabinet still remain, as Disraeli put it, "The work of great time, great labour and great responsibility." After the elections to the parliament are over, the KKKing summons the leader of the majority party as the Prime Minister and asks him to form the Council of Ministers and the Cabinet. It is now a well established convention since 1923, that the Prime Minister must belong to the House of Commons and it is for this reason that Baldwin was preferred over Lord Curzon in 1923 and Churchill over Halifax in 1940. After his appointment, the Prime Minister then forms the Ministry from among the members of his own party from both the Houses of the parliament. A non-member may be appointed as a Minister, but he has to become the member of parliament either by getting himself elected to the House of Commons or by the grant of peerage which enables him to become a member of the House of Lords. Although theoretically the Prime Minister is free to choose anybody as a Minister, but he is not that free in the selection of the Cabinet. In the interest of party solidarity and unity he has to include important leaders of his party whether he likes them or not. For getting the support of the entire rank and file of the party the Prime Minister has to make certain compromises. According to law three Ministers have to be taken from the House of Lords, because it is a convention in England that Ministers can only address that House to which they belong as members. It is to be admitted, however, that a strong Prime Minister can exercise a good deal of his discretion in selecting his team of Ministers. It may be mentioned that although the King has to choose the Prime Minister and appoint the other Ministers with the consent of the Prime Minister, he has no personal choice in the matter, when a single party has got majority in the House of Commons. But the King may have a say when no party gains an absolute majority or when the Prime Minister is removed from office by death or resignation. The King may also play an important role when a National Government is formed.

## Powers and Functions of the British Cabinet

The British Cabinet constitutes the real authority in the state and exercised the authority vested in the Crown, both in the executive and the legislative spheres. The King is just a constitutional head and all his powers are in fact exercised by the Cabinet in the name of the Crown, with the approval of the parliament. As the king can do no wrong, he has also no right to authorise any wrong-doing and the Ministers are responsible to the parliament for all acts of omission and commission. It is one of the important principles of British parliamentary system that the King can only act on the advice of his Ministers. Thus in the course of history there has been the democratisation of Monarchy and this process has added to the powers and importance of the Cabinet. The Cabinet has monopolised not only initiative but also taking final decisions in legislative, executive, financial and many other spheres. The Cabinet brings a synthesis between the political soverign, i.e., the parliament and the legal soverign i.e., the king. It is also the Committee of the House of Commons and as such represents and embodies its mandates in its activities, while exercising all state powers in the name of the Crown. In terms of strict theory it is the parliament which has the power to control and supervise the activities of the Cabinet, but in practice it is the Cabinet which control over it owing to its never failing majority in the House of Commons. There is thus no doubt that the Cabinet is the most powerful organ of government in Great Britain.

The important powers and functions of the British Cabinet are analysed under the following heads:

## The Executive Powers

The Cabinet plays a key role in the excutive sphere, as it is primarily an executive organ of the country. The Cabinet in its collective capacity formulates the policy of internal administration. Each Minister individual is in charge of one or more departments of the government and is responsible to guide and supervise the administration. All important appointments to the departments are also controlled by the Cabinet Ministers. Co-ordination of the activities of the various departments is also done by the Cabinet. It is the duty of the Cabinet to ironout differences and disputes among the various departments. The Cabinet formulates the foreign policy of the country and plays an important role in this sphere. On behalf of the Cabinet, the Secretary for Foreign Affairs negotiates all treaties and agreements with the foreign countries. Although the policies following by the Cabinet in respect of internal and foreign affairs are subject to review and approval of the parliament, the cabinet is able to follow its own course and get policies approved because of its ever dependable majority maintained under strict party discipline. The party always extends its unfailing support to the Cabinet and maintains it in power.

### The Legislative Powers

In addition to its executive powers, the cabinet also exercises vast array of legislative powers.The parliament is being summoned and prorogued by the King on the advice of the Cabinet. Even after a vote of noconfidence is passed against his government, if the Prime Minister feels that he enjoys the confidence of the nation, he may advice the King to dissolve the House of Commons and order for fresh elections. However, the Prime Minister can exercise this power only once. The speech which the King delivers, at the beginning of each session of parliament, is prepared by the Cabinet and in this speech the policies of the government are out-lined. Most of the bills which are initiated, steered, explained, defended and ultimately passed in the parliament are government bills, prepared by the Cabinet. As such most of the time of legislative business is consumed by government bills. Private bills or Private Members' bills have no chance of passage in the parliament, if they are not supported by the Cabinet.

### The Financial Powers

The budget is prepared by the Chancellor of the Exchequer, who is an important member of the Cabinet. The various departments of the government sumbit their estimates and on that basis, the Cabinet decides the outlines of the budget. The budget is presented before the

House of Commons by the Chancellor of the Exchequer. The House can only move a cut, but cannot add anything to the budget. But this is also not possible as the Cabinet as a matter of principle insists that the budget should be passed as it was presented without any addition or alteration, because the passing of a cut motion would tantamount to lack of confidence in the Cabinet.

### The Judicial Powers

The judges of the important courts are appointed by the King on the advice of the Lord Chancellor, who is an important member of the Cabinet. The King's powers of granting pardon and reprieve are exercised on the advice of the Secretary of State for Home Affairs. However, some writers are of the opinion that the King's power of exercising prerogative and mercy is not subject to discussion in the Cabinet.

The foregoing survey is evident that the Cabinet exercises vast range of powers which are executive, legislative, financial and judicial in nature. This concentration of powers in the hands of the Cabinet amounts to the violation of Montesquieu's theory of separation of powers which strangely enough was inspired by the British political system. Due to this vast range of powers of the Cabinet and the concentration of authority Lord Hewart described it as a 'new despot'.

### Control of House of Commons over the Cabinet

There are different views regarding the relationship between the Cabinet and the House of Commons. According to strict theory of parliamentary government, the Cabinet is a committee of the parliament, taken out of it and accountable to it. The House of Commons is the master and the Cabinet is its servant. Even though, the cabinet is elected for a period of five years, it can be driven out of office by a vote of no-confidence for its acts of omission and commission. It is answerable to the House of Commons for all its actions and the House exercises this power by asking questions, supplementary questions and moving censure or cut motions. This is known as the juristic view-point and is advocated by Dicey. Thus legally speaking the Cabinet is a subservient body and its very existence depends on the will of the parliament or more specifically the House of Commons.

But what is true in theory is not true in practice. In reality the tables have been turned and it seems that now the Cabinet has become the master and the House of Commons has become its servant. In reality the Cabinet is supreme and it dominates all spheres of governmental activity. Due to its ever loyal majority support it can get any bill passed and the parliament has been reduced to the position of a weak and ineffective critic. It is rightly said that the bills are passed in the parliament but not by the parliament. Due to majority support behind the Cabinet, it is also not possible on the part of the parliament to drive out the Cabinet, irrespective of its performance. Now the parliament has been relegated to the background and the Cabinet has acquired supreme powers. The Prime Minister's power to advice the King for the dissolution of the House of Commons has silenced the House as members do not want to be deprived of their privileges and to be thrown into political uncertainty. Thus from the stand-point of practical politics the Cabinet dominates all activities and the House of Commons only registers its will. Due to the practice of delegated legislation, in addition to its executive, legislative and financial powers, the Cabinet has also assumed some judicial powers. Both Harold Laski and Ramsay Muir are critical of these almost arbitrary powers of the Cabinet in Great Britain. They have expressed the view that the Cabinet is supreme and the House of Commons is just a dittoing body. They are, however, not unanimous on the extent and impact of Cabinet supremacy. Ramsay Muir is of the opinion that the concentration of legislative, executive, financial and judicial powers in the hands of the Cabinet has led to Cabinet dictatorship. Further, this Cabinet dictatorship leads to the dictatorship of the civil servants, who work under the protection of the Ministers. Consequently there is a steep deterioration and degeneration in the democratic processes. On the otherhand, Laski is of the opinion that concentration of power has led to Cabinet supremacy but this cannot be called as dictatorship of the Cabinet. According to him in the interest of the smooth functioning of the parliamentary government, the House of Commons should be controlled by the Cabinet, otherwise there will be uncertainty, instability and political chaos in the country. However, Lord Hewart was in agreement with Ramsay Muir when he branded the Cabinet as a 'new despot'.

## Factors Responsible for Cabinet Supremacy

There are several factors which are responsible for enhancing the powers of the Cabinet so as to make it a dictator. This has been made possible due to the cumulative effect of a number of factors which may be analysed as follows:

### *(i) The Amateur Character of House of Commons*

With the progress of time, governmental problems are becoming more and more complex and it is not possible on the part of the members of the House of Commons, who are just laymen, either to understand or deliberate upon them. The Ministers make the confusion worst confounded by flooding the House with vast statistics and technical data, which they are able to set with the help of the civil servants. This utter helplessness and ignorance of the Members of the House of Commons lead to supremacy of the Cabinet.

### *(ii) Pressure of Work and Delegated Legislation*

England has now become a welfare state from a laissez faire state and the pressure of work of the House of Commons has tremendously increased. Even during the days of Queen Victoria, Bagehot, complained that the House of Commons was over-worked. In view of this pressure, the House is not in a position to take legislative business seriously and it goes on skipping over. Thus the Cabinet assumes the power to do things in its own way. Another development of this pressure of work is that, the House delegates legislative authority to the Cabinet. Taking advantage of this power the Cabinet frames such rules and regulations which would help it to aggrandise its own powers even in the judicial sphere. This kind of Cabinet intrusion into the judicial field, under the cover of delegated legislation is considered as arbitrary and despotic by Lord Hewart.

### *(iii) The Bi-Party System*

Due to the existence of bi-party system in England, after the election, one of the parties is able to get absolute majority in the House of Commons. This absolute majority of the ruling party in the House of Commons is the most important cause of Cabinet supremacy. Absolute majority support behind the Cabinet makes it arbitrary and despotic and it can behave as it pleases. It can initiate any bill in the parliament and can get it passed. It can make the House of Commons dance to its tune and can function without much regard for the wishes of the House.

### *(iv) Rigid party Discipline*

There is rigid party discipline in England and the members are bound by the whip issued by the party on each issue before the parliament, irrespective of their personal likes or dislikes. As deserters from party are not easily accepted by the other parties, a member who is ousted from one party on the grounds of violation of party discipline may have to ruin his political future. Due to this once a party gets majority, it can be sure of having the party support at its back and call. This makes the Cabinet go in its own way.

### *(v) The Desire to Remain in Power*

Once a party forms a government, the importance of that party increases. Some of the members get Ministerial berth and have direct access to power and other members also occupy privileges due to their proximity to the corridors of power. They can get things done more quickly than members of other political parties. It is due to this reason despite many discussions and difference of opinion among them, they are interested in the continuance of the government in office. They support the Cabinet on all questions–right or wrong.

### *(vi) The Impact of National Emergencies*

The Cabinet in England, today, outshines the House of Commons. In the course of history national emergencies have been responsible for increasing the powers of the Cabinet. During the First World War (1914-18) vast powers were given to the Cabinet to meet the challenges of the War. The Cabinet's authority and prestige were enhanced and even after the War was over the Cabinet exercised most of these extraordinary powers to deal with industrial depression and labour unrest etc. that followed in the wake of the War. The National Government of England in 1931-35 was also endowed with almost dictatorial powers to meet the internal crisis. Parliament delegated huge powers to the Cabinet, again during the Second World War (1939-45). The Cabinet retained most of these powers even after the War was over. There is no wonder, therefore, that it has emerged in the 20th century, as one of the most powerful organs of government in the whole world.

### *(vii) Collective Responsibility*

The collective responsibility of the Cabinet gives it added strength and support. The members of the Cabinet either sail or sink together. If one Minister is successfully impeached in the House of Commons, then it will tantamount to a vote of noconfidence against the entire cabinet. Thus on all issues, the Ministers give a united fight and in this fight they are supported by the rank and file of the party. As such the principle of collective responsibility forms a solid bed-rock for Cabinet dictatorship. The Cabinet can give the threat of collective resignation to silence a dissentient House of Commons.

### *(viii) Leadership of the Prime Minister*

The Prime Minister is at one and the same time the Head of the Government as well as the leader of the House of Commons. As the leader of the House of Commons, he can use his position to enhance the supremacy of the Cabinet. He also works as a cohesive force to maintain the unity of his party. By issuing directives through the party whip the Prime Minister procures the unanimity among his party members on important governmental issues.

### *(ix) Prime Minister's Power of Dissolution*

The House of Commons has the theoretical or legal right to drive out the Cabinet by passing a vote of noconfidence against it. But it is difficult to translate this into action as long as the Cabinet is supported by majority in the House of Commons. On the otherhand, the conventional right of the Prime Minister to advice the King to dissolve a too much harrassing and refractory House, is a real power. Elected Members of the parliament both belonging to the party in power and the opposition do not want to face fresh election, as it is a big gamble in so far as it costs money and its result is uncertain. So in their own enlightened self-interest Members of the House of Commons extend their support to the government and do not want unnecessarily to thwart the government in its actions. Thus the eagerness on the part of the Members of the House of Commons to cling to their seats and avoid the uncertainty of costly elections, contribute to the supremacy of the Cabinet.

## Desirability of Cabinet Supremacy

Cabinet supremacy has become a controversial issue and in it some writers visualize a great danger to the democratic system of Great Britain. No doubt in England supremacy of the Cabinet has posed a great problem, but it would not be proper to say that it has led to 'dictatorship of the Cabinet'. The Cabinet is a temporary body elected for a definite period of time, after which it has to go to polls to seak the mandate of the people. The people will throw it out if it crossed its bounds during the period when it was in office. Thus the fear of the coming defeat keeps the Cabinet on its bearings and it cannot behave like a dictator. In the words of Laski, "responsible government lives in England under the shadow of coming defeat".

Ramsay Muir is of the opinion that Cabinet supremacy makes it play into the hands of the civil service. These bureaucrats act arbitrarily and go scot free as the Ministers serve as a buffer for the irresponsible works of their civil servants. In the words of Ramsay Muir, "Bureaucracy thrives under the cover of ministerial responsibility". There is no doubt an element of truth in the allegation of Ramsay Muir, but it is sure that no Minister would blindly follow the advice of the civil servant, if it is detrimental to the public interest, because ultimately he has to defend it before the parliament and face its consequences. Muir also takes exception to the exercise of certain powers by the Cabinet which ought to have been exercised by the parliament. In this regard it is not the Cabinet which is to be blamed, but the parliament which has itself delegated these powers to the Cabinet. In the absence of the Cabinet's control over the parliament, legislation would become 'atomistic' with members competing with each other to meet the requirements of only their constituencies. When decisions are taken by the House of Commons instead of the Cabinet, they would be guided not by the expert advice of the civil servants but by the lay wisdom of the Members of the House. Another point that is to be noted is the unwidely size of the House of Commons which makes it unfit to take serious decisions or determine policy. Due to its vast strength it is also not in a position to shoulder responsibility which is likely to be divided, shelved and lost. If this situation takes place then it will appear to be 'an appeal from knowledge to ignorance and from responsibility to irresponsibility'. Laski, therefore, observed that, "The secret of the success of Parliamentary government lies in the control of the House of Commons by the Cabinet".

## The Office of the Prime Minister

The office of the Prime Minister of Great Britain is very important. He performs multifarious duties. He is the leader of the nation; he is the leader of the House of Commons; he presides over the Cabinet meetings and is its chairman; he is the link between the King and the Cabinet; he is the indirect nominee of the electorate and also he is the first adviser of the Crown. The King selects the leader of the majority party in the House of Commons as the Prime Minister and on his advice he appoints the other Ministers. The Prime Minister exercises a general control over the work of his Cabinet colleagues. The Prime Minister is their leader and not their boss. The Ministers perform their duties, under the direction of the Prime Minister and in case of a difference of opinion among them, the Prime Minister acts as an umpire.

The Prime Minister selects his Cabinet colleagues and sumbits their names to the King for his formal approval. He consults the King before entering into new discussions in the Cabinet. It is his duty to keep the Crown informed about all the happening and to convey the decisions of the Cabinet on various matters. He is the chief exponent of cabinet policies and as such he is considered as "the Key Stone of the Cabinet arch", by Lord Morley. In the Cabinet, the Prime Minister is the central figure and the Ministry remains in office so long as the Prime Minister enjoys the confidence of the House of Commons. The Prime Minister can also resign on his own and can bring dissolution for the Ministry. The Cabinet continues in office with him and falls along with him. He has the power to shuffle and reshuffle his pack of cards–the Council of Ministers. He is the keyman as he is the person who is central to the life and death of the Cabinet. The whole cabinet may decide to continue but if the Prime Minister resigns, the government is dissolved. Similarly the whole Cabinet may resign, but if the Prime Minister decides to continue in office then the government will be deemed to be in office.

No Minister can continue in office, if he does not pull on well with the Prime Minister. It is rightly said that a Minister keeps a letter of resignation in his pocket because in case of disagreement with the Prime Minister, he has to resign. But in the context of democratic politics and party government obtaining in England, the Prime Minister cannot ride roughshod over his Cabinet colleagues as he has to carry the entire party with him. It will be difficult for him to carry on the administration smoothly if he does not keep rapport with his Cabinet colleagues. He has to be loyal both to the King and his Cabinet. But despite all these, he is the real ruler of the country and enjoys enormous powers. Ministers do the routine work of the departments on their own responsibility, but consult the Prime Minister when they are confronted with some problems. They consult and confer with the Prime Minister on all important matters. The Cabinet as a whole never meets to discuss routine matters. The Prime Minister is the sole adviser to the King and can advise the Crown even if the majority of his cabinet colleagues are not in favour of such a measure. But it is expected that a Prime Minister who is interested to maintain the solidarity of his party will not usually take recourse to such a step.

According to some writers the Prime Minister is just 'Primus Interpares' or first among his equals. But in the opinion of Ramsay Muir, far from being the first among the equals, the Prime Minister is the boss of the Cabinet Ministers and enjoys such vast powers that he may be called a dictator. However, in the estimation of Laski, although the Prime Minister is more than 'Primus Interpares', he is certainly not a dictator. The British parliamentary system will not permit any Prime Minster to become a dictator. He is some times forced to take in his Cabinet even those persons whom he might not be liking at all. But a Prime Minister with a dominating personality can certainly act in his discretion in appointing his Cabinet colleagues and in distributing the portfolios among them.

The Prime Minister summons, prorogues and presides over the meetings of the Cabinet and plays an important role in the day-to-day administration of the country. The general policy in respect of the various departments of the government is formulated by the Prime Minister and the Ministers are required to work out the details in confirmity with the directives issued by him. He co-ordinates the work of his colleagues and exercises general supervision over their work. In all matters affecting the general policy and the efficiency of administration in the country, his decision shall be final.

The Prime Minister takes keen interest in formulating the foreign policy of the country. Even when he does not hold the portfolio of foreign affairs, he actively participates in shaping the foreign policy and controlling the relations of England with foreign countries. Ambassadors accredited to England by foreign countries are received by him and British Ambassadors and High Commissioners are appointed on his recommendation. Exchange of public messages with Heads of other states is done by him. During the time of war, the Prime Minister's power to deal with foreign countries is further increased. At the time of the Second World War, Churchill became the 'War-Lord' and assumed almost dictatorial powers. International treaties and agreements are negotiated and completed by the Prime Minister. In International Conferences, the Prime Minister, represents his country. Lord Beaconsfield attended the Berlin conference, Llyoyd George took part in the Paris Peace Conference and Chamberlain participated in the Munich Conference. In international parleys and negotiations, the Prime Minister may make secret commitments.

The Prime Minister's power as head of the foreign office is in consonance with his supreme status which also makes him the ex-officio chairman of the Committee of Defence, Imperial and Commonwealth Committees etc.

The Prime Minister also has got the power to control the purse strings through the Chancellor of the Exchequer. It is interesting to note that the office of the Prime Minister found its first mention in the preamble to the Treaty of Berlin in 1878, when Beaconsfield was referred to as "First Lord of Her Majesty's Treasury and Prime Minister of England". The Prime Minister now plays a key role in determining the shape of the budget.

As the constitutional position stands today, the Prime Minister is the sole advisor to the Crown. He is the only channel of communication between the King and the Cabinet. The distribution of honours and distinctions by the Crown are made on the basis of his recommendations. All high appointments like the Ambassadors, High Commissioners, Governor-General of Dominions and appointment to higher ecclesiastical offices are made on the advice of the Prime Minister. The King is advised by him in the exercise of his powers in general and the dissolution of the House of Commons in particular to ascertain the will of the electorate on certain issues.

The Prime Minister also plays an important role as the leader of the House of Commons. While Ministers can speak about their respective departments, the Prime Minister can intervene to speak on any issue concerning any department or the general policies pursued by the government. His words are taken to be final on every issue in parliament. He alone is competent to make public statements on government policy and other important national and international issues. He keeps all informations about all government bills in the parliament. Thus the Prime Minister is the most leading figure of the Cabinet, the leader of the House of Commons and the undisputed leader of the nation. He is not only, as Laski described "central, both to the life and death of the Cabinet", but also central to the entire system of administration. It is due to this ever increasing dimension of the powers of the Prime Minister, which has eclipsed the other institutions like the Cabinet and the parliament, there is a reference to the development of Prime Ministerial system of government in England. It is believed that the Prime Minister has assumed almost dictatorial powers.

A careful scrutiny of the powers of the British Prime Minister bears out the statement of Ramsay Muir. "The Cabinet is the steering wheel of the ship of the state and the Prime Minister is the steer-man". The British system of parliamentary government makes allowance for the development of the office of the Prime Minister with concentration of powers and exercise of discretion. The Prime Minister is certainly all in all and more than 'Primus Interpares', but he is not a dictator.

The British Prime Minister with a stable majority in the parliament can exercise powers which no head of state in any country of the world can dream of. But this does not mean that he is a dictator. He cannot ride roughshod over his Cabinet colleagues, as they all have great following in the party and if they are all united, they can dislodge him from office. He is their leader, but not their boss. The Prime Minister also cannot afford to ignore the sentiments of the members of the House of Commons. If he shows disrespect to the House or is indifferent towards public opinion, he along with his party will be thrown out of office in the coming election. Hence, the British Prime Minister cannot afford to be a dictator or behave in an irresponsible manner.

# 6

# The Civil Service

With the proliferation of governmental activities due to the transformation of England from a laissez faire state into a welfare state, the role of the Civil Service has increased to a very great extent. The Civil Servants are required to perform different kinds of work at present, which in the past was considered out of the purview of governmental activities. The Civil Servants are recruited through competitive examinations conducted by Public Service Commissions and have a permanent tenure. The Civil Servants represent merit, stability and continuity. As he has a permanent tenure, a civil servant in course of time acquires experience and wisdom and becomes an expert. It is the function of the legislature to provide guidance for the formulation of policy and that of the Cabinet to determine those policies. Once these policies are formulated it is the duty of the Civil Servants to implement the policies without any personal predilections. In a parliamentary system of democracy, where different political parties are likely to form governments at various times, the civil servants should be politically neutral and should carry out their duty, without any partisan spirit.

## Relation between the Ministers and Civil Servants

In the British parliamentary system the Civil Servants are required to work under their political masters, who come and go like seasonal flowers. They are lay men having no claim to any kind of expertise. Their portfolios are very frequently changed. Thus the Ministers are amateurs and although they may have the breadth of vision, they do not have the intensity of gaze. The Ministers represent the democratic element in the administration and are required to translate the wishes of the poeple into action. They are politicians and their tenure of office depends on the mandate of the people and the confidence of the electorate and the parliament. It is due to their amateur character they depend on the Civil Servants for advice and are very often guided by such advice. This amateur-expert reactionship between the Minister and the Civil Servant is one of the moot points of parliamentary system of government or for that matter any form of democratic government.

The Civil Servants should not be politically committed to any party in power. A committed bureaucracy is dangerous for the proper functioning of the parliamentary system of government. It is antithetical to the very concept of parliamentary government which presupposes change of party government from time to time. But unfortunately there is an alarming tendency on the part of the party government to get the bureaucracy more and more politically committed by distributing powers and privileges among the civil servants on the basis of their loyalty and political commitment. This has resulted in the reintroduction of the much criticised spoils system, through the back door. Due to this practice some unscrupulous civil servants view with each other to be closer to the party in power.

In the interest of democracy the civil servants must be politically noncommitted. They should not identify themselves with their political masters. They should have the freedom to point out the genuine defects in the policies and the nature of their implementation, made by the Ministers without any consideration of fear or favour. However, since the ultimate responsibility in a parliamentary system, is that of the Ministers, who head the departments, if the Ministers insist even after being made aware of the lapses, the Civil Servants have to carry out the orders.

It is also to be noted that the Ministers change very frequently and most of them do not possess the qualification essential for understanding the highly technical matters pertaining to general administration and other complicated matters, needing specialised knowledge. This has led to the total dependence of the Ministers on the civil servants and it is observed that some of them "sign on the dotted lines", without understanding anything about the file.

The government depends totally on the civil servants for the implementation of policies and enforcing the laws passed by the legislature. The civil servants communicate to the government the defects in a particular legislation and the reaction of the people to it. Their recommendations inspire amendments to the existing laws and initiation of new laws for meeting the requirements of new situations.On the basis of the data and statistics provided by the civil servants, the

Ministers formulate the policy of the government. The Ministers are only confined to the issuing of broad directions and general supervision of administration, but actual execution of the work is done by the civil servants.

The power of the civil servants to make rules and regulations under delegated legislation has also been responsible for the enhancement of their influence and importance. They work behind the screen and the ultimate responsibility is that of the Ministers. The Ministers may either get lavels or be dismissed for defending a policy formulated by a civil servant on his behalf. Thus it is rightly said that 'bureaucracy thrives under the clock of ministerial responsibility'.

The smooth working of parliamentary institutions requires co-operation and understanding between the Ministers, who are the political heads of the various departments and the permanent civil servants. The Ministers are responsible to the parliament for all their works and policies. They are also public men whose political career depends on the support of the people. In their eagerness to promote public good, they may like to introduce far reaching changes, breaking the old conventions, precedents and the usual red-tapism. But the civil servants are, by training and temperament, conservative and have a tendency to stick to tradition and precedents. This may give rise to serious conflict between the political head and his civil servants who are deeply entrenched in the department. Due to the increased importance of the Civil Service in Great Britain, Ramsay Muir has rightly observed that, "Bureaucracy has become a far more potent and vital element in the British system of government than the text books realise. It has become indeed the effective operative part of the British system".

## The Role of Ministers as Amateurs

Critics of the British constitution focus on the issue of the amateur character of the Ministers in Great Britain and their consequent weakeness in relation to the civil sevants, who are in the position of experts. Referring to the growing importance of the civil servants Laski is of the opinion that the Parliament is a tool in the hands of the Minister, and the Minister is a tool in the hands of the permanent officials. The amateur character of the Ministers is an accepted fact. A Minister is given a portfolio according to his political influence and following in the party and no importance is given to his specialised knowledge. Sidney Low has observed, "The youth must pass an examination in Arithmetic before he can hold a second class clerkship in the Treasury; but a Chancellor of the Exchequer may be a middle aged man of the world, who has forgotten what little he ever learnt about figures at Eton or Oxford and is innocently anxious to know the meaning of 'those little dots' when first confranted with treasury accounts worked out in decimals". Winston Churchill, who was a politician and soldier was appointed as Chancellor of the Exchequer in 1924. Robert Lowe wrote his brother, "I am Chancellor of the Exchequer with everything to learn". Such appointments are bound to make them amateurs. Munro has rightly observed that, "The British War Office has been headed at times by a philosopher or a Journalist, an Admirality by a merchant or a Barrister and the Board of Trade by a University Professor". It is interesting to note that the Ministers have also accepted their position as amateurs and think that this amateur-expert combination is desirable for better administration which is responsive to democratic public opinion. Bagehot has said that a Minister's business is "not to work his department, but to get it worked".

As the representatives of the people, the Ministers should keep close contact with the people. This role can probably be played better by the amateur Ministers. Their work is primarily to democratise the action of the government and administration so that the interest of the people is protected and promoted. The Ministers are chosen from among the people and neither it is desirable nor possible to expect that they would be of extraordinary character. In the words of Laski, "A Cabinet of extraordinary men is always liable to the danger that, just because members are extraordinary, they fail to think as the man in the street thinks. They lose, as it were, the common touch". Experts are likely to prefer seclusion and avoid meeting people, for whose frailities they express contempt. They indulge in armchair theorising and do not have direct knowledge about the problems of the people. The amateur Ministers due to their close contact with the people and sympathy for their needs and aspirations, would provide both democratic and pragmatic touch to the administration. In the words of Ogg, "The Ministers must serve as the intermediary between the department and the House of Commons, keeping the one in touch with public opinion and the other informed of administrative needs and problem". The Ministers play a valuable role as mateurs, which they may not play so well if they were experts. Instead of the broad outlook, they would have developed a 'frog in the pond' attitude, which is a common characteristic of most of the experts. Sir William Harcourt was of the opinion that the Minister who knew the likes and dislikes of the people was duty bound to "tell the civil servants what the public won't stand". This would act as a check against the arbitrary authority of the civil servants. The role of Ministers as amateurs and civil servants as experts could be summed up in the following words of Munro: "The former provides the democratic element in administration; the latter the bureaucratic. Both are essential–one of them to make the government popular, the other to make it efficient. And the best of a good government is its successful combination of democracy and efficiency".

The amateur Ministers serve many useful purposes in the British parliamentary system. As amateurs, they do not suffer from narrow departmentalism as they are free from the superiority complex of the experts, who look down other departments. The amateur Minister instead of thinking only in terms of his subject or department like an expert, thinks about administration as a whole. This attitude helps in avoiding inter-departmental conflicts and promotes co-ordination which is very vital in administration. The spirit of mutual give and take is being fostered between the various departments of the government.

The Minister is a very busy person and he has to attend to several works of varying and complicated nature and has little time to devote to study the files and the problems confronting the department. As departmental head, he has to look to the work of the department. He is a member of the Cabinet and has to attend several meetings. He has to actively participate in the legislative procedings of the parliament. As a party leader he has to take part in party activities and he should maintain close link with the people as a public leader. All these multifarious functions and engagements compel the Minister to depend on his Civil Servants more and more.

The Ministers are taken for maintaining their political popularity so as to ensure a bright for themselves and their party and therefore, they are not prepared to take any risk. Due to this they prefer to follow the matured advice of the civil servants, based on experience. Moreover, the problems with which the Ministers are confronted do not originate only during their own regime. Most of them are problems with past history, which might have originated during the time of their predecessors. The civil servants alone can give a proper picture of the problem by presenting its past history and the earlier step taken for its solution. This enables the civil servants to influence the Ministers, by enlightening him about the pros and cons of the steps taken in the past and the desirability of the step to be taken at the present monent. The knowledge and experience of the civil servant adequately compensate the ignorance of the amateur Minister.

**Discretion of the Ministers**

Despite all the importance and influence of the civil service, it will be too much to assume that the Ministers have become mere tools in the hands of the civil servants and that they have lost their independence and discretion. The art of government is not that technical and complicated, which a Minister cannot understand at all. The generalist Ministers with their strong common sense can certainly analyse the good and bad points of the advice tendered by the civil servant. They reject the advice which they think would not be in the general interest of the people, because it is they who have to take the ultimate responsibility for any act of omission or commission on their part, although the advice might have been given by somebody else. It is the duty of the Minister to democratise the government and the administration and promote and protect the interest of the people. He shall have to apply his discretion in accepting or rejecting the advice given to him by the civil servants, keeping the general interest of the people as his main objective.

It is also not proper to assume that the Ministers are absolutely amateurs. They have a long period of apprenticeship in the House of Commons as active members either on the side of the opposition or the party in power and have come into the limelight before becoming Ministers. Thus they know the problems of the country very well and have thought about their pros and cons and the possible solutions. It is not easy on the part of the civil-servants to hoodwink them on such issues of national importance.

The Ministers belong to a political party and have to follow a party line with regard to the important problems confronting the country and as such they cannot blindly accept the advice given by the civil servants. Another important fact of which we have to take notice is the accountability of the Ministers to the Parliament. If they fail to properly control and supervise the work of the civil servants and are blindly guided by them, then there will be bitter criticism in the parliament and more specifically in the House of Commons.

Although very often the civil servants are men of far greater ability than the Ministers, it is also true that Ministers like Llyod George, Churchill, Morrison, Sir Kings Leywood, Atlce Handerson and the like, have dominated the civil servants by their vast knowledge of administration and towering personality. Earl Altbee has rightly observed that, "It is the business of the ministers to bring in the common touch". The democratic character of the government and the direct accountability of the Ministers to the Parliament and through it to the people takes away to a great extent, the evil impacts of bureaucracy. It will also be proper to say that the civil service in England like any other institution is imbued with the national spirit and knowingly it would not give any advice detrimental to the interest of the country.

## Organization of the Civil Service

In Great Britain, the civil servants were appointed by nomination in the first half of the 19th century. As this system of recruitment was not satisfactory, there was a demand for recruiting the civil servants through competitive examinations, in the manner it was done by the East India Company for India. This resulted in the end of the spoils system which was in practice in England and gradually the merit system was introduced. Competitive examinations were held to recruit civil servants for different branches of government service as per the decision made in 1854. A Civil Service Commission consisting of three Members was appointed in 1855, by an Order-in-Council, to conduct the examinations.

In the beginning the rules of selection through competitive examinations were not satisfactory. In 1870, Gladstone made open competitive examinations compulsory for all categories of posts and the powers of the Civil Service Commission were increased to a very large extent. Thus slowly but steadily the path was prepared for the introduction of fair and open competition based on merit alone.

It is needless to say that at present all the civil servants belonging to different branches are selected under Civil Service Rules. But this rule is not applicable to the appointment of some permanent Under Secretaries, the Assistant Secretaries, Chiefs of Bureaus, etc., whose work is of a specialised or confidential nature. These posts are generally filled up promotion from lower posts on the basis of the experience and competence of the incumbents.

There are three Members in the Civil Service Commission, who are appointed by the Crown. There are different grades in the Civil Service and for each grade separate examination is held. As regards the appointment of all the civil servants of the higher rank, it is the Secretary of the Treasury, who advises the Prime Minister. However, his advice is not always binding and the Prime Minister is free to apply his own discretion. But the Treasury has got the power to issue general regulations, orders-in-council and other instructions and exercises an over all control on the civil service.

The civil service in Great Britain can be divided into the following four categories:

### (i) The Adininistrative Category

The administrative class occupies the top most position and is divided into Permanent Secretaries, Deputy Secretaries, Assistant Secretaries, Principals and Assistant Principals, etc. Graduates of the universities with best possible liberal education are recruited. The civil servants belonging to this class play a vital role in the formation and the execution of policy. Besides open competition, there is also provision of promotion to this class from the lower executive, professional and clerical cadres. The officers of this category issue orders to their subordinates for the execution of policy and exercise supervisory control over them. They are also entrusted with the work of co-ordinating the functions of several branches in their own departments as well as between several departments. They are responsible for improvement of administration in the country in general and their departments in particular. The officers of this class are liable to be transferred from one department to another.

### (ii) The Executive Category

In the British civil service, next below the Administrative class, there is the Executive class, which is recruited partly by open competition and partly by promotion from the clerical level. Candidates with education upto the Higher Secondary School level within the age group of 18 and 19, compete for this category of civil service. In the departmental administration the civil servants of this class play an important role. They deal with internal control and organisation of the department. Officers of the Administrative class issue directions and the Executive class is concerned with the execution of policies, in accordance with the instructions received from above. The Administrative class depends upon the Executive class for the execution of policies and matters of importance and gives great weightage to such actions and implimentations.

### (iii) The Lower-Grade Class

This class occupies the third position in the hierarchy of the

British civil service and has been rightly described as "the working class of the administrative section of the service". This category consists of two classes; the clerical and the clerical assistant class. Posts in this class are filled up partly by open competition and partly by promotion from clerical assistant and short-hand typist grades. Candidates in the age group of 16 and 17, having education upto Intermediate Secondary School level, generally compete for this class. The clerical assistants class is open to women and is concerned with such work as type-writing, preparation of simple cards, maintenance of card index, handcopying, transcribing of records etc.

**The Professional Class**

Strictly speaking the professional experts like engineers, doctors, scientists, lawyers, architects and professors do not belong to the hierarchy of the civil service. The people of this class are not required to appear for any written test and are recruited through a system of interviews with the help of the experts.

**An Assessment of the British Civil Service**

Ramsay Muir admitted that the British civil service "has become indeed the effective and operative part of the British system". It is playing a very dominant role in the management of administration, legislation and finances of the country. But from this it cannot be concluded that it has become so very dominant that the Ministers have become tools in its hands. As public men the Ministers are accounable to the people and by virtue of being in public life and in the parliament as members, before inducted into the Ministerial office, they have sufficient political experience and knowledge about the problems confronting the country. It is therefore, not an easy task for the civil servants to use the Ministers as their willing tools.

**Arguments in Favour**

The British bureaucracy has got many strong points in its favour. There is a highly organised and efficient civil service in England which works according to the general policies laid down by the Ministers. With the enormous increase in the powers of the government, there is a corresponding increase in the power and influence of the bureaucracy. The acceptance of the welfare concept of the government has increased the responsibility of the government as it has to perform a large number of functions which were considered out of its purview in the 19th century. For the implementation of the policies of the government and the execution of work, the government depends on the civil service. Max Weber rightly observes that, "However, much people may complain about the evils of bureaucracy, it would be sheer illusion to think for a moment that continuous administrative work can be carried out in any field except by means of officials working in office".

Due to the concentration of powers in the hands of the civil servants, the British system of civil service is known as bureaucracy. According to Laski, bureaucracy is a term usually applied to a system of government where the officials exercise complete control over all branches of administration and their excessive powers threaten the liberties of the ordinary citizens. But despite the enhancement of its powers and prestige, the British bureaucracy has not been able to jeopardise the liberties of the poeple. The civil servants are guided by national spirit and keep the interest of the nation above all considerations. They function under the control of popularly elected Ministers who provide the democratic touch. The Ministers are very often capable people and in everything, the ultimate responsibility has to be shouldered by them, they therefore, have to control the civil servants and rejected their advices which are likely to adversely affect the interest of the people.

The British civil service has a reputation for its efficiency and high quality of men and women are attracted to this service. In the words of Ogg, "some are impelled by a sense of civil duty, some are drawn by the prospect of a career in a field in which the way is open for talents and industry, irrespective of family connections, some no doubt, are appealed by a profession which promises a steady and assured income, without much risk instead of worry and competition for the glittering prizes or doleful failures, common to the outside world".

The British civil service is very responsive to public opinion. The civil servants carry out the policy of the government honestly and diligently and change according to the requirements of time and the party in power.

The civil servants in England take pride in maintaining high ideals and traditions with which the civil service has been identified. The British civil service has displayed excellent esprit de corps and sense of responsibility, rerely noticed among the civil servants of other countries.

## Weakness of British Civil Service

The over-dependence of the Ministers on the civil servants has led to the development of bureaucratic tendencies in the British system of administration. An agitation was spear-headed in Great Britain against the rising bureaucratic tendencies in the government. In his epoch-making book, 'The New Despotism', Lord Hewart, warned the people against the growing bureaucratic control over the government in 1929. In 1930, Ramsay Muir also launched a massive campaign against bureaucracy. In 1931, Prof, C.K. Allen, published his sensational book, 'Bureaucracy Triumphant', in which be pointed out that in the so-called parliamentary democracy of Great Britain, the real powers were vested with the bureaucrats and not the popular Ministers. In this context the remarks of Ramsay Muir deserve to be quoted: "In a majority of cases, he (minister), has no special knowledge of immense and complex work of the department over which he has to preside. He has to deal with a body of officials who may be and often are, men of far greater ability than himself, and who have been giving their wholetime to the study of the problems of the office, during the years when he has been making his position in the world of taking hot air on platforms. They bring before him hundreds of knotty problems for his decision, about most of them he knows nothing at all. They put before him their suggestions supported by what may seem the most convincing arguments and facts. It is most obvious that, unless he is a self-important ass, or a man of quite exceptional grasp, power and courage, (and both of these types are uncommon among successful politicians) he will, in ninetynine cases out of hundred simply accept their view and sign his name on the dotted line. On the whole, the policy of the office will nearly always prevail, its power of quiet persistence and of quite obstructions, its command of all the facts, are irresitible except to a man of commanding power".

Due to a growing consciousness among the people that the civil service must play a more democratic and constructive role, the Fulton Committee was appointed on 8th February, 1966 to "examine the structure, recruitment and management, including training of the Home Civil Service, and to make recommendations". In its report the Fulton Committee has pointed out the following six main defects of the British civil service, due to which it has failed in the most efficient discharge of the present and prospective responsibilities:

(a) It is still too much based on the philosophy of the amateur (or 'generalist' or 'all-rounder'). This is most evident in the

Administrative class, which holds the dominant position in the civil service.

(b) The present system of classes in the service, results in unnecessary stratification and seriously impedes its work.

(c) Scientists, engineers and members of other specialist classes are frequently given neither the full responsibility and opportunities nor the corresponding authority, they ought to have.

(d) Too few civil servants are skilled managers.

(e) There is not enough contact between the service and the community, which it is required to serve.

(f) Personnel management and career planning are inadequate.

The Fulton Committee observed that, "For these and other defects the central management of the service, the Treasury, must accept its share of responsibility".

In addition to the aforesaid shortcomings, the British civil service also suffers from the evils of red-tapism. There is under emphasis on rules, file work, cross reference etc. This leads to delay and loss of efficiency.

The competitive examination through which the civil servants are recruited is defective as it only gives emphasis on academic knowledge, but not the knowledge of the department to which they are being recruited.

Another defect of the British civil service is the tendency on the part of the civil servants to grab more and more power and authority. In the words of Lord Hewart, "No doubt in the main unjudicial, the permanent Civil Service is becoming more and more impatient of the sham facade of democracy behind which it works, and is showing progressively greater skill in using the forms of parliament and the convenient doctrine of ministerial responsibility, has a cover for steady increase of the power of the departments".

The British civil service is becoming more and more conscious of its growing importance and power in administration and is operative as a powerful pressure group for achieving the goal of self-aggrandisement. In the opinion of Ogg as the members of the permanent civil service "become more organised, and more group conscious, they will be increasingly tempted to make use of their power as unionised employees and as voters to force unjustifiable legislation concerning pay, hours, pension and other matters of interest to them as a class".

The growth of the evil spirit of departmentalism has led each department to think about itself as an autonomous unit in complete isolation of the other departments of the government. The smooth working of the government depends on co-operation and co-ordination among the various departments and this is being adversely affected due to the growth of departmentalism. Ramsay Muir suggested that inorder to check this departmentalism, there should be firm control and criticism to ensure efficient co-ordination and to avoid the waste of effort and money.

# 6

# The Parliament

The British parliament is sovereign in real sense of the term. There is practically no limit to its powers and it can do anything. Sir Edward Coke observed that, "Of the power and jurisdiction of the parliament, for making laws, it is so transcendent and absolute, as it cannot be confined either for persons or causes within any bounds". While trying to give expression to the unlimited powers of the British parliament De Lome said, "Parliament can do everything but make a woman a man, and a man a woman".

The parliament consists of the King, the House of Lords and the House of Commons. The supreme legislative power is vested in the parliament and it can pass any law as its legislative competence is outside the purview of any judicial or legal authority. The courts in England have no power to set aside a law passed by the parliament. The British parliament has got the power to make legal Acts illegal or illegal ones legal; it can declare legitimate children illegitimate or illegitimate ones legitimate. It can change the British constitution in any manner it likes. It has been pointed out that, "England is not governed by logic, she is governed by parliament". Referring to the supremacy of the parliament Ogg and Zink have observed that, "parliament remains ultimately supreme and legally omnipotent". The British parliament can do everything that is not naturally impossible. No power on earth can undo what has been done by the parliament.

The supremacy of the parliament can be divided into two parts, namely, functional and supervisory. As far as the functional aspect is concerned, the parliament is omnipotent and omnicompetent. The parliament enjoys unrivalled legislative jurisdiction. The parliament is both a law-making and constituent authority. There is no difference between ordinary and constitutional laws and the parliament can pass both these laws with the same ease and competence. The laws passed by the parliament are not subjected to any judicial review and no court can declare a law passed by the parliament as unconstitutional. In addition to these factors, the unitary system of government in England also facilitates the growth of parliamentary sovereignty. There is no other legislative body to legislate side by side with the parliament as is the case in federal states.

The British parliament, in its supervisory capacity, plays the role of the director and co-ordinator of the cabinet, which is accountable to it for all its acts of omission and commission. The cabinet is also a committee of the parliament and is created by it. The parliament adopts the methods like the vote of no-confidence, censure motion, questions, supplementary questions, cut motions etc. inorder to exercise its supervisory power.

The evolution of democracy out of its monarchical past, when the King was all powerful, and is still all powerful in theory, over all branches of government, accounts for the sovereign omnipotence of the parliament.

But the omnipotence of the British parliament is not so ıeal as it appears in theory. The powers of the parliament are limited by customs, traditions, canons of religion and mortality, conservative nature of the British people and force of public opinion. The legal sovereign that is the parliament has to be afraid of the political sovereign namely, the electorate. The parliament cannot dare to pass a law which the people would not like. Munro has rightly said that the parliament cannot do anything as to bind its successors. It cannot interrupt or put an end to the process of constitutional changes. It has no power to pass a law, declaring that the future parliament cannot change it.

## THE HOUSE OF LORDS

The House of Lords is the upper chamber of the British parliament and is a heterogeneous body.

### Composition

It is the oldest legislative chamber in the world. It is called the second chamber, through it is the oldest legislative body in the world. It is the outcome of the Great Council and is an integral part of the political and judicial system of Great Britain. Its membership varies from time to time.

The House is composed of the Princes of the Blood Royal, Hereditary Peers, 16 Representative Peers from Scotland, elected for a single parliament, 28 Representative Peers from Ireland elected for life. After the creation of the Irish Free State in 1922, the provision of creating new Peers in Ireland has been abolished. As a result the number of Irish Representative Peers has been reduced to five. There are 26 Ecclesiastical Lords (2 Arch-Bishops and 24 Bishops), and 9 Law Lords or Lords of Appeal, appointed for life. The Lord Chancellor is the President of the House, but has no such power like the Speaker of the House of Commons. The quorum for the meeting of the House is 30 members. It holds sessions simultaneously with those of the House of Commons.

## Functions of the House of Lords

The House of Lords had supreme powers until 1911 and it could reject any Bill including a money Bill. However, the House had lost this power by non-use. The House of Lords had also lost by non-use its power of amending any money Bill. Prior to 1911, the House exercised the power of rejecting and amending Bills other than money Bills.

## Legislative Power

A money Bill must originate in the House of Commons, but any Bill other than a money Bill can be introduced in the House of Lords. The Parliament Act of 1911 empowered the Speaker of the House of Commons, to decide whether a Bill is a money Bill or not. After a Bill is passed by the House of Commons, it is sent to the House of Lords for its approval. The House, at that time plays an important role in the revision and improvement of the Bill. A money Bill can be delayed by the House for one month only, after which the Bill is sent to the King for his consent. The House of Commons may or may not agree to the amendments suggested by the House of Lords, but it becomes an Act after receiving the consent of the Crown, which is formal.

According to the Parliament Act of 1911 an ordinary Bill could be delayed by the House of Lords for a period of two years. After the lapse of two years and after having been rejected twice by the Lords; if it was passed for a third time by the House of Commons, it became an Act after receiving the assent from the King, despite the disapproval by the House of Lords. The Parliament Act of 1949, further reduced this delaying power to a period of one year only. After the lapse of one year from the date of its passage by the House of Commons it becomes an Act, after receiving the King's approval irrespective of its approval of disapproval by the House of Lords.

## Judicial Power of the House of Lords

The House of Lords is the Highest Court in Great Britain and North Ireland. It exercises both appellate and original jurisdiction. It exercises its original jurisdiction, when it tries its own members for felory or treason. The House also acts as a Court of Impeachments brought by the House of Commons.

The House of Lords is also the Supreme Court of Appeal. But these functions are not exercised by the whole House sitting as a Court. These functions are now exercised by the Lord Chancellor and the nine Law Lords, who may be occasionally assisted by other Lords who have held high judicial office.

The judicial power of the House of Lords is a special power of the House, which the House of Commons does not possess. The Power of Impeachment is with the Lords since the days of 'The Witan', but this power is not being exercised now.

## The Parliament Act of 1911

Prior to 1911, the House of Lords exercised real powers of amending and rejecting any Bill other than money Bills. The First Reform Bill of 1831 and the Second Irish Home Rule Bill of 1893 had been rejected by the House of Lords. Under such circumstances, the House of the Commons had no power to override the decisions of the House of Lords. It however, used the method of putting the pressure of public opinion on the House so as to compel it to give in. When a government measure was rejected by the House of Lords, the Prime Minister used to advice the Monarch to order for fresh election on the issue. If the same Ministry was returned to power by the electorate, the House of Lords usually gave in.

A serious conflict took place between the House of Lords and the House of Commons in 1909, when the House of Lords rejected the Finance Bill introduced by Lloyd George, the then Chancellor of the Exchequer in the Liberal Ministry. The Bill proposed to levy new taxes particularly on land and would have adversely affected the interests of the owners of large estates. The Lords were opposed to it as they themselves were owners of large estates. The House of Lords had also rejected some other Bills and the House of Commons was not prepared to take it lying down. The House of Commons adopted a resolution which declared the action of the House of Lords as undemocratic and violation of the provisions of the constitution. The House of Lords remained adamant and as a result a general election was held in 1910.

The Liberals were again returned to power by the electorate, which vindicated the stand of the House of Commons. The same Finance Bill was again passed by the House of Commons and was sent to the House of Lords for the second time. But this time the House of Lords gave in.

This bitter experience made the Liberals determined to curb the powers of the House of Lords for all times to come. There was also popular demand for "clipping the wings of the House of Lords". Accordingly the Parliament Act of 1911 was passed, which is a very important constitutional document. It defines the legislative and financial powers of the House of Lords and determines the relations between the two chambers.

The important provisions of the Bill are discussed below:

(i) The Act laid down that a money Bill, if passed by the House of Commons, would go to the House of Lords, and would become an Act after one month of its introduction, irrespective of the consent or the refusal of the House of Lords. It would be sent for Royal approval, which is formal and then it will become a law, whether the House of Lords has considered the Bill or not.

(ii) The Act defines money Bills and in cases of disagreement, the decision of the Speaker of the House of Commons shall be final. This has also proclaimed the supremacy of the House of Commons over the House of Lords.

(iii) As per the Act, any other public Bill, passed by the House of Commons in three successive sessions, with an interval of at least two years between its first and final passage, will become an Act on receiving Royal assent, notwithstanding the dissent of the House of Lords. The Parliament Act of 1949 further curtailed the powers of the House of Lords and reduced the delaying power of the House from two years to one year. Instead of the Bill being passed in three successive sessions as provided by the Act of 1911, now it was to be passed only by two successive sessions of the House of Commons before sending it to the House of Lords.

(iv) Another significant achievement of the Parliament Act of 1911 was the reduction of the duration of the Parliament from seven years to five years. Now it could be possible for the parliament or more specifically, the House of Commons, to come in closer touch with the public opinion and reflect the same more frequently.

**Appraisal of the Act of 1911**

It is an important constitutional document which democratised the British political system by establishing the supremacy of the House of Commons, through constitutional changes of great magnitude hither to unknown in England. It reduced the powers of the House of Lords both with regard to Money and Public Bills. The paramountcy of the House of Commons both in the legislative and financial matters was proclaimed by the Act. In strict legal theory the House of Lords was relegated to the background and it not only became the second chamber, but also the secondary chamber from the point of view of its relative importance. But prior to the passage of the Act of 1911, the House of Lords was a very important chamber and it exercised tremendous powers. In the British political system, at present, the House of Lords is one of the most criticised institutions.

But it would be wrong to presume that the Parliament Act of 1911, has reduced the House of Lords to "a mere shadow of its former self". It still plays a prominent role in the British political system and despite several attempts to abolish it, the House continues with the support of British conservative public opinion. It also justifies its position by the performance of certain judicial functions denied to the House of Commons.

It will, however, be pertinent to point out that leaving aside the money Bill, the House of Lords still enjoys considerable powers with regard to the public Bills. As per the provisions of the Act, the House of Lords theoretically enjoyed only suspensive veto for a period of two years, but two years period was a considerable time. Very often during this period either the Ministry was changed or fresh elections were ordered after its dissolution. The changed Ministry or the new Ministry formed after the General Elections was not as interested as its predecessors for the passage of the Bill. Thus most of the Bills to which the House of Lords was opposed died their natural death. As the average life of a Ministry in England is only 3½ years, it is likely that while the Bill is delayed for a period of two years by the House of Lords, the tenure of the Ministry is over. Thus the delaying power of the House may result in the negation of the Bill. Referring to this Ogg has pointed out that, "the terms required for placing such measures on the statute book without the Lords' assent are admittedly not easy to meet and it is interesting to observe that in all 28 years, from the passage of the Act, no single measure financial or otherwise has become effective without the Upper Chamber's consent".

It is also wrong to conclude that the House of Commons has gained the powers lost by the House of Lords. Now all the powers have been assumed by the Cabinet and it dominates the process of law-making in England. No Private Bill or Private Member's Bill has any chance of passage in the parliament, without the support of the Cabinet. Ogg is right when he says that behind the sheer legal powers of the House of Commons to enact legislation unilaterally, the give and take of law making goes on pretty much as before.

## Appraisal of the House of Lords

The Members of the House of Lords enjoy certain privileges. They enjoy the freedom of speech and freedom from arrest, while the House is in session. The Peers were, previously only tried by their fellow Peers, but this privilege has now been abolished. The members of the Peerage cannot be elected to the House of Commons, but this is not applicable to the Irish Peers who are not Irish representatives in the House of Lords. During the life time of the Peers, their elder sons can be elected to the House of Commons, but they have to vacate their seats on succession to the father's title.

Meetings of the House of Lords are held in its own chamber at Westminster and its sessions are coincident with those of the House of Commons. The Lord Chancellor, presides over the meetings of the House and puts motions for voting, but he has no disciplinary powers. He does not possess the speakers power to recognize a Member who desires to speak.

The Members of the House of Lords are extremely apathetic and the attendence is very thin. However, when matters of importance are taken up for discussion, there is considerable increase in the attendance. At least thirty members are required to pass any Bill. In the House of Lords, very rarely there are full-dress debates. But whenever such debates are there, they are characterised by high quality of deliberation, because the Members of the House have ripe experience and some of them are able orators. The House of Lords is an undemocratic House and it is rightly said that a British Peer, represents no one but himself. The principles of heredity and nomination rather than merit and election are followed in appointing the Members of the House of Lords. The House only represents the upper class of the society. Ramsay Muir described it as the "fortress of wealth". In the words of Sidney and Beatrice Webb, "it is the worst representative assembly".

In the House of Lords, always there is the dominance of the Conservative Party. The House safeguards vested interest and is opposed to radical ideas. It is not in tune with the changing time and the needs of the people. Lord Balfour was of the opinion that the House of Lords was in favour of seeing the Conservative Party permanently in power.

The House of Lords is a much criticised institution. Rt. Hon'ble J.R. Clyms made the cynical comment that, "In our view the House of Lords is an institution which cannot well be reformed; it cannot be mended, it must be ended". In general they do not subscribe to the view of J.R. Clyms, although they agree that this House needs to be mended. The House has not yet outlived its utility and is still considered essential for the democratic system of government.

It is argued that the House of Lords gives breathing time to the people to examine the pros and cons of a Bill passed by the House of Commons. The Members of the House of Commons are too progressive and radical and in their zeal to achieve progress, they may hurriedly pass certain legislative measures, which might not be in the interest of the people. The House of Lords can check such ill considered and hurriedly passed legislation by the House of Commons by focusing public attention on its lapses through its power of suspensive veto.

It is argued by some that the House of Lords is required to preserve the rights and liberties of the people in the absence of guaranteed fundamental rights. As there is no provision of fundamental rights in the British Constitution, the party in power may act arbitrarily which may trample the rights and liberties of the people. The existence of the House of Lords is also justified on the ground that it is not safe to concentrate so much powers in the hands of one chamber. M.C. Kechie has observed that, "Powers so tremendous and unexampled cannot safely be entrusted to the arbitrary decisions of the fluctuating majorities of any single chamber".

The House of Lords helps in improving the process of legislation by pinpointing the defects of the Bills which might have been hurriedly passed by the House of Commons. It also relieves the burden of the House of Commons as many less important Bills are generally introduced in the House of Lords.

The House of Lords also serves as a reservoir of talented persons. Many talented persons, who fight sigh of direct politics and elections may be nominated to the House of Lords and their services may be utilised for the benefit of the country.

## Proposals for the Reform of House of Lords

The British people have expressed themselves in favour of the House of Lords in a changed form. For that purpose from time to time several reform proposals have been submitted, but very few of them have been taken seriously by the British people.

In 1869 Lord Russel suggested the creation of Life-Peers, but this proposal was rejected. In 1888, Lord Salisbury proposed the gradual creation of 50 Life-Peers, but his plan was also not acceptable.

It was also proposed to discontinue the issue of writ of Summons to the undesirable Members of the House of Lords. This was dubbed as the Black Sheep Bill and was rejected.

The Lansdowne Plan of 1909, proposed a House of Lords of 330 members–100 Peers to be chosen by the whole body of Peers, 100 persons to be appointed by the Crown, 123 persons to be selected by the House of Commons, sitting in regional groups and 5 Bishops to be chosen by the whole body of Bishops. This scheme was also rejected.

In 1918, the Bryce Committee was constituted by taking 15 Members from each House of the Parliament to recommend reform proposals. According to the suggestion of this committee the total membership of the House of Lords was to be reduced to 327, out of which three-fourths were to be elected by the House of Commons by means of proportional representation. No sitting Member of the House of Commons was to be elected to the House of Lords. A Joint Standing Committee of the two Houses was to select the remaining Members. The scheme was to be implemented in stages. The Members of the House of Lords were to be elected for a period of 12 years, one-third retiring after every four years. A Joint Committee of the two Houses was to decide whether a Bill was a money Bill or not. In the case of difference of opinion, the matter was to be referred to a further Joint Committee consisting of 60 Members–30 from each House.

In 1922 the Cabinet Committee submitted five resolutions. In addition to the Peers of the Royal Blood, Spiritual Peers and Law Lords, there were to be some elected Members, either elected directly or indirectly, a few Hereditary Peers elected by their order, and a few Members nominated by the Crown. The number of the Lords was to be fixed by law. Excepting the Peers of Royal Blood and the Law Lords, the terms of other Members was also to be fixed by law. The total membership of the House was to be about 350. A Joint Committee of 7 Members from each House was to be appointed at the beginning of each parliament to decide whether a Bill was a money Bill or not.

The Speaker of the House of Commons was to be the ex-officio Chairman of the Joint Committee. The House of Lords was not to have any power of amending or rejecting money Bills. The procedure prescribed by the Act of 1911, was not to be applied to any Act which intended to change the constitution or the power of the House of Lords. This plan was also shelved.

In 1925, Lord Birkenhead gave certain proposals for the reform of the House of Lords which were also shelved.

In 1928, Lord Clarendon gave a plan that the House of Lords should consist of 150 Members elected by the Peers and 150 Members, nominated by the Crown in accordance with the strength of various parties in the House of Commons. A few Members were to be appointed by the Crown as life-Peers.

Lord Salisbury gave a proposal in 1932, for the reform of the House of Lords. According to his plan, the House was to consist of 300 Members, out of which 150 were to be elected by Peers for 12 years and 150 were to be nominated by the Crown for the same period. The Crown's power to create new Peers was to be restricted to 12 per year. The powers of the House of Lords were not to be changed. Only the definition of a money Bill was to be decided by a Joint Committee, presided over by the Speaker of the House of Commons.

Prime Minister Altbee gave another reform proposal in 1947. According to this the House was to consist of 300 Members of all sexes. The Members of the House were to be paid remuneration. The Members were to be declared disqualified if they neglected duty or were found to be incompetent. But this proposal was also rejected.

Thus the House of Lords continues to remain without much change. Now it can only delay legislation and its other powers have been so considerably reduced that it cannot act as an obstacle to democracy. Due to this the reform proposals are not viewed seriously.

## THE HOUSE OF COMMONS

The House of Commons in England is the oldest representative chamber and is so very powerful that very often people consider it to be synonymous with the parliament. But it is not the correct picture as despite its weakness, the House of Lords plays many significant functions and cannot be called a chamber of no consequence. The House of Commons, however, represents the people directly and rightly it has got the claim to supremacy over the House of Lords. The House of Lords has not only become the second, but also the secondary chamber from the point of view of its importance. The essential business of law-making is carried out in the House of Commons and it also exercises control and supervision over the executive. The House exercises control over the formulation and implementation of public policy. It is in the House of Commons that the policies of the government are discussed and debated and these debates have far reaching consequences as the government is directly accountable and responsible to the House of Commons. The Cabinet in theory exists on the basis of a day-to-day accountability of its actions. Although elected for a period of five years the Council of Ministers can be driven out of power by passing a vote of no-confidence in the House of Commons. Thus the importance of House of Commons is a recognised fact and in this connection Newmann has rightly observed that, "Sovereignty of Parliament resides in the House of Commons".

**Democratisation of the Electoral Process**

Before we discuss the organisation the House of Commons, it is proper to analyse briefly how the system of representation and the mode of election have changed during the course of time. Before the passage of the great Reform Act of 1832, election to the House of Commons suffered from many limitations and the House of Commons of those days cannot be called as a fully representative House. There were many "rotten boroughs" and "pocket boroughs". A "rotten borough" was one which used to send the same number of representatives although a major section of its population had migrated to big industrial townships, after the Industrial Revolution. The seats from such "rotten boroughs" were usually purchased by some rich men and they converted these boroughs into their "pocket boroughs", which they sold at high prices. Even in boroughs and counties having large populations, the votes were sold. The members who were elected to the House through such manipulations, acted against the interest of the people as a whole by opposing the process of democratisation through widening of suffrage or redistribution of seats on the basis of population. There were nearly 24 millions people in England and Ireland in 1831, and less than a million people had the right to vote, i.e., only 4 per cent of the population. Thus the upper classes alone had the access to the corridors of power and the common people were deprived of their role in the political process of the country.

After the Napoleonic War in 1815, England has become industrialised. The new industrial towns had become over-crowded and conditions in the factories and the newly developed urban areas had become intolerable. Inorder to meet the requirements of the war there was heavy taxation. People resented these conditions and demanded for socio-economic reforms. But the House of Commons which was the citadel of all kinds of vested interests, was not in favour of any reforms. So in the first instance it was felt necessary to adopt political reforms for the purpose of reorganising the House of Commons. It was thought that a reformed House of Commons would be in a position to pass laws for improving the socio-economic conditions of the people.

The Whigh Ministry came to power in 1832 and passed the Reform Bill in the House of Commons. This was however, turned down by the House of Lords. The Bill was again repassed by the House of Commons and this time the House of Lords gave in. The great Reform Bill of 1832, which was passed in this way is considered to be a significant landmark in the constitutional history of England. Seats were redistributed and the pocket and rotten boroughs were abolished from the list of constituencies. The Reform Act of 1832 remedied some of the problems and widened franchise by extending suffrage to about a million people. Uniform suffrage was provided by enfranchising all "rate-paying occupants who were assessed on a rental value of ten pounds or more per annum".

In 1867 the Second Reform Bill was introduced by Disraeli who headed the conservative Ministry and got it successfully passed. There was further extension of suffrage by this Act.

In 1872, the system of secret ballot was introduced and the elections were to be confined in each constituency to a day only instead of the previous practice of keeping the polls open for a whole week. The Suppression of the Corrupt Practices Act was passed in 1883, inorder to make the conduct of elections free and fair.

Gladstone, the Liberal Prime Minister, succeeded in getting the Third Reform Act, passed in 1884. There was further extension of suffrage and this time house-holders in the countries got the right to vote. There was also considerable redistribution of seats by the Reform Act of 1885. The whole country was divided into several electoral districts and every district was allowed to return one Member to Parliament. Despite all these Reform Acts, large number of farm labourers, domestic servants and sailors etc. did not enjoy the right to vote. The women were still denied voting right.

During the regime of Lloyd George as Prime Minister, in 1918, the Representation of the Peoples Act was passed by the parliament. For the first time uniform qualifications were prescribed for members of county and borough constituencies for enjoying the right to vote. Every person above the age of 21 years got the right to vote. For the first time in the history of England, the Act of 1918, gave the right to vote to women, with certain limitations. The shortcoming was, however, removed in 1928 when the Conservative Party got the Equal Franchise Act passed by the Parliament. By this Act all women of 21 years or above got the right to vote. This Act provided for the principle of universal adult suffrage.

Business premises and university franchises were abolished by the Representation of Peoples Act of 1948. In 1949, the Representation of the Peoples Act, provided for registration of electors. Thus it took nearly one hundred years for democratising the electoral process and making it universal.

## Composition of the House of Commons

The House of Commons consists of members from all sections of the society and at present it is a truely representative body. At present there are 635 members who are directly elected from the single member constituencies. There is universal adult franchise for the citizens of 21 years of age or more. Members are elected for a period of five years subject to the right of the King to dissolve the House of Commons before the completion of its tenure.

The Boundary Commission which acts under the Chairmanship of the Speaker of the House of Commons, demarcates the parliamentary constituencies. The demarcation is made on the basis of population by dividing the total population by the number of seats, allowing a plus or minus margin of 25 per cent. The persons who are residents in a constituency on the qualifying date and who are British subjects or citizens, have the right to vote.

Infants, aliens, peers (unless they renounce the peerage under the 1963 Peerage Act), bankrupts, idiots, lunatics, certain kinds of convicted persons, the Clergy of the Church of England, the Church of Scotland, the Roman Catholic Church and persons convicted of corrupt and illegal practices at elections are dis qualified to become members of the House of Commons. Holders and undertakers of contracts or commissions for or on account of public services, office-holders, pensioners of the Crown, except for those in civil, military and diplomatic services are also excluded from the House of Commons.

However, under this provision, the Ministers are not considered as office-holders.

The Parliament Act of 1911, provided that the duration of the House of Commons shall be for five years and this provision cannot be changed without the constent of the House of Lords. But the parliament has the right to extend its own life and the parliaments of 1910-1918 and 1935-45 lasted for more than five years due to the involvement of Great Britain in the two World Wars. It may however, be pointed out that during normal times, the House of Commons rarely completes its five year term as the King has the power to dissolve it on the advice of the Prime Minister, if it becomes hostile or too refractory a critic to be tolerated by the government.

These days the duration of parliamentary sessions has increased because of pressure of work. There is no statute to regulate the number or duration of the parliamentary sessions. The meetings of the House take place on every day of the week, except Saturdays and Sundays. On Mondays, Wednesdays and Thursdays the sessions begin at 2.30 P.M. and usually continue upto 10.30 p.m. There are also whole night sessions when important matters are tabled for discussion. On Fridays, the House sits at 11.00 a.m. and closes the session at 4.30 p.m.

## The Office of the Speaker

The Speaker occupies the most significant position in the British House of Commons. Although, he is called the 'Speaker', he never speaks and whenever he speaks, he speaks for the House and not to it. Commenting on the Office of the Speaker Herman Finer said: "The endeavour of the last 150 years has been to make the Speaker the objective embodiment of the rules and laws of the Commons, purging from him the last milligram of partisanship. He is the impartial presiding officer of the House, with the weighty functions of seeing that debate is orderly, that the authority of the House is respected, that procedure for the making of laws and control of policies is maintained. He must speech free, with special concern for the minorities in the House". Thus the British Speaker is characterised by impartiality, neutrality and objectivity and is in sharp contrast with the position of the speaker in the House of Representatives in the U.S.A. The British speaker is politically neutral and after becoming the Speaker he even ceases to be the primary member of the party to which he belonged on the other hand, the American Speaker is the leader of the majority party in the House of Representatives and continues his party position and affiliation, even after he is elected as the Speaker. He presides over the party caucus and participates in party meetings and conferences to decide the strategy of his party. He utilises his position as speaker to favour his own party as against the other parties in the House of Representatives.

The powers and functions of the British Speaker are discussed under the three following broad heads:

***(i) As Representative of the House of Commons***

The Speaker represents the House in relation to the outside world i.e., to the King, House of Lords and outside authority. He is the only link between the King and the House of Commons. At the time of the joint session of the two Houses, he leads the House of Commons to the House of Lords and is being received by the King, along with the Members of the House. The Crown's messages to the Commons are conveyed through the Speaker. On ceremonial occasions, the messages of the House of Commons are carried to the King by him. The Speaker also presents the Money Bills to the King for his assent. The Parliament Act of 1911 has increased the powers and functions of the Speaker. He is the only competent authority to decide whether a bill is a Money Bill or not and his decision shall be final in the matter. The Speaker informs the outside authorities about the decisions of the House and has the power to issue them instructions for the proper enforcement of the orders and directives of the House. The petitions and opinions of the outside authorities are communicated to the House by the Speaker.

***(ii) As Presiding Officer of the House***

In consultation with the Leader of the House, the Speaker allots time for the discussion of various matters before the House. The admissibility of resolutions and questions is determined by him. He can disallow any question or motion. No motion for adjournment or a debate on a bill can be taken up without his consent. No member can address the House without the consent of the Speaker. When a Member raises a point of order on any issue, the Speaker shall give the ruling and his ruling shall be final. He can reprimand a Member for using un-parliamentary or defamatory language and can order for expunging the same from the proceedings of the House. He can suspend the business of the House and can also adjourn its meetings, if he thinks it proper. The entry of outsiders into the House is regulated by him. He can ask them to leave the House and can refuse entry to anybody into the House. The Speaker's signature is necessary before sending a bill to the House of Lords or to the King for his assent.

It is the duty of the Speaker to see that whenever the House meets to transact its business the quorum of the House is there. If there is no quorum, he is empowered to suspend the House till the quorum is complete. The Speaker is the guardian of the privileges of the Mambers of the House.

The Speaker, or anybody working in his place, has only a casting vote in case of a tie. The Speaker has no right to vote as an ordinary member of the House except when the voting is on a resolution to remove him from office.

When the Speaker rises, others must sit down as a mark of respect, and must not leave the House, when he is addressing.

### *(iii) As Administrative Officer of the House*

As the Chief Administrative Officer of the House, the Speaker appoints the Editors, and Printers of the Journals of the House. It is his responsibility to see that the speeches of the Members are reproduced correctly in the journals of the House. Thus the office of the Speaker is an office of dignity, power and responsibility. He symbolically represents the democratic values and traditions of Great Britain.

## A Review

The British Speaker ceases to be a party man after his election to that office. He is allowed to continue as Speaker as long as he is a Member of the House, provided that he is wlling to serve. The changes in the party complexion in the House of Commons do not affect the office of the Speaker. The Speaker is returned unopposed from his constituency at the time of the General Election. He gets a pension and peerage after his retirement. These provisions are very much essential for maintaining the neutrality and impartiality of the office and to keep it above any political controversy.

The Speaker as the symbol of the authority and the dignity of the House, should not allow anybody to impair the dignity of the House. He must guard the House against the arbitrary high-handedness of the Government. The Speaker must possess the capacity to know the collective mind of the House, and if he fails to do so, he wll be out of tune with the currents of thought in the House. This might lead to pandemonious situations in the House.

## Legislative Procedure in the British Parliament

The British Parliament generally deals with three kinds of bills, such as, Public Bills, Private Member's Bills and Private Bills. Public Bills aim at the general welfare of the people and are introduced by the Ministers. Public Bills dealing with financial matters are called Money Bills. Bills which affect the general interest of the people, but are moved in the Parliament by ordinary Members and not Ministers, are called Private Member's Bills. A Private Bill is one which affects the private interest of an area or a group of people and is usually moved on behalf of a petition by the local organisation.

Before Bill becomes an act it has to go through several stages which are discussed below:

### *(i) Introduction and the First Reading*

Before the Bill is introduced, the mover gives information about the Bill to the respective House. Then he is formally called by the Speaker to introduce the Bill. The Minister himself or the clerk of the House reads about the title of the Bill. Then a vote is taken and if the majority is in favour of the Bill, it is considered to have been moved. Then it is printed in the journal of the House. Generally at the stage of the first reading of the Bill no formal speeches are made. The introduction and first reading are supposed to be over after the motion is carried out by the House.

### The Second Reading

During the second reading stage a full debate takes place on the Bill for a period of three days and the Bill is discussed as a whole. The general principles of the Bill are discussed in details, but it is not discussed word by word or clause by clause. At this stage the Bill may be accepted or rejected by voting in the House. The Bill may be rejected directly by voting against the motion. There is also a polite way of proposing the reintroduction of the Bill six months hence, when the Parliament shall not be in session. By adopting this method the Bill may be killed for all practical purposes. The rejection of the Public Bill at the second reading stage will tantamount to be a vote of noconfidence against the Government and it shall be forced to resign from office.

### The Committee Stage

The Second reading stage of the Bill comes to an end when its fundamentals are approved. After this stage the Bill comes to the third stage which is known as the Committee stage. During this stage the Bill is usually referred to a Select Committee which consists, among other Members of the House, the sponsor of the Bill or those who are incharge of the Bill. The Chairman of this Committee is nominated by the Speaker and if the Deputy Speaker is the member of any Select Committee, he becomes its Chairman. There is a thorough and clause by clause discussion of the Bill during the Committee stage. The committee collects all information regarding the Bill and its pros and cons are critically examined. After a thorough examination of the Bill the Committee proposes such amendments, as it thinks necessary. Herman Finer rightly observes that, "In Committee the government is prepared to do business–that is, to accept amendments in order to produce a better bill; that is technically better to wipe out a flaw and better in that it satisfied the bigger number as being in the general interest".

### The Report Stage

The members of the Committee are free to express any opinion on the Bill and every individual member may give his report separately. Usually there is a majority report and a minority report. The House proceeds to consider the Bill clause by clause, as it has emerged from the Select Committee. During this stage Members are free to move amendments to any clause under consideration. If there are too many amendments, the Speaker shall decide as to which amendments are to be considered and which not. Finally, the clause with such amendments as many have been accepted by the House is put to vote. Votes may be taken after every clause or many clauses are discussed together and vote may be taken on all of them at one time. The defect of this stage is that it takes too much time. In the words of Herman Finer, "Here is always the tendency of a parent body to reconsider the discretion it gave its offspring. To save the time of the House of Commons it is necessary to withstand it".

### The Third Reading

The third reading is the final stage of the Bill in the House of its origin. The Speaker moves that the Bill be now read for the third time. Then the Bill as a whole is discussed and arguments in favour and against it are expressed by the different members. The third reading stage is a formal one and no substantial changes are allowed at this stage. However, certain verbal amendments may be suggested by the Members to clear certain ambiguities or defects in the form of the Bill and the suggestions may be accepted by the House. If the Bill is passed by a majority of the Members present and voting, then it shall be deemed to have been passed by the House of its origin and after receiving a certificate to this effect, from the Presiding Officer of the House, the Bill goes to the other House, where the same procedure is again repeated. Generally important Public Bills are introduced first in the House of Commons and then sent to the House of Lords.

### Passage of the Bill in the House of Lords

When a Bill comes to the House of Lords, the same procedure is adopted as in the House of Commons. However, in this House, at the Committee stage, the use of the Committee of the Whole is made. The Bill is not referred to a Standing or a Select Committee. The House of Lords has got the power either to pass a Bill or reject it or amend it. If the Bill is passed by the House, then it is sent for Royal assent after which it becomes an Act. In case of amendments by the House, it is again sent back to the House of Commons for reconsideration. If the House of Commons rejectes the amendments, then the House of Lords has to yield. The House of Lords has the power of delaying a Bill for a maximum period of one year and if in the meanwhile the Bill is passed in two consecutive sessions, after its rejection by the House of Lords, it shall become an Act with the assent of the Crown.

### The Royal Assent

This marks the last stage of the Bill and is a formal affair. In the presence of the Speaker in the House of Lords, the titles of the Bills are read out, and a representative of the King proclaims the King's consent on batches of Bill which are submitted for the royal consent. After this the Bills become Acts.

A detailed study of the legislative procedure in England reveals that it is a scientific and elaborate method, which is followed with a view to perfect the Bill in all respects before it finally becomes an Act:

### Procedure in Respect of Money Bills

Money Bills are passed by the British Parliament by adopting different procedures. The peculiarities of the procedure are duscussed below:

(i) Public Bills other than Money Bills can be introduced in any House of the Parliament, but Money Bills can be introduced only in the House of Commons, which is the sovereign representative chamber of the people.

(ii) Other Public Bills may be introduced on behalf of the private members also. But Money Bills are introduced by the Chancellor of the Exchequer as a government measure. Money Bills need the prior consent of the Crown and this can only be accorded to a government measure moved by a Minister. Royal assent to the Money Bill has, however, become just a formality.

(iii) After the second reading is over, all the Money Bills are sent to the Committee of the Whole House while other Public Bills normally go to either Standing Committees or Select Committees.

(iv) The Committee of the Whole House is called the Committee of Supplies, when it discusses the estimates part of the Bill and the grants of money. On the other hand it is called the Committee of Resources, when the Committee of the Whole House discusses the question of resources to provide for the estimates, passed by the Committee of Supplies.

(v) The power of the House of Lords to delay a Money Bill has been very much limited as it can delay it only for a period of one month. After the lapse of one month period of time, the Bill shall be sent for the Royal assent, on receipt of which it shall become an Act. However, Public Bills other than the Money Bills can be delayed by the House of Lords for a period of one year as per the Parliament Act of 1949.

## The Procedure in Respect of Private Bills

The procedure of passage of Private Bills in the Parliament is different from that of Public Bills in the following respects:

(i) Before the beginning of a parliamentary session, the petition pleading for the introduction of the Private Bill together with its draft, has to be submitted to the Private Bills Office. It is notified in the Gazette that the Bill may be introduced in the Parliament and concerned government departments are also served with the copies of the notice for information and necessary action at their level. The petitioners are required to submit an estimate of cost involved and deposit certain amount as security money. The Bills are then examined by the Examiner of Petitions of Private Bills, who is himself an officer of the House. On the receipt of a favourable report from him that the Bill is in order, it is introduced in the House.

(ii) At the second reading stage, the Bills are examined closely and voting takes place. If passed unopposed, the Bill is referred to the

Committee on Unopposed Bills which thoroughly examines it, clause by clause and word by word. Then it reports to the House with or without amendments. In case the Bill is opposed by Members of the House or by representatives of vested interests, outside the House, it is sent to a Private Bills Committee, which has got quasi-judicial power. A trial takes place in which the parties can appear in person or through their Barristers to put forth their own case. There is a detailed cross-examination of witnesses. After hearing all the parties to the case, the Committee decides regarding the desirability of the Bill. The Bill is killed if the committee gives an unfavourable report on it. If however, the committee after hearing all the parties, gives a favourable report and sends it back with or without amendments to the House, the same procedure is followed, as with regard to the Public Bills.

### The Procedure in Respect of Private Member's Bills

There is no difference in the procedure adopted for passing the Private Member's Bills and the Public Bills. But a Private Member's Bill has very little chance of passage in the Parliament without getting government support in favour of it. As it is difficult for a Private Member sponsoring the Bill to get the support of the Government, the whole exercise becomes a wastage of time and energy.

### The Committee System in England

The legislative bodies throughout the world are overburdened with work and have no time at their disposal to discuss a Bill in all its details. Moreover, in Parliamentary systems debate over a Bill becomes a prestige issue and on the floor of the House, even genuine amendments suggested by the opposition are not acceptable to the party in power. Thus large part of the preliminary work of the legislative bodies is assigned to the various Committees. The Committees assist the legislative bodies to acquire legislative competence on the one hand and on the other to save time on discussion of details. The Committee System was organised in England on a scientific basis in the year 1882. Since then the Committees have acquired great importance in the legislative process of Great Britain.

The more important among the Committees are discussed below:

#### *(i) The Committee of the Whole House*

When the entire House sits in the form of a Committee, it is called the Committee of the Whole House. But there are some differences between the House and the Committee of the Whole House. When the House sits as the Committee of the Whole House, instead of the Speaker, the Chairman or the Deputy Chairman of the Committee of Ways and Means presides over it. The Chairman sits in the Chair of the clerk of the House and the mace, which represents the authority of the Speaker is placed beneath the table. This indicates the relaxation in the rules of discipline and procedure of the House. Members have the liberty of speech and can speak as many times as they like.

All Money Bills are referred to the Committee of the Whole House. It is called the 'Committee of Supply' when it considers the question of demand of money and when the question of resources are discussed in the Committee, it is called the 'Committee of Ways and Means'. Controversial Bills and Bills of an urgent nature are also referred to the Committee of the Whole House.

There is the criticism against this Committee that it consumes too much time on deliberations. It is further criticised that the party in power controls its deliberations.

***(ii) Select Committee on Public Bills***

Usually there are fifteen members in a Select Committee, who are experts on the subject of the Bill. The Select Committee may be created before a Bill is introduced in the Parliament or after it is passed there. They are classified into two categories. *Ad hoc* Select Committees and Sessional Select Committees. The *Ad hoc* Committees are temporary in nature and go out of existence as soon deliberations on a particular Bill are over. On the other hand the Sessional Select Committees are created by the House at the beginning of a Session, and they continue till the end of the session. The Select Committee and its Members are proposed and accepted by the House. The Select Committees are most powerful and can invite public opinion on a certain issue. The Summons issued by the Select Committee are binding in nature and no body can refuse to attend Summons of the Committee. Any Bill that requires technical skill is under the absolute control of the Select Committee.

***(iii) Standing Committees***

At the beginning of a session, the Standing Committees are appointed and they remain unchanged, until the Parliament is prorogued. There is a peculiar Standing Committee known as the Standing Committee on Scottish Bills. There are five other Alphabet

Committees marked as A.B.C.D and E. The members of these committees are classified into regular and non-regular members and do not have any expertise. The regular members are 20 in number but when a Bill is referred to the Committee, temporary members varying between 20 to 30 are added to the membership of the Committee. The term of the temporary members is over as soon as the deliberation on a particular Bill comes to an end. The non-regular members are taken as members to render expert advice to the Committee. The Committee on Scottish Bills deals with those Bills that pertain to Scotland and it consists of seventy one members who come from Scotland. The Speaker forms the panel of Chairmen and the Standing Committees appoint their Chairmen from among the members of the panel. The Standing Committees try to eliminate the shortcoming of the Bill and give it the best form as far as possible. It may change the Bill by amending it, but has no power to kill the Bill.

The Standing Committee is criticised for its unwieldy size which is not conducive for a calm, sober and rational deliberation. It is too busy and overburdened with work as the number of Standing Committees is limited. It is also criticised as the regular members do not have expert knowledge.

### *(iv) Private Bills Committees*

In the U.S.A. and France, there are no Private Bills Committees as in those countries there is no distinction between Public and Private Bills. So the Private Bills Committees are peculiar to England only. They deal with the particular interest of a group or an area. The Private Bills Committee in the House of Commons consists of four members and in the House of Lords it consists of five members. It has got quasi-judicial power and its decisions are invariably accepted by the House of Commons.

### *(v) Joint Committees*

Matters or Bills in which both the Houses are interested are referred to the Joint Committees. These Committees are constituted by taking equal number of members from both the Houses. They are similar to the Select Committees as they consist of those members of both the Houses who have special interest in the matters under discussion.

Thus it is evident that these Committees play a great role in the legislative process of Great Britain.

# 7

# The British Judicial System

The British judicial system is famous for its independence, promptness, fairness, impartiality and incorruptibility. England is the classic home land of Rule of Law and this has been able to guarantee liberty and rights to the British people. The judges in England enjoy considerable independence. The English system of law has enabled the people to maintain their liberties without any interference by the Government or other agencies. In Great Britain there is no provision of Judicial Review as is the case in the U.S.A. Laws enacted by the British Parliament cannot be declared as null and void by the judges in England. Parliament has got the power of change any existing law by a new enactment. In the past judges in England used to hold office during the pleasure of the King. But now they are appointed by the Crown and hold office during good behaviour. They hold office for life. The judges can be removed from office only when an address is presented to that effect by both the Houses of the Parliament.

The British courts do not tolerate the dilatory tactics of the lawyers and cases before the courts are disposed off promptly and speedily. Appeals are allowed only in cases in which the judges are satisfied that good reasons exist for doing so. English Courts have also earned a reputation for the fairness with which cases are heard and decided.

The England judicial system is also characterised by the high standards of the British lawyers. In England there are two kinds of lawyers–Solicitors and Barristors. It is the duty of the Solicitors to deal with the clients and prepare the cases. Then they engage Barristors to present and argue the cases in the courts. The efficiency of the British judicial system is enhanced by this division of labour. The Jury system in England is working extremely well and it has not been abused till to-day. This system has also helped the Englishmen to safeguard their liberties.

Besides the Rule of Law, three other kinds of the law also operate in England. These are discussed below:

### *(i) The Common Law*

The British system of laws are greatly influenced by the Common Laws, which form the bulk of the laws in England. Customary rules as interpreted and applied by the judges in specific cases over a long period of time, have taken the shape of Common Laws. These laws own their origin to customs and tradition. These are neither enacted by the Parliament nor laid down by the King. There is no comprehensive codified document consisting of all the Common Laws of England and they are scattered in the decisions of the judges.

The genesis of the Common Laws can be traced back to the normal period. Prior to this local courts tried the cases according to local customs and tradition. But an attempt was made in the 12th century A.D. to centralise the judicial system, when travelling judges were appointed to be associated with the administration of justice by the local courts.

The travelling judges appointed by the King, travelled all over the country and administered justice as per the local customs and traditions, which differed from place to place.These judicial decisions based on local customs became centralised and gave birth to the system of Common Law, which were applied throughout the country.

### *(ii) Equity*

Equity consists of legal precedents, traditions and maxims which satisfied the conscience or discretion of the judges in respect to a case where Common Law was either absent or it failed to provide the proper remedy. As a matter of fact the shortcomings in the system of Common Laws helped the growth of the laws of Equity. About the middle of the 13th century and thereafter the Common Laws became an inflexible mass of customary rules. These laws suffered from many lapses and were inadequate to meet all the requirements of the judicial system. Thus the vaccum created by the Common Laws in the legal system was filled up by the laws of Equity, which also have the support of history behind them.

In ancient times when the people failed to get justice in the hands of the judges, they appealed to the King to grant justice in the name of conscience or principles of morality. The Lord Chancellor who was the 'Keeper of the Kings conscience' and was also the head of the Court of Chancery examined the cases on the basis of the petitions of the people and decisions were given by the Court of Chancery. This practice gave birth to a system of law which is known as 'Equity' to-day. Thus it is evident that both the Common Law and the system of Equity have resulted out of judicial decisions.

Judicials decisions have contributed to the growth of both the Common Laws and the laws of Equity. While the decisions of the King's travelling judges have contributed to the growth of the Common Laws, the judicial decisions of the Court of Chancery have helped the growth of the laws of Equity. Custom is the basis of Common Law, but in the case of Equity conscience, discretion and moral code of the community have provided the basis for development. The system of Equity is complementary to the system of Common Law, the former providing remedies in cases where the latter could best provide for a penalty. Only civil cases come within the jurisdiction of the laws of Equity; it does not criminal cases. In the past there were different courts which administered the Common Laws and the laws of Equity separately, but at present this difference has been eliminated.

***(iii) Statute Laws***

Now-a-days the statute laws have acquired a predominant position in the legal system of England. These are the laws enacted by King-in Parliament. The Statute Laws are unambiguous, clear and cogent and there is no difficulty in ascertaining the existence of the Statute Laws in any particular field. They have also filled up the gaps which were left unfilled by the Common Laws of the Country. In the ancient times the King's words were the laws. But now the laws are made by the Parliament, concerning all walks of the life of the individual and the society, and the King has no power to withhold assent from a Bill which has been passed by the Parliament.

The Common Laws have been at times changed by the Statute Laws and at times their scope has been enlarged by Parliamentary Acts. The Statute Law shall supercede the Common Law in case of conflict between the two. Both the Common Laws and the laws of Equity have emerged as a result of customary laws, born of judicial decisions and hence are unwritten, the Statute Laws are enacted by the Parliament and as such are fully codified. Despite the fact that in England the importance of Statute Law is on the increase, still the Common Laws constitute the backbone of the British legal system. It is difficult to think of administration of justice in England without the Common Laws.

### *(iv) Rule of Law*

Rule of Law guarantees liberty and equality to the British people. They are treated as equal before the eyes of law and no arbitrary punishment can be meted out to any body without the charge being substantiated in an ordinary court of law and without a verdict of the court. This has been remarkably enunciated by Dicey in the following words: "Everyman what ever his rank or condition is subjected to the ordinary law of the realm and is amenable to the jurisdiction of the ordinary tribunals. Every official from Prime Minister down to a constable or a Collector of Taxes is under the same responsibility, for every act done without legal justification as any other citizen". The Rule of Law has greatly influenced the British legal system.

## Organization of Courts

There is a well organised system of law courts in England. The Judicature Acts passed between 1873 and 1876 have reconstructed the present day organization and procedure of the English Courts. The organizational defects of the old judicial system have been rectified and now there is a uniform judicial system in the whole country. There were separate sets of Courts–one set to administer the Common Law and the other to administer the Law of Equity. There was no clear cut demarcation between the jurisdiction of the two sets of courts and this gave rise to conflicts of jurisdiction. Litigants who brought their cases to a wrong court from the point of view of jurisdiction had to suffer heavy pecuniary losses. In addition to this, he was put to lot of inconvenience and delay in getting due justice. After the passage of the Judicature Acts, nobody is allowed to suffer due to overlapping or conflict of jurisdiction.

The cases are classified into two categories–Criminal and Civil cases. The organisation of the English judicial system is based upon this division and there are two sets of Courts for criminal and civil cases. The prosecution is conducted in the name of the Crown in the Criminal cases. But the civil cases are brought by private individuals or Corporations etc., against one another.

## Criminal Courts

In the Criminal cases, justice is being administered by the following courts :

### *(i) Justice of Peace and Stipendiary Magistrate*

Justice of Peace and Stipendiary Magistrates administer justice in criminal cases in the local areas of England. The justice of peace serve in an hononary capacity and can try only petty offences. They are appointed by the Lord Chancellor. They do not have the power to award a punishment of imprisonment for more than 14 days or a fine which may exceed 205 pounds. They can be removed from office at any time if they are found unfit for the job, for which they are appointed. The Stipendiary Magistrates perform the functions of the justices of peace in the large cities.

***(ii) The Court of the Petty Sessions***

Over and above the court of the justice of Peace or Stipendiary Magistrate, there is the Court of the Petty Sessions. Its functions can be divided into two categories. Firstly, it has to try cases where there is no necessity of trial by jury. Minor offences like theft, cruelty, breach of traffic rules etc. come under this category of offences. In such cases it cannot give a sentence of imprisonment for more than six months or a fine exceeding £50 per month. Secondly, in respect of cases which are to be referred to a High Court for jury trial, the Court of the Petty Sessions, acts as a Court of Investigation.

***(iii) The Court of Quarter Session***

The Court of Quarter Session is just above the court of the Petty Sessions. It consists of all justices of peace in a country. Two judges form the quorum and all the justices of peace do not take part in the sittings of the Court. The cases come to the Court of Quarter Session on the basis of the report of the Court of the Petty Session in its capacity as a Court of Investigation. However, this court is not competent to try cases involving death or cases involving highly complicated issues.

***(iv) Assizes***

Assizes are must above the Court of Quarter Sessions and deal with serious offences which are beyond the jurisdiction of the Court of Quarter Sessions. Travelling Judges of the High Court who visit the country towns twice or thrice a year, preside over the Assizes. Cases in the Assizes are tried by a single judge together with a jury. Assizes have their sittings thrice a year in each country and four times in certain cities.

***(v) Court of Criminal Appeal***

Cases can be taken in appeal from the jurisdiction of the Court of Quarter Session or Assizes to the Court of Criiminal Appeal. The Lord Chief Justice and the Judges of the King's Bench are members of this court and the court hears appeals, that are instituted by the defendants only. It is thus obvious that the prosecution cannot put up criminal appeals where cases are usually tried before three judges.

## The Civil Courts

The organisation of civil courts in Great Britain is made as per the following details:

### *(i) The County Courts*

The County Courts are at the bottom of the judicial hierarchy of Civil Courts in England. These Courts were established in the year 1848 with a view to bring justice within the easy reach of the people. The whole country is divided into 500 districts or Counties and there is a Court in each County. Claims of more than £200 were referred to the jurisdiction of these courts. There are about 30 circuits into which the Counties are divided on the basis of work load and in each circuit there is a Circuit Court. Generally each circuit court is managed by one circuit judge.

### *(ii) The High Court of Justice*

The High Court of Justice has three divisions, viz., The King's Bench Division, presided over by the Lord Chief Justice; the Chancery Division, presided over by the Lord Chancellor and the Probate, Divorce and Admiralty Division under a President and another judge. Cases from the county courts can be taken in appeal to the High Court of Justice. Each division deals with the cases assigned to it by law. It may be mentioned here that cases involving large amounts do not go to the county courts and go directly to the High Court of Justice. Both Civil and Criminal cases are tried by the King's Bench. The Court of Appeal, which is the upper chamber of the Supreme Court of Judicature, hears appeals from the High Court. In theory the Judges of the High Court are free to sit in any Division and can be allotted any case. But in practice they are allotted work on the basis or their specialisation.

### *(iii) The Court of Appeal*

The Court of Appeal is there over and above the county courts and the High Courts to which cases are taken in appeal from the lower courts. The Court of Appeal is presided over by the Lord Chancellor and consists of 5 Lords Justices of Appeal and 3 Presidents of the three Divisions of the High Court and some other judges. Right of appeal is restricted only to those cases in which the interpretation of law by the lower Courts is in dispute.

## Top Appeal Tribunals

The foregoing analysis represents the organisation of Civil and Criminal Courts in England. But in addition to these courts, there are also two important appeallate tribunals which are endowed with supreme powers. They are discussed below:

### *(i) House of Lords as the Highest Court of Appeal*

The judicial committee of the House of Lords is the highest court of Appeal in civil as well as criminal cases. Appeals in civil cases from the decisions of the Court of Appeal can be taken to the House of Lords only on the recommendations of the Attorney-General. In theory all the Peers have the right to participate in the discussion when the House of Lords sits as a Court of Appeal, but in practice only the nine Law Lords take part in such discussions. The Judicial Committee of the House of Lords is presided over by the Lord Chancellor. The Law Lords are men of great legal distinction and they are made Peers for life. Remuneration is paid to them for their specialised nature of work. This highest Court of Appeal gives judgements and does not make recommendations. Peers who are charged with treason or felony are also tried by the House of Lords. Impeachments brought forward by the House of Commons are heard by the House of Lords in addition to its other judicial functions. The decisions of the House of Lords are supreme and final as it is the highest Court of Appeal in England.

### *(ii) The Judicial Committee of the Privy Council*

It is the last and highest Court of Appeal for cases from Dominions, Colonies, Ecclesiastical Courts in England, Courts of the Channels Islands, the Isle of Man and from Prize Courts during the time of war. All the members of the Privy Council do not sit when it meets as a Judicial Court. Its judicial committee only functions as the Court. It consists of about twenty members–Lord Chancellor, nine Law Lords, the Lord President of the Privy Council and some other members of the Privy Council and some judges appointed from the higher courts of the Dominions. The Lord Chancellor and the nine Law Lords, however, do not actual work. The Judicial Committee of the Privy Council makes only recommendation and does not give judgements. After the receipt of these recommendations these may be passed by the Crown as Orders-in-Council. The importance of the Privy Council was gradually reduced as more and more of the Common Wealth countries opted for self government on the Republican model and cut off all their connections with the judicial system of England. Even the Statute of Westminister of 1931 gave the power to the Dominions not to prefer appeals to the Privy Council, if they so desired.

From the foregoing survey it is evident that the judicial system in England is characterised by efficiency, impartiality and fairplay.

# 8

# Party System

Well organised political parties are the *sine qua non* for the smooth functioning of democratic institutions in a country. We cannot imagine a free country having democratic institutions without the existence of political parties. In the words of Burke: "Party is a body of men united for promoting, by their joint endeavours, the national interest upon some particular principle on which they are all agreed". According to Gettle, a political party is "a group of citizens, more or less organized, who act as a political unit, and who by the use of their voting power aim to control the government and carry out their general policy". In democratic countries, the political parties play a predominant role and the governments are party governments. The party which secures the majority in the Parliament or to be more specific, in the House of Commons forms the government in Great Britain. The other parties remain in opposition and they are said to form the 'shadow government'. The opposition tries to keep the government on the track by constant criticism. Political parties mobilise public opinion and make politics issue-oriented by focusing the attention of the people on the major issues confronting the nation. When the party in powers loses its majority support, it is forced to resign from office. Then the opposition is ready to step into the shoes of the out-going party. This helps the process of continuity in administration. In most constitutions, there is no reference to the political parties, yet the parties are indispensable for the proper working of the constitutions in the democratic countries. Responsible government and political parties are both of British origin and both are inseparable. Parties of one kind or the other have developed in England over the last five hundred years or so. There were the Lancastrians and Yorkists, Cavaliers and Roundheads, Whigs and Tories and now there are the Liberals, the Conservatives and the Laborites.

In the strict sense of the term the Lancastrians, the Yorkists, the

Cavaliers and the Roundheads were not political parties. The introduction of the Exclusion Bill in 1679, during the reign of Charles II, led to the formation of two political parties in England–the Whig Party and the Tory Party. The Whigs were opposed to the King's prerogatives, but the Tories supported the Royal prerogatives. Subsequently the Whigs and the Tories fought elections and in the course of time the Whigs came to be known as the Liberals as they followed a more liberal and progressive policy and the Tories came to be known as the Conservatives, because they were more conservative in their policies and attitudes. At the initial stages the Liberal Party was in favour of reforms, but the Conservative party was opposed to reforms. Ironically, in later years when reforms were introduced by the Conservative party, the Liberal party opposed these reforms in the Parliament. The Conservatives extended full support to the prerogatives of the Crown, the powers of the Upper Chamber, and the interests of the upper classes in the society. On the other hand the Liberal party was opposed to such vested interests and had its hold on the middle class. The Liberals were in favour of free trade and free competition, extension of suffrage etc.. The Irish Nationalists formed a party of their own during the early 19th century. This party was opposed to the union of Ireland with England and it wanted to restore Irish Home Rule. In the year 1900, the various Trade Unions, Co-operative Societies and Socialist Organisations formed themselves into a Labour Party.

In England at almost every time only two political parties have acquired the place of prominence and the other parties have been relegated to the background. First there were the Whigs and Tories, then the Liberals and the Conservatives took their place. At present the Conservative party and the Labour Party are the two major political parties in Great Britain. The popularity of the Liberal party has been very much reduced and it has got very few seats in the Parliament.

In England the party system has helped the process of growth and development of ministerial responsibility and the parliamentary system of government. In the words of Sir Courtenay, "The Cabinet system presupposes a party system, and more than that, a two-party system". Public opinion is reflected in a clearcut way in a two-party system. It is also conducive to maintaining the stability of the government as the party in power can always command a comfortable majority in the parliament. This will enable the Ministers to bring forward measures based on the programmes of their party in the legislature and can easily get them passed by the legislature. In a parliamentary system the legislature should exercise control over the executive, but it is also the duty of the legislature to support the government in carrying out the administration smoothly and efficiently. In a parliamentary system the opposition also plays an important role as it exercises constant vigilance on the government. It should also be able to oust the government from office and come to power when such a political contingency arises in the country. It is the duty of the opposition to ventilate the grievances of the people and to make constructive criticism of the lapses of the party in power.

The bi-party system in England facilitates the smooth working of the parliamentary system of administration. The two-party system, however, has got some disadvantages. Under this system, usually the interest of the minority is neglected. It leads to the tyranny of the majority party as it becomes supreme in respect of law-making, regulation of finance and administration, etc. The majority party develops an overbearing tendency and is not prepared to make any compromise with the opposition, even when the opposition is right. Sometimes party interest gets priority over the national interest. This amount to the violation of the true spirit of the representative government.

The above analysis should not make us blind to the short-comings of the multiple party system. In this system generally after the election, no single party is able to get a clear majority. This results in the formation of a Coalition Ministry, having representatives from all the parties or the majority of them in the legislature. A Coalition Ministry may be based on the principle of compromise, but it lacks stability. It may lead to frequent changes in the government, which will hinder the continuation of the policies and the programmes of the government. Thus the country's interests are bound to suffer under a multiparty system.

### Organization of Political Parties

Democracy and political parties had almost a simultaneous growth in Great Britain. Thus the political parties played a very significant role in the growth and working of the British constitution. Basset rightly observed that, "The British system of government–the product of British experience–is largely the product of British party life". People sharing the same ideas and a common political programme, organise themselves in a party and make endeavours to win political power in the state. In the words of Ramsay Muir, "organised co-operation among those who broadly think alike is the essential condition of achievement and organised co-operation in a party". General Elections are held in England in regular intervals and all the political parties try to win maximum popular support so as to come to power. Even after coming to power a party is interested to maintain the popular backing. To reach the people and to maintain the political communication, the parties need to be organised. Without a strong organisation a party cannot win in the election. Even if it wins by chance, it will fail to run the administration smoothly and effectively. Referring to the party organisation Bagehot has said that–"There never was an election without a party".

The British political parties follow a more or less similar pattern of organisation, which is discussed below:

***(i) The Local Committee***

In each Parliamentary constituency, there is a local committee belonging to each party. The local committee organises meetings, debates and discussions inorder to encourage peoples participation in party affairs and mobilise public support in favour of the party. There is a close collaboration between the Central party office, the elected members of the party to the parliament and the local committee of the party. The part prepares the support-base for its organisation through its local committee. The strength and efficiency of the party ultimately depend on the successful working of the local committee.

***(ii) The Parliamentary Party***

This is a very powerful party unit and consists of all the members of the party, elected to the parliament. It formulates the policy that the members of the party have to follow on the floor of the parliament. It also maintains the unity of the party by issuing directions and whips to the members to act in a concerned manner. No body is allowed to deviate from the party line on the important policy matters. It enforces discipline in the rank and file of the party and compels the party-members to work as a team.

***(iii) National Organisation***

Each party also has a national organisation for the purpose of presenting an integrated national image of the party. The central organization of the Liberal Party is known as the National Liberal Federation and that of the Conservative Party, the National Conservative union. The central organisation of the Labour party is known as the Annual Conference. The central organisations of the parties have supreme power over their respective party organisations. It is interesting to note that, the leader of the party is elected by the party members in the House of Commons and not by the Conference. Party officials are elected in the annual meetings of the national organizations. The party programme or the manifesto is also prepared by the national organization. It has got the power to review the work of the party during the year and to give constructive suggestions.

**The Party Programme**

Each political party has its own programme. It may be worthwhile to mention that at times the Liberal party brought forward reforms, which were opposed by the Conservatives and likewise the Liberals opposed the reforms introduced by the Conservatives. There are some common goals which are pursued by all the three major political parties of England. There is unanimity among all the parties regarding the continuance of constitutional monarchy as well as the retention of the Commonwealth of Nations. The parties also unanimously support the United Nations.

The Conservative party, which is the outcome of the Tory party, is supported by nobles, high ranks, clergymen, landed aristocracy, commercial and industrial interests. People of the middle class, small manufactures, tradesmen and shopkeepers also extend their support to this party. In the past these people gave their support to the Liberal Party. The Conservative party is opposed to socialism and nationalization. It stands for "the protection of property and the maintenance of the British Empire under the Crown".

The Labour party has assumed an important role in the political process of England due to the multifarious problems pertaining to trade, industry and labour. It secured the largest number of seats in the Parliament in the 1945 elections. Trade unions, Co-operatives and socialist societies extend their whole hearted support to the Labour party. Majority of the workers and members of the Trade Unions are included in the ranks of the party. The Labour party stands for socialisation and "the common ownership of land and capital, and the democratic control of all economic activities". The party is committed to the establishment of Socialist Commonwealth in Great Britain. It advocates the nationalisation of key industries and services and compensation to be given for the same. India got her independence when the Labour party was in power in England.

The Liberal Party is the outcome of the Whig Party. In the past it was a very strong party and formed Ministry in England on several occasions. This party is mostly supported by the middle class and at present has got very few seats in the parliament. It advocates social security, trade policy, full employment and development of agriculture.

In addition to these major parties there are small parties like the Communist Party, the British Fascist Party and the Independent Labour party in Great Britain.

The opposition is being constitutionally recognised in England and it plays a very important role in the British political system. It is called His Majesty's loyal opposition and its leader is paid from the Treasury. It is the duty of the Opposition to criticise the shortcoming and the lapses of the Government and to offer constructive suggestions. It is always prepared to step into the shoes of the party in power.

# Constitution of United States of America

# 1

# Growth and Development of the American Constitution

The United States of America is a very vast country with an area of 3,022,387 square miles. It occupies about one nineteenth of the land surface of the globe. In its physical size it would be nearly as large at all the countries of Europe taken together and a little larger than the continent of Australia. It is deep from North to South and rectangular in shape from East to West. It consists of nearly one-sixth of the earth's population. It is thinly populated having only 54 persons to a square mile and has got plenty of rich natural resources. It has got an excellent climate as it lies mid-way between Tropical heat and Arctic cold. It has got varied and vast lands suitable for all kinds of crops and agriculture is equally flourishing in the U.S.A. as is the case with trade and industry. It is at present one of the most affluent countries of the world and a Super Power, whose views and decisions have wide ramifications and far reaching consequences all over the wrld. Mineral resources like gold, silver, lead and zinc are in abundance and they contribute in no small measure to the affluence of the United States of America. The Industrial Revolution and the consequent urbanization greatly affected the distribution of population after 1850. There was a very fast growth of urbanization as a result of which at present more than three-fourth of the people in the U.S.A. live in the cities.

It may be out of place to analyse the entire history of the growth and development of the American constitution, but emphasis should be given on some major historical events inorder to have the right perspective of the political system of the U.S.A. America was inhabited by the socalled Red Indians, before the arrival of the European immigrants in a ship called–Mayflower. They were persons who were frustrated because of religious persecution both in England and the other European countries and had decided to leave for the U.S.A. with new hopes and expectations. These were the first original settlers of America who imbibed in them the spirit of liberty and rights and were detemined to fight for their rights at the cost of their life.

American colonists had founded thirteen colonies, in North America on the Atlantic Coast, during the 17th and 18th centuries. In 1607 the first colony, Virginia was founded and the last one–Georgia was founded in 1732. The people of the thirteen colonies enjoyed absolute internal autonomy although they were under the control of Great Britain. By Acts passed by the British Parliament, the people of the colonies were exploited for the benefit of the mother country. Exploitation of the American colonies under British imperialism was very much resented by the people of America. The American colonists from England were aware of the fact that the British who were oppressed under absolute. Monarchy could enjoy liberty and rights, because of the constitutional documents like the Magna Carta, the Petition of Rights. The Bill of Rights, the Habeas Corpus Act and other rights granted by the British Common Law. Thus, there was nothing unusual on the part of the American Colonists when they wanted to take a share in the making of laws in their own territories; the right of trial by jury; the right of self-taxation; the right of petition; the right of speech and assembly; and the right to be treated as equal before the law.

However, as long as there was the danger of being swallowed up by the French in Canada, the colonists never wanted to agitate vigorously against the mother country. This fear was removed from their minds after the end of the Seven Years War (1756-63), and the colonists started agitating against the unpopular and unjust laws passed by the British parliament for their exploitation. The Stamp Act, the Declaratory Act, New Duties, Duty on Tea etc., were some of these unjust Acts against which the people articulated their resentment.

"No taxation without representation", became the war-cry of the colonists. The colonists wanted to assert this principle in their future war against the mother country. The colonists were very much agitated against the enhanced duty on Tea, which was deliberately increased to grant protection to the tea locally produced in England. In 1773, an important incident took place, known as the 'Boston Tea Party', which dramatically transformed the whole situation. In this incident some of the colonists, disguised themselves as Red Indian Coolies, boarded the ship and threw all the tea chests into the sea. The British Government was very much annoyed due to this incident and it wanted to punish the colonists. The Boston Port Bill was passed and the Port of Boston (in Massachusetts), was closed to trade and the Charter of Massachusetts was suspended. This became a turning point in the history of the North American colonies. They wanted the fight against British exploitation and imperialism in a united manner.

On September 5, 1774, the meeting of the first Continental Congress took place consisting of all colonies except Georgia to discuss the common problems confronting the colonies and to present a united front against Great Britain. This Congress adopted several resolutions and decided to call a similar Congress in the following year. But things took a different turn and open clash of arms between the colonists and the imperial army of the mother country took place in April, 1775 at Lexington and later at Concord (Massachusetts). These events may be rightly described as the beginning of the American War of Independence.

On may 10, 1775, the Second Continental Congress met in Philadelphia to review the whole situation. George Washington was appointed as the Chief Commander of the Armed Forces for the purpose of successfully conducting the War of Independence against the mother country.

The Declaration of Independence adopted on July 4, 1776 was a historic document and the spirit of John Locke reverberated through the pages of this famous documents, an extract of which is given below:

"We hold these truths to be self-evident, that all men are created equal; that they are endowed by their Creator with certain unalienable rights; that among these are life, liberty and the pursuit of happiness. That to secure these rights, governments are instituted among men, deriving their just powers from the consent of the governed; that whenever any form of government becomes destructive to these ends, it is the right of the people to alter or to abolish it, and to institute a new government laying its foundation on such principles, and organizing its power in such form, as to them shall seem most likely to affect their safety and happiness".

Thus the 'Declaration of Independence' proclaimed the birth of the new nation of the United States of America and set forth the philosophy of human freedom and rights. Oppressed people all over the world accepted this as an idea model for starting their own respective movements against the away of imperial authority. People were inspired by the fundamental principles of the 'Declaration of

Independence' and decided to carry on the struggle against the oppressive regimes till they got their freedom and independence. The British colonies on the North Coast of the Atlantic declared themselves as independent of the Crown and also politically independent of each other as a result of the "Declaration of Independence'. But these thirteen independent States separately did not have the capacity to fight against the mother country and hence each one of them could have been easily subdued and reconquered by the mother country. This realisataion forced the erstwhile colonies to unite for the purpose of common defence and in 1777, the Continental Congress adopted, "Articles of Confederation and Perpetual Union". On November 15, 1777, the American Confederation was founded by the united effort of the erstwhile colonies. The 'Articles of Confederation', were sent to the States for ratification and the states ratified the provisions. The confederal congress decided to fight the war, under the leadership of George Washington.

Although the American States entered into a League of Amity and joined hands to fight the battle for independence in a united manner, they maintained their sovereign status and were free to decide their future course of action. It was a weak confederation. The congress was the central organ of the Confederation having delegates ranging from two to seven from each States. However, each State had only one vote. The Congress was empowered to fight the War of Independence and to look after foreign affairs and also to make peace.

It may be mentioned that a short time before the adoption of the 'Declaration of Independence', the Congress passed a resolution advising the colonies to form new governments "such as shall best conduce to the happiness and safety of their constituents". After the Declarataion of Independence on July 4, 1776, ten of the thirteen States had each adopted a new constitution within a year. The remaining three States also adopted their new constitution by 1780. As per the new constitution of each State it was to have an elected governor as the head of the State; an elected legislature to make laws for its administration and an independent judiciary to decide disputes. A Bill of Rights, incorporating the Fundamental Rights of the citizen such as right to speech, right to assembly, right to trial by jury and other rights was added to each State constitution subsequently.

Despite all these democratic provisions in their constitutions, the States did not make a real union and the confederation was a weak organisation. Munro has rightly observed that, "It was weak because it lacked four things which every strong national government must possess: the power to tax, to borrow, to regulate commerce and to maintain an army for the common defence. Now it is significent that these were the four powers given to the Congress of the United States by the new Constitution, which in 1787 replaced the old Articles of confederation.".

## The Process of Transformation to a Federal Constitution

As usual certain disputes cropped up between the States of Maryland and Virginia over trade and navigation. At the request of Virginia, a conference of all the States was convened to discuss inter-State trade relations. It met at Annapolis in 1 1786, but was attended only be delegates of five States. The need of calling another conference at Philadelphia in 1787 was emphasised by Alexander Hamilton, a delegate from New York. This conference was to discuss the question of strengthening the bonds of unity of the American Confederation.

As per the earlier decision a conference of all the American States was held in the Philadelphia State House in May, 1787. Fiftyfive delegates from twelve states, who had distinguished themselves in different walks of life attended this conference to discuss the question of strengthening the confederation. George Washington was unanimously chosen as the President of the Convention. The Rhode Islands was not represented in the convention. The rules of procedure were adopted by the convention and each State had only one vote. The members were pledged to maintain secrecy of the proceedings. Although the members of the convention were only authorised to discuss the ways and means to strengthen the confederation, the delegates after a vote, decided to go ahead with the consideration of a new forn of government.

Two separate plans such as the 'Virginia Plan' and the 'New Jersy Plan', containing various proposals of federation, were brought forward. There was dispute regarding the number of delegates from the big and the small states, to the proposed federal Congress. This was solved by the 'Connecticut Plan', which provided for representation in proportion to the population of the States in the Lower House of the proposed Federal Congress and equal representation irrespective of the size of the population in the Upper House. It was also proposed that the Money Bill should be introduced in the Lower House. The convention wanted that the powers of the Federal Government should be clearly defined and stated. The Philadelphia Convention recognised the need for giving the powers to coin money, to regulate commerce, to declare war and make peace to the Federal Government inorder to make it strong and effective.

On September 17, 1787, the New Constitution was signed by the delegates at the end of sixteen weeks of deliberations and discussions. The constitution was to come into force as soon as it was approved by conventions. Soon as it was approved by conventions in nine of the thirteen states. The required number of nine states adopted the constitution by the middle of 1788 and by the Spring of 1790, the remaining four states also ratified the constitution.

Under the provisions of the constitution, the presidential election was held and George Washington was unanimously elected as the first President of the United States of America. He took the oath of office to faithfully carryout the duties of the President of the U.S.A. to the best of his ability and to "preserve, protect and defend the Constitution of the United States". On April 30, 1789, the New constitution of the United States of America came into force.

The American War of Independence came to a close in 1781. In November 1782, preliminary treaties were signed between the governments of England and the U.S.A. and these provisions came into force after the signing of the Treaty of Versailles between France and Great Britain in 1783. The independence, freedom and sovereignty of the U.S.A. was recognised by the Treaty of Versailles.

Slowly but steadily the number of American States was increased from thirteen to fifty and the U.S.A. has risen to the position of being the world's most giganitc power.

The original American constitution did not include the fundamental rights, but the first ten amendments to the constitution appended a Bill of Rights to the Constitution, which guaranteed to all Americans religious freedom, freedom of speech, freedom of press, the right of trial by jury, the right to assemble peaceably for any purpose, to petition the government for the redress of grievances and the right to bear arms. The American citizens are also provided the right to security against unreasonable search and seizure of persons or property and the right to a fair public trial, in case he is charged with crimes. Thus like the British constitution setting the example of the Rule of law which was the bulwork of individual freedom and rights, the American Bill of Rights inspired the imagination of the lovers of freedom and democracy to incorporate in their own constitutions a chapter on fundamental rights. It is needless to say that the makers of the Indian Constitution were also greatly influenced by the constitutional experience of the Americans.

# 2

# Development of the American Constitution

The Constitution of America has been steadily developing during the last two centuries and it has celebrated the 200th anniversary of the constitution, in 1987. The constitutional system of America has come a long way since it was inaugurated in 1787. Although formally only twentyseven amendments have been received into the original framework of the American constitution, still the constitution has been metamorphosed without formal amendments. It is interesting to note that almost all the amendments so far have been brought about by Congressional initiative and not by any convention, called at the initiative of the States. Due to this process of change which was very often imperceptible, but was vital to the working of the system, the Congress was able to make laws on many topics, for which it was not authorized by the Constitution. In the past the American Congress has made laws on the banking and credit system, stock exchange, social security, guarantee of bank deposits, fixation of the price of food etc.

But Strictly speaking the original framers of the constitution never wanted to make the Congress so powerful as to be able to enact laws on most of these topics. They wanted that the federal government should have enumerated and specific powers so that it did not become too much overbearing in its dealings with the states. It was their intention to give more powers including the residuary powers to the States. This was deliberately planned to have a weak centre and relatively strong States to facilitate the growth and working of a decentralised federal polity. With this purpose in view, the constitution did not authorize the Congress specifically to legislate on the above mentioned topics. But the American constitution has adopted itself to the new conditions and it has gone through a process of healthy change and transformation inorder to meet the requirements of time. At present the American constitution is madeup of the Original Constitution, 27 amendments, statutes passed by the Congress and State Legislatures, judicial decisions interpreting the Constitution and the Statutes, administrative rulings, executive orders, conventions, usages, customs, precedents and traditions.

## Development by Amendments

Formal amendments are required to enable the constitution to adapt to the changing requirements of the time and clime of a country. A constitution is a document providing for the power-relationship among the various organs of the government as well as between the government and the governed. If a constitution is unable to change with time and does not provide for sufficient elbowroom for its growth and development, it will become outdated. Instead of being an asset, itwill become a liability and there is the apprehension of its being thrown out by a violent revolution. Since the time of the making of the American constitution and the establishment of its national identity, socio-political and economic life has undergone a sea-change. From the position of a weak confederation, it has grown in stature, beyond the most daring dreams of its founders. Most of these changes were never conceived by the framers of the constitution. Thus changes are inevitable to a constitutional system.

The American constitution also has been developed by way of amendments. The framers of the constitution did not want too many and too frequent changes to take place in the constitution. But they were aware of the fact that the constitution should not aid the minority in blocking the process of constitutional change, if that was the desire of the large majority of people. Due to this they provided for a rigid and difficult procedure of amendment and during the period of nearly 200 years there have only been 27 amendments accepted to the original framework of the American constitution. The process of Amendment which is incorporated in Article V of the Constitution is given below:

"The Congress, whenever two thirds of both Houses shall deem it necessary, shall propose amendments to the constitution, or, on the application of the legislatures of two-thirds of the several states, shall call a convention for proposing amendments, which, in either case, shall be valid to all intents and purposes as part of this constitution, when ratified by the legislatures of three-fourths of several states, or by conventions in three-fourths thereof, as the one or the other mode of ratification may be proposed by the Congress....."

The Congress proposed the first ten amendments, and they were ratified by the State legislatures. These ten amendments constituted the American Bill of Rights and they guaranteed fundamental rights and basic freedoms to the American citiznes. The congress also took the initiative in proposing the next ten amendments, which were also quickly ratified by the States. There was however, an exception is case of the 21st amendment, which was ratified by conventions in the several States, instead of the State legislatures. The power of amendment is not unlimited and certain provisions cannot be altered through the procedure of amendment. The provision of equal representation of the states in the Senate cannot be changed by amendment without the consent of the concerned States. Division or amalgamation of a State, without the consent of its legislature is also prohibited by the constitution.

The American constitution is not specific whether two-thirds majority of total membership, is necessary for amendment to the constitution and therefore two-thirds majority of the Members present is only taken into consideration, at the time of passing the Amendment Bill. The Supreme Court in its ruling has made it clear that the assent of the President is not necessary for proposing a constitutional amendment by the Congress.

A State legislature after ratifying a proposed amendment cannot go back on its decision. But there is no bar to ratify an amendment later although it might have refused ratification at an earlier stage. The State legislature's right of ratification of a proposed amendment is not subject to the veto power of the governor. There is no time limit for ratification of the amendment by the States. However, a seven year limit was fixed by the Congress in case of the ratification of 18th, 20th and 21st amendments and the Supreme Court upheld this decision.

## Development by Law

The Congress has helped the process of development of the American constitution by passing innumerable statutes from time to time. Without enacting these laws, it would not have been possible to run the administration in the country smoothly and effectively. These statutes have filled the gaps in the constitution. The organization and functions of the Supreme Court were provided by the constitution, but the structure and procedure of the sub-ordinate federal courts, were provided by statutes passed by the Congress. The constitution does not make any mention regarding the President's Cabinet and the various executive departments of the government.

These have been created by statutes. The laws passed by the Congress have provided for the national budget, although there was no reference to this in the Constitution. It is also interesting to note that the American constitution is silent about the Committee system, which was subsequently created by the statutes. The entire procedure of law-making by the congress has developed as a result of enactments adopted by the Congress. The American Constitution itself was silent on many vital aspects. The American federal system would have either become inoperative or ineffective in the absence of statutes, which have filled up the gaps in the constitution. The framers of the American constitution drafted a very brief constitutional document on the accepted notion that 'brevity is the soul of wisdom' and deliberately left out the details to be filled up by laws passed by the congress. In addition to the statutes, the executive officials issued many executive orders and there are also many administrative regulations which are also based on the statutes. These regulations and executive orders have the sanctity of laws and are highly essential for running the administration in the U.S.A.

## Judicial Decisions and Interpretations

Judicial decisions and interpretations have also played a great role in the development of the American constitution. In this connection the role of the Supreme Court in actual law-making is worth mentioning. The American Supreme Court has given a new meaning and dynamism to the phrases, provisions and words of the Constitution by its liberal interpretation. By this the small document of the Original Constitution has become vibrant with new life and purpose. Article I of the Constitution declares that, "The Congress shall have powers to regulate Commerce with foreign nations and among the several states". Through a very liberal interpretation of this constitutional provision by the Supreme Court, the congress has got complete power to make laws for railroads, motor stages, telegraph and telephone companies, steamship lines, airplanes, stock exchanges, radio broadcasting stations and so many other things. Originally the Congress was granted only 18 powers by the constitution, but through the liberal interpretation of the Constitutional provisions, a large numbe of powers have now been acquired by the Congress.

In the case of Marbury V. Madison, the Supreme Court gave the judgement that since it was the final arbiter of constitutional disputes, it ultimately reserves the rights to decide the constitutional validity of any congressional legislation and to declare it null and void if it is violative of the provisions of the constitution. This gave the Supreme Court not only the power to decide the constitutional validity of laws passed by the Congress, but also absolute power to interpret the Constitution. It is in this sense that the American Supreme Court was called as the 'Third Chamber' by Harold J. Laski, So long as the court did not outrage public opinion, it was free to change the constitution in any manner through its interpretation and apart from the constitutional amendment, this was the major factor which helped the development of the American Constitution.

**Conventions, Usages and Customs**

The role of the conventions, customs and usages in the development of the American constitution cannot be minimised. These factors have been able to change the very spirit of the Constitution. For example, the Constitution provided for the indirect election of the American President, but since the development of party system in American politics, by usage the election of the President has become direct. The Constitution did not provide for the Cabinet of the American President, but this has come into existence by means of usage and now weekly cabinet meetings are held and the Cabinet of the President has become an inseparable part of the administration.

The American Speaker has also derived his powers from usages. Another important Convention has developed that no President will stand for reelection for the third term. This convention was violated, when President Roosevelt was elected for the third term and the fourth term But now this tradition is followed very meticulously. The House of Representatives elects the Speaker, but he is the nominee of the majority party and its leader in the House. The executive and the legislative organs of the government which were desired to function separately from each other, have been linked up due to the growth of the party system in the U.S.A. The Constitution does not bar the President and the Vice-President from being elected from the same State. But in actual practice, the President and the Vice-President have never been elected from the same state. It may be mentioned that most of the rules and regulations of Congress are also the products of Customs.

Thus the development of the American Constitution has been both positively and negatively affected by the above mentioned factors.

# 3

# Characteristic Features of the American Constitution

Like the British Constitution which is famous for its parlimentarism, Rule of Law, bicameralism, responsible government, flexibility of the constitution and unitary government, the American constitution has been universally recognised for its contributions to federalism, presidential system of government, judicial supremacy, republicanism and rigidity of the constitution. It is innovative in many ways and has become an ideal model to be emulated by many countries of the world. It satisfied the aspirations of people having religious, ethnic, linguistic, racial and cultural diversities to join together in the creation of a political entity that protects their individual identity while uniting them under a sovereign state.

Some of the salient features of the American constitution are discussed below:

***(i) Popular Sovereignty***

The principle of sovereignty of the people is recognised by the American constitution. This has been enshrined in the Preamble of the Constitution in the following words:

"We the people of the United States, in order to form a more perfect union, establish justice, insure domestic transquility, provide for the common defence, promote the general welfare, and secure the blessing of liberty to ourselves and our posterity, do ordain and establish this constitution for the United States of America".

As per Article II, the Constitution of the United States of America is "the supreme law of the land". It is supreme over everything. The provisions of the American constitution are binding on all irrespective of their position or status.

The above mentioned provisions in the Preamble of the Constitution marked a clear departure from the Articles of the Confederation. Now sovereignty was transferred from the States to the poeple. This concept of popular sovereignty runs throughout the constitution and puts emphasis on the principle that there is no limit to the legal powers of the people. The American constitution also made specific reference to the right of revolution of the people, whch is a corollary of the concept of popular sovereignty. It was elaborated in the 'Declaration of Independence', in the following words:

"We hold these truths to be self-evident. That whenever any Form of Government becomes destructive of these ends, it is the Right of the People to alter or to abolish it, and to institute a new government laying its foundations on such principles and organising its powers in such form, as to them shall seem most likely to effect their safety and Happiness".

But the right of revolution, which is a corollary of the concept of popular sovereignty is no longer given any importance in the United States. The American Supreme Court has rejected this right in the case of Dennis Vs. United States in 1950. It was emphasised in the majority decision that, "It is within the power of the Congress to protect the Government of the United States from armed rebellion. Whatever theoretical merit there may be to the argument that there is a right to rebellion against dictatorial governments, is without force where the existing structure of the government provides for peace and orderly change".

### *(ii) Written Constitution*

In America there is a written constitution, which was adopted in 1787 and came to force in 1789. It was famous for its brevity and contained 4000 words which could be read in half an hour time. The constitution is the pivot of the American political system and though small it is a relatively sound and sufficiently detailed document. It contains the principles according to which the country is governed. In addition to the original principles of the Constitution it also consists of 27 amendments, the statutes of the American congress and of State Legislatures, Judicial decisions, usages, precedents administrative decisions etc., which have become part and parcel of the Constitutional Law of the country. In the words of Munro: "The architects of 1787 built only a basement. Their descendants have kept adding walls and windows, wings and gables, pillars and porches, to make a rambling structure which is not yet finished".

### *(iii) The Rigidity of the Constitution*

One of the salient features of the American Constitution is its rigidity. A rigid constitution is one which distinguishes between the ordinary law and the fundamental law of the country and provides for a difficult method for the amendment of the fundamental law as enshrined in the constitution.

In the last nearly two hundred years there have been only 27 Amendments to the Constitution. The first ten Amendments were adopted in 1791, and are collectively called as the "Bill of Rights". These are considered as part of the American constitution itself. There are two methods for proposing amendments to the Constitution and two methods of ratification. A constitutional amendment can be proposed by two-thirds majority of both Houses of Congress. On the applications from the legislatures of two-third States, the Congress has also to summon a national convention, for the purpose of drafting amendments to the Constitution. The constitution provides that Amendments may be ratified either by legislatures or by conventions in three-fourths of the States. Although previously there was no time limit, a time limit of seven years is now provided within which the ratification must be completed. The rights of the States to equal representation in the Senate cannot be denied by amendment, except with the consent of the States concerned. The division or amalgamation of the States, without the approval of the concerned legislature, is prohibited by the American constitution.

### Brevity of the Constitution

The brevity of the American constitution is one of its most striking characteristics. Together with all the amendments, it spreads over some dozen pages of an average book. It is a very small document in comparisons to the constitutions of other countries. On the question whether the constitution should be short or long, we are reminded of the controversy between Napolean and Talleyrand. Napoleon once told Talleyrand, his leading political adviser, that a "Constitution ought to be short and clear". But the latter replied, "No Sire, it ought to be long and obscure." This controversy has not yet been solved and the debate continues till to-day. The framers of the American constitution have preferred to follow the dictum of

Napoleon in framing a short constitution for their own country. But whether bravity and clarity go together, it is doubtful to come to any categorical conclusion. The American constitution has not been free from litigations and conflicting interpretations of its provisions. One thing, however, is certain that its brevity has provided ample scope for flexibility and adaptation. The fact that the constitution has survived for a period of more than two hundred years with very little change is an evidence of its strength and stability. The times have changed and challenging new situations have called for new measures to tackle them. Significantly enough, the constitution has been able to adapt and accommodate the gradual but decisive political evolution that has taken place during the past two centuries. It has provided for growth and development in response to new needs of a vast governmental structure. It never tried either to define, or prescribe or specify the details of governmental organisation in the country. It provided only the minimum essential conditions for the maintenance of liberty and efficiency.

The same constitution which at the beginning was used as an instrument of a laissez-faire state was transformed into an instrument of a welfare state. In the absence of the adaptability of the constitution, the development of modern industry and communications and the consequent problems faced by the government, would have led to a major constitutional upheaval. The brevity of the constitution facilitated the liberal interpretation of terms like "commerce" and "inter-state" by the Supreme Court and a whole range of powers were allowed to come under the jurisdiction of the federal government, may be against the intention of the original framers of the constitution. In so doing the Supreme Court was guided by the requirements of the community and the principle of maintaining governmental efficiency.

The American constitution did not make any specific reference either to the detailed organisation of the executive or the cabinet of the President. This has been subsequently done by Congressional legislation. In case of violation of the constitutional provisions by the legislature, executive or any state government, who shall have the power to declare such acts as unconstitutional or ultravires was not specified by the Constitution. This was decided in 1803, in the case of Marbury Vs. Medison, wherein the Supreme Court asserted this power. Since then it has exercised the power of declaring any law, executive decision, order or decree as unconstitutional if it was violative of the constitution. In the beginning there was some resistance to this assumption of power by the Supreme Court; but now it has become firmly established as a Constitutional usage. The constitution only gave the power to the Congress to admit new states into the union, but the laying down of conditions of membership and the nature of organisation or creation of the new States was determined by the Congress for which it did not have any specific constitutional support. Most of these problems were solved by political action as in all such matters consulting the constitution would have been meaningless. Thus the brevity of the American constitution has allowed it scope for expansion and adaptation to new circumstances and developments.

**Federalism**

The American constitution inaugurated the concept of federalism as an administrative contrivance to suit to the requirements of a large population having diversities due to geography, climate, resources, economic facts and social conditions. The heterogeneity of race, nationality, ethnic origin, language or religion presupposes that special protection and attention should be given to the different groups and their separate identity should be recognised. The essence of federalism lies in the fact that the federating units are recognised as separate and sacred entities deriving their power from the constitution. They have to maintain their separate identity at any cost. Dicey has rightly observed, "Federation is a contrivance for harmonizing local autonomy with national union". Federation implies union but not unity. While joining hands for common defence and increased power to implement common programmes, the States must be able to preserve their separate identity.

The constitutional relationship between the union and the States is inherent in a federal system. As the federal system provides two sets of government–one at the centre and the other in the periphery – so for the purpose of avoiding possible conflicts of jurisdiction, it must provide, for the definite relationship between the federal government and the government of the periphery, in their different spheres, namely, legislative, administrative and financial. America is accepted as the ideal model of a federal polity. Prior to the creation of the American federation, there wer 13 sovereign states, which surrendered parts of their sovereignty and created a federal state by granting it certain common powers through a Constitution. Thus in the American federation the centripetal force was responsible for its development. This has been responsible for making it an "indestructible union of indestructible units". The 13 States which started the revolution and succeeded in liberating their country from British imperialism were in need of maintaining their unity and solidarity, because they had to defend their new republican state against the onslaught of rival foreign states. They had to develop a sense of community consciousness and commonness of interest for maintaining the unity and the solidarity of the federal state. Due to these reasons, despite their eagerness to maintin the separate identity they had to develop a sense of legalism, faith in the constitution and should have a general willingness to yield to the authority of the Law courts which have to act as arbitrators in case of conflicts.

According to the provisions of federalism of the American Constitution, certain specified powers have been granted to the Federal Government and residuary powers are left with the States. The constitution also provides certain limitations. There are certain things which neither the Federal Government nor the State governments can do. They have no power to pass Bills of Attainder or grant titles of nobility. Power of coining money, issuing of paper currency and entering into treaties with foreign countries are the exclusive powers of the Federal Government. There are also certain powers which are exclusively exercised by State governments such as, controlling the local government.

The American Constitution provides for division of powers between the Federal Government and the State Governments. These Governments are supreme in their respective spheres. The powers which have been granted to the Federal government by the Constitution can be exercised by it without interference by the States. Similarly, in the sphere of specified and residuary powers, which have been granted to the States, they can exercise these powers without any interference by the Federal Government. According to the 10th Amendment of the Constitution: "The powers not delegated to the United States by the Constitution nor prohibited by it to the states, are reserved to the states respectively, or to the people." Thus the States occupied a preponderant position in the American federal system and the residuary powers were granted to them by the Constitution.

The following main powers were granted to the Federal government by the American Constitution:

(1) To lay and collect taxes for federal purposes – such as payment

of debts and provision for the common defence and general welfare of the United States.

(2) To borrow money on the credit of the United States.
(3) To regulate commerced with foreign nations and among the several states.
(4) To coin money.
(5) To establish post offices.
(6) To raise and support armies and to provide and maintain a navy.
(7) To declare war.
(8) To fix the standard of weights and measures.
(9) To look after foreign relations and to make treaties.
(10) To admit new States to the union.

The important residuary powers left with the States are:– (1) To lay and collect taxes for State purposes; (ii) to borrow many on the State credit: (iii) to regulate commerce within the State; (iv) to make civil and criminal laws; (v) to exercise control over the educational system; (vi) to control the local government, (vii) to have its own militia and (viii) to regulate industry and labour etc.

Thus despite enumeration, the powers of the States were indefinite and numerous.

The American federalism was the result of political expediency. The desire for the union was motivated by several factors. Professor K.C. Wheare observes that; "Communities have been led to desire union from a variety of reasons. But in the modern federations some factors seem always to be present. A sense of military insecurity and the consequent need for common defence, a desire to be independent of foreign powers, and a realization that only through union could independence be secured, a hope of economic advantage from union, some political association of the communities concerned prior to their federal union either in a loose confederation, as with the American States, and the Swiss Cantons or as parts of the same Empire, as with the Canadian and Australian colonies, geographical neighbourhood and similarity of political institutions–these half-dozen factors all operated in the United States, Switzerland, Canada and Australia, to produce a desire for union among the communities concerned."

The Constitutional convention at Philadelphia was aware of the weakness of Confederation. There was a desire to have a Stronger federal government but no unit was prepared to surrender the existing arrangement. They were afraid of the powers of the Federal Government and thought that it would be prejudicial to the interests of the States. The new constitution of the United States of America came into force on April 30, 1789, but very few and defined powers were given to the Federal Government. The Champions of the States' rights were not prepared to grant more powers to the Federal Government at the expense of the State Governments. In the words of James Madison, "The powers delegated by the proposed constitution to the federal government are few and defined. Those which are to remain to the state governments are numerous and indefinite. The former will be exercised principally on external objects as war, peace, negotiation, and foreign commerce with which the power of taxation will, for the most part be connected. The powers reserved to the several states will extend to all the subjects, which in the ordinary course of affairs concern the lives, liberties and properties of the people, and the internal order, improvement, and prosperity of the State".

But despite all these restrictions on the powers of the Federal Government, in the course of time its powers have increased immensely and there has been a constant tendency towards greater and greater centralisation of authority. Centralisation has become a universal tendency with all systems of government and the federal government is no exception to it. Several factors like the world wars, economic depression, urbanization, industrialisation and the rise of the welfare state have made it indispensable for the state to exercise more and more authority so that it can solve the problems of the people and meet the challenges of the changed circumstances. But it is interesting to note that this expansion of the powers of the Federal government has taken place not because of formal constitutional amendments but by the liberal interpretation of the constitution by the judiciary.

It was chief justice Marshal who popularised the doctrine of implied powers by his famous interpretation of the constitution in the case of McCulooch vs. Maryland (1819). By a new and broad interpretation of the Constitution, he allowed large powers to the American Congress, which were not specifically mentioned in the Constitution. In the words of Chief Justice Marshal, "We admit, as all must admit, that the powers of the government are limited and that its limits are not to be transcended. But we think the sound construction of the constitution must allow to the national legislature that discretion, with respect to the means by which the powers it confers are to be carried into execution, which enable that body to perform the high duties assigned to it, in the manner most beneficial to the people. Let the end be legitimate, let it be within the scope of the constitution and all means which are appropriate, which are plainly adopted with the letter and the spirit of the constitution, are constitutional".

This interpretation of Marshal opened the floodgates for the transformation of the constitution leading to ever-increasing centralisation of authority, during his time (1801-1835) and during the New-Deal period of Franklin D. Roosevelt. K.C. Wheare has also referred to the centralising tendency in most political systems of the world, particularly the federal ones due to the operation of the following factors: (i) the two World Wars; (ii) the Economic Depression of 1930; (iii) planning; (iv) welfare programme of the government; and (v) revolutionary change in the means of transport and communication. All these factors have shown very powerful and unmistakable tendencies towards centralization. In view of phenomenal centralization in America, some writers on the American political system have also described it as "quasi-federal".

Centralisation of powers in the American federation took place more vigorously after the Civil War of 1860-65. The agricultural southern States were having limited resources and wealth in comparison to the industrially advances States of the North. This was the basic reason of bickering and badblood between the North and South. The people of the South and their agricultural economy largely depended on Negro captive labour for growing cotton, tobaco, tomatoes, oranges and other commodities. Thus the people of the South were conservative and had a limited outlook, while the people of the heavily industrialized Northern States were liberal and progressive. The abolition of slavery in America by President Abraharm Lincoln led to a Civil war which went against the South. The victory of the Northern States was a victory for the forces of centralisation as it settled the question or secession for all times to come. Afte this incident the American Federal Government did not hesitate to implement progressive welfare measures and in bringing reforms in the socio-economic sphere of the country. Thus we can say that history has also played a decisive role in the centralizing process of the U.S.A.

Another factor which has helped in enhancing the powers of the Federal Government is the economic assistance given by it to the States for running the various projects. In most of the States projects like housing, urban renewal, sanitation, parks and recreation, job-training programmes etc., are managed with the help of federal assistance. It is therefore, quite natural that these States would concede to central supervision and direction in the management of the projects which are aided by the Federal Government. In recent years States have vied with each other to get more and more grants-in-aid and other types of financial assistance for their various developmental programmes.

In this connection one is reminded of the adage, 'he who pays the piper, controls the tune.

The Congress was given the power to receive more States to the union as members and to create new States out of the territory in the United States. The 13 original States who fought for indepndence and were equal partners in the making of the constitution were enthusiastic champions of States' rights and they insisted on limited powers of the Federal Government. But the new States which were created subsequently by the Congress, naturally owed their allegiance to the Federal Government, because they were created by it. In comparison to the number of the old States, the number of the new States became substantially large enough to neutralise any resistance to the increased powers of the Federal Government.

Another factor responsible for centralization in the American Federation is the planning process. Although it is not all-embracing and total as in the former Soviet Union, China or India, yet the planning process has enhanced the powers of the Federal Government in determining financial outlays and exercise of review and supervisory powers over the States. The financial assistance and grants-in-aid given by the Federal Government to the States have resulted in financial and administrative constraints and controls by the Federal Government over the States.

Wars and National Emergencies have also added to the process of centralizatioin in America. During the Second World War period the States surrendered large amount of their power, authority and initiative to the Federal Government. In order to make it more efficient and effective. Although supposedly this surrender of power was only temporary, the State governments never regained these powers after the war was over. National emergencies like the Economic Depression of 1930s have also greatly increased the powers of the Federal Government. Due to this Depression, prices, production and the economy collapsed and people became panic-striken. President Roosevelt acquired tremendous powers to deal with this grave situation and he inaugurated the New Deal–a multi dimensional economic programme. The American economy recovered very quickly as a results of the extraordinary measures, but in the process the Federal Government acquired immense powers in the administrative, economic and political spheres. The Federal Government continued to execise these powers even after the crisis was over.

It is needless to say that the development of America as a welfare state in the 20th century has changed the entire concept of state functions. The laissez faire attitude to state functions was discarded and the new philosophy approved the participation of state in ever increasing activities of the society to give a better deal to the underprivileged and provide social justice to all. This process enhanced the powers of the Federal Government and centralisation became the order of the day.

The revolution in the means of transport and communication has also transformed the federal system in America and has changed the pattern of federal-state relations. As a result of this there was a shrinkage in the size of the political system in terms of distance and it increased the effective control of the Federal Government over the federating units.

The tendency towards the emergence of co-operative federalism has also increased the dependence of the States on the Federal Government. By a legal interpretation of the Supremacy Clause as laid down in Article VI of the American constitution, some writers have expressed the view that supremacy of the Federal Government is inherent in the consitution. But this aspect is no longer insisted in the American political system as the purpose is wonderfully served through the process of co-operative federalism.

American federalism has been criticised by Professor Harold J. Laski as an 'obsolescent federalism' as it is not sufficiently positive in character. He observes: "It does not provide for sufficient rapidity of action, it inhibits the emergence of necessary standards of uniformity, it relies upon compacts and compromises which take insufficient account of the urgent category of time; it leaves the backward areas a restraint at once parasitic and poisonous, on those which seek to move forward". But most of these alleged short comings of the American federalism have either been remedied or eradicated. It may be mentioned that co-operative federalism in America has both helped the process of centralization and has also acted as a substitute for centralisation. As a result American federalism has become a living and developing instrument of government.

## Separation of Powers

The principle of separation of powers forms the basis of the American constitution. This theory was propounded by Motesquiu, the French political philosopher as a bulwork of individual freedom and rights. He was of the opinion that the legislative, executive and the judicial powers of the government must be separated from each other inorder to safeguard the liberty of the individual because the concentration all these powers in one and the same hand would lead to arbitrariness. Montesquieu was of the view that because all these powers were concentrated in the hands of the French Monarchs they behaved in a despotic manner.

The makers of the American constitution were very much influenced by this doctrine of Montesquieu in drafting their own constitution as they were predominantly concerned with the preservation of the liberty and rights of the individual. They provided for the election of the President and the Members of the Congress by the people. Although originally the constitution provided for the indirect election of the President, in the course of time, because of the development of party system, in practice the Presidential election has become direct. The President appoints the judges of the Supreme Court, but after their appointment, they hold office during good behaviour for the whole life. The President and Members of his cabinet are neither Members of the Congress nor they are responsible to it. The President has no power to dissolve the Congress. The President cannot be removed by a vote of noconfidence as is the practice in the Parliamentary system of government. His office goes by the Calendar and once elected, he continues for a period of four years. This is how in the American political system, the executive, legislature and the judiciary maintain their independence and are separate from each other in their composition and functioning.

## Checks and Balances

It is known to every student of government that absolute separation of powers among the different branches of government is neither possible nor feasible. Government is an organic whole and its different branches cannot be separated into watertight compartments. Any such separation would be detrimental to the working and the efficiency of the government.

Thus inspite of the separation of powers, the three organs of the government of the United States are not fully independent of each other and a system of checks and balances is in operation. The President's power of appointment has to be ratified by the Senate, the upper chamber of the American Congress. He cannot declare war without the approval of the Congress. The laws passed by the Congress are sent to the President for his approval. The President has got the power of veto with the help of which, he can exercise a check on the legislative powers of the Congress. The Congress also is empowered to override a Presidential veto, by passing the Bill again by a two-thirds majority. Through his power of sending messages to the Congress, the President has got the power to influence the legislative process in the Congress. The treaty-making power of the President is subject to ratification by the Senate. There is judicial independence in America, but the judges of the Supreme Court are appointed by the President. Although the judges have a life tenure, they can be removed from office by impeachment. The President has a fixed tenure of office, but he can also be removed from office by the Congress by the means of impeachment. Laws passed by the Congress, executive decisions and decrees of the President can be declared as unconstitutional or ultravires by the Supreme Court. Thus it is clear from the above analysis that the principle of separation of powers has been provided in the American constitution with a system of checks and balances.

## Judicial Supremacy

The American constitution provides for the supremacy of the judiciary. A federal system provides for distribution of powers between the Central Government and the federating units and the constitution is the main source of authority for the respective governments. No government is expected to transgress the jurisdiction of another. In case of such transgression there must be some independent authority to decide the dispute and give the final decision. Then there may also be disputes regarding the interpretation of the provisions of the Constitution and rights guaranteed by the constitution to the individuals and the States might be violated. In all such cases people look to the Supreme Court as the final arbiter and the decisions of the Court are final and conclusive. In England there is a different system. The laws passed by the British Parliament are final and no court in England has got the power to challenge the constitutional validity of the laws passed by the parliament. But in America, the judiciary is endowed with the power of supremacy to nullify the laws passed by the Congress, even after the President has given his assent to these laws. Laws passed by the State Legislatures and any executive decrees, orders or decisions can be declared unconstitutional by the Supreme Court, if they are violative of the provisions of the Constitution. The American Supreme Court can even declare a law as unconstitutional, if it is violative of the provisions of Natural Law. The American Supreme Court assumed this supreme power in the year 1803 and since then this power is being exercised by the court without any challenge. In this respect John Marshall, Chief Justice played a very vital role in asserting the supremacy of the judiciary in matters of the interpretation of the constitution and quashing down in its opinion was unconstitutional.

### Republicanism

The State where the Head is elected is called a republic. The American Constitution provides for the election of the President, who is the Head of the State. The American had the bitter experience of imperial rule by England and were against any kind of concentration of power. Thus they provided for an elected President with limited or defined powers. The Constitution provides for the indirect election of the President by an electoral college. The electoral college consists of representatives called 'electors'. Their number is equal to the number of Members in the House of Representatives and the Senate. These electors vote in their respective State capitals. Although the constitution provided for the indirect election of the American President, since the year 1800, it has become direct in practice after the development of political parties. The 12th Amendment of the American constitution provided to designate votes for the President and the Vice-President separately. This election procedure to elect the President and the Vice-President has worked with success till to-day.

### Presidential System

The American Constitution provides for a Presidential system in which there is a clear distinction between the executive and the legislature. In the United States the President is the Chief Executive and he is both the nominal and real executive Head of the State. He is the Head of the State as well as the government. The American Congress cannot ordinarily remove the President by a vote of noconfidence as is the practice in the Paliamentary system of government. The

American President remains in office for the fixed term of four years as provided by the Constitution. In the American Presidential system, due to separation of power among the different organs of government, the Congress is primarily responsible for law making and the President is in charge of implementing the laws. The President and his Secretaries are neither Members of the Congress, nor do they play any role in its deliberations and the passage of the laws.

In the American Presidential system, the Secretaries of the President are not appointed strictly on party lines. Efficiency and experience are taken into consideration at the time of the appointment of the Secretaries. Since collective responsibility is not an essential pre-requisite of the Presidential government, political homogeneity of the executive is not insisted upon. The President and his Secretaries are not the Members of the Congress and are not accountable to it as is the practice in the Parliamentary system of government.

In the American Presidential system the President is the master of his cabinet. The Secretaries are his servants. The Cabinet is known as the 'President's Family'. The Secretaries are individually responsbile to the President for the acts of omission and commission on their part. The President dominates over the Cabinet and he has the power to override the decision of the Cabinet without any hesitation.

## Secularism

Secularism means that the State should not give patronage to any particular religion and there should be no state religion. People should enjoy religious freedom and equality. No body should be discriminated or should be made ineligible for any benefit or privilege merely on the ground of his religious faith. People must be given the right to freely preach, profess and propagate their religion without any interference. In many countries secularism identified with anti-clerical attitude and the extreme form of it was represented in the form of atheism. On the basis of secularism, some people rejected the value of organised religion and carried on an active campaign against faith in God. Now also there is a notion in some quarters that a secular state is an irreligious state. When the American constitution was drafted, it was the common practice on the part of each State to have its official religion. But the 1st Amendment of the American constitution provided that, "Congress shall make no laws respecting an establishment of religion and the free practice thereof". This amendment incorporated the basic principle of religious freedom of the individual. The constitution also provides that, "no religious test shall be required as a qualification in to any office or public institution in the United States". Thus the American Constitution guarantees freedom of conscience and religious practice for all. No body shall be discriminated in any manner in the holding of public office, on the basis of religious beliefs. American secularism prevents it from establishing any official or state religion. Despite American secularism, religion plays a predominant role in the life of the individuals. No political leader can get himself elected to any political office, if he is a pronounced atheist. There is a remarkable religious element in the American political traditions. Harold J. Laski was very critical of the religious element in the American political traditions as it was antagonistic to any radical social philosophy.

# 4

# The President of United States

America has a Presidential system of government and the American constitution provides for a President as the Head of the State and government. According to Article II of the Constitution, "The executive power shall be vested in a President of the United States of America. He shall hold office during the term of four years, and together with the Vice-President, chosen for the same term". The Constitution did not provide for any limit to the number of times a person could be elected to this august office. A limit on the number of Presidential terms, however, has been fixed due to the growth of a usage according to which, no president was to stand for reelection for the third term. In 1940, this tradition was broken when President Roosevelt was reelected for the third successive term and again in 1944 for the fourth term. He, however, died in April 1945. The limit on the Presidential tenure is now fixed by the 22nd Amendment of the American Constitution which has restricted the tenure of office to two terms.

The American Presidency has been described by Lord Bryce, as the greatest office in the world, to which any person can rise by his own efforts. The President occupies one of the most powerful offices ever created in a democratic country. He is the Head of the nation, Head of the government, the leader of his political party, the chief custodian of national interests. He also plays a great-role in influencing the legislative process in the Congress. Not only the American national but also the whole focusses its attention on the statements and actions of the President. "Almost his thoughts become news. The difference between a good Congress and a bad one is largely the difference between a Congress which accepts his leadership and one which seeks to refuse the initiative he tries to communicate". This however is not a true picture of the present day situation. The Congress is taking now far greater initiative in translating into action the just and radical aspirations of the people as against the conservative and outdated policies of the Presidents. In recent times the American Congress radically differed from the views of President Reagan on the question of economic and political sanction against the racist government of South Africa. A Bill providing for more stringent sanctions against South Africa, which was passed by the Congress, was voted by the President. But the Congress took a historic stand in over-riding the Presidential Veto, by repassing the Bill by a two-thirds majority in each House. On this vital issue the international public opinion and the support of an overwhelming majority of the people in America are with the American Congress. It is proved that, the Congress does not always accept the initiative of the President just only to become a 'good Congress'.

But there is no doubt that the American President influences very aspect of policy and action in the federal sphere. In the words of Harold J. Laski: "From one end of the scale to the other, it is the presidential attitude which, on the government side, can alone make a universal impact on public opinion. The President is one man in the United States, the expression of whose opinions is certain to receive attention".

The American President combines in himself the prestige and halo of the King with the powers and authority of the Prime Minister. He represents the dignity and the strength of the nation and symbolizes the aspirations of the people. Despite his party affiliations, he is the undisputed leader of the country and its chief spokesman. He represents America in major international conferences and gatherings. His key role in natioinal politics, his undeniable influence in the sphere of international politics, his power of Veto, the power of sending messages to the Congress recommending legislative measures, his vast powers of patronage and his special position in determining the foreign relations of the country have projected his image in a manner that he is considered not only the most powerful person in the United States, but also the whole world.

## Qualifications for Office

Only the natural born citizens of America who have completed at least 35 years of age and are resident in the United States for fourteen years are eligible to contest for the office of the President. The salary of the President is fixed by statutory law and cannot be increased or reduced during his term of office. In 1949, the salary was fixed at one lakh dollars per year plus fifty thousand expense allowance. Now this is made taxable.

## Presidential Succession and Inability

The 25th Amendment of the constitution (1967), provides that, on the death or resignation of the President, the Vice-President shall become the President. Whenever such a situation arises, the Vice-President becomes the President and not the acting President. In case of vacancy in the office of the Vice-President, the President nominates a Vice-President, who assumes office on confirmation of both Houses of the Congress. As far as succession to the office of the President is concerned, as per Article 2 of the Constitution, the Vice-President exercises the powers and duties of the President in the event of the death, resignation or disability of the President or his removal from office. It is provided by the 20th Amendment that in the event of the death of the President elect before inauguration, the Vice-President elect becomes the President. In the event of the death of both the President and the Vice-President, according to the new law of 1947, the Speaker of the House of Representatives and the President Protempore of the Senate will be in the line of succession and preference given earlier to the Secretary of State and then down the line of Executive Departments as per the Act of 1886 has been cancelled. This has been done with a view to give priority to elected office-bearers in matters of succession, in preference to others.

## Privileges of the President

The President gets the salary and allowances as fixed by the congress. The President is above law and enjoys certain constitutional immunities as Head of the State. He cannot be arrested for any crime. He cannot be sued in any Court and cannot be made a witness against his wishes. It is very difficult to enumerate all the privileges of the President as he occupies one of the most exalted offices ever created by a democratic constitution. He stays in a luxuriously furnished mansion, known as the White House. He is also entitled to a Secretariat, a suit of offices, a private car, a yacht and an aeroplane. He is the Commander-in-Chief of the Army, Navy and Air Force, and of the Militia, when in the service of the Union.

## Impeachment of the President

Despite all his vast powers and privileges, the President can be removed from office by impeachment for the crimes of treason, bribery or other highcrimes. In the impeachment is passed by the House of Representatives by two-thirds majority of votes, then it is sent to the Senate. The whole Senate sits as a Court of Impeachment and if the resolution is passed by the Senate by two-thirds majority also, then it will have the effect of removing the President from office with immediate effect. It may be mentioned that no President has so far been removed by impeachment although there was once a case of unsuccessful impeachment against President Andrew Johnson.

## The Presidential Election

The American Constitution has provded for indirect election of the President by presidential electors. According to the procedure of election prescribed by the constitution, each state was required to "appoint in such manner as the legislature thereof may direct, a number of electors, equal to the whole number of senators and representatives to which the state may be entitled in the Congress."

In their turn the presidential electors from each state meeting in a group were to give their votes in writing for two persons and one of the persons was not to be an inhabitant of the state of the electors. Previously the person getting greatest number of votes was to be the President, provided this was also clear majority of all the electoral votes, and the person getting the next highest number of votes was to be the Vice-President. In case more than one person had such majority and also had equal number of votes, then the House of Representatives decided by ballot as to who among the five highest on the list would become the President. But the 12th Amendment of the American constitution provided to designate votes for the President and Vice-President separately inorder to avoid the complications of the procedure of election.

Laski observed that, "The founders of the Constitution were especially proud of the method they adopted for choosing the President, none of their expectations has been more decisively disappointed". This took place due to the emergence of political parties by 1800. The American Constitution did not provide anything regarding the nomination of the Presidential candidates.

The American President is elected by an electoral college consisting of Presidential electors from each State which is equivalent to its strength in both the Houses of the Congress. Each of the parties selects a full state of candidates for the seats to which a State is entitled in the electoral college. The Presidential electors are pledged to vote for the party's nominee. Members of the electoral college are chosen by popular vote on a general ticket basis. The Presidential candidate either wins a state or loses it completely, and secured all the votes allocated to the state for the electoral college.

The members of the electoral college vote mechanically for the party candidate and hence voting for the President by the electoral college is just a formality. Generally from the composition of the electoral college one can easily guess as to which party is going to get its nominee elected as the President.

The members of the electoral college meet on the second Wednesday of December in their respective state capitals and cast their votes for the President. The votes are opened in the presence of the members of the Senate and the House. The President of the Senate counts and declares the result. As it is mentioned earlier, if no candidate for the presidency receives the necessary electoral majority on Election Day, the issue is referred to the House of Representatives, where each state has but one vote to cast, regardless of its size of population. Such exigency has taken place three times in American history–1800, 1824 and 1876. The elected President assumes office on January 20 at noon, as per the provisions of the 20th Amendment of the American constitution.

The method of election of the American President as provided in the constitution has considrable significance in American politics. Inorder to win the presidential election, one has to get considerable support in at least two or the three regions–the Industrial and Commercial North East, the Agricultural and Industrial Middle West, and the South with its peculiar traditions, each of which commands a substantial number of votes. Merely having more supporters in the electoral college is not sufficient as the votes of each State are cast en bloc, the candidate should not only think of his supporters throughout the nation, but also he must get a majority in a number of populous states. This means that he must be able to combine wide popular appeal with the emphatic support of certain regions and interests.

"The conflicting regional interests, the special loyalties of the many racial and national groups of whch the population is composed, and the factor of class-conflict, might have produced a Keleidoscope of small sectional parties to the injury and division of the nation. The nature of the Presidential election obliges the parties to become broad coalitions seeking support from many different groups and anxious to offend as few as possible. If, in the result, there are such strange bedfellows inside each party that it is hard to say what principles or beliefs unite them, America is atleast seved from the bitter strife that might result if every racial, regional or class grouping fought in the political battle for its own undiluted interest. In Britain, fundamental national unity is taken for granted; America has still to keep in mind the need to preserve it".

## Criticism of the Electoral System

In America, the first short coming of the electoral system is the possibility that the members of the electoral college may break their pledge to vote for a particular Presidential candidate. If the pledges are broken even by a few members, it can put the presidential election in a situation of great disorder.

According to the provisions of the existing system, it is also likely that the winning candidate might have obtained fewer popular votes than the losing candidate. This happens due to the operation of the election by general ticket where the winner in a particular state, wins all the electoral votes of the state. It is a sort of 'unit rule' under which the winner of a plurality in each state takes all and the national total of popular votes counts for nothing. Thus the proportionate division of electoral votes is prevented.

The third shortcoming of the Presidential election is that, when no candidate gets the required majority, the matter is referred to the House of Representatives with strange possibilities. When there are more than two strong candidates and no body secures the required majority of votes than the mattter is referred to the House of Representatives. In the House voting takes place by States, with one vote for each state and not by members. It is likely that a minority party may have control in the House over a majority of the State delegations and in that case the candidate who is elected as President might have stood second in both the popular and the electoral votes.

## Powers and Functions of the President

The American President derives his powers from many sources, but the constitution is the main source of his power and authority. He enjoys vast and far-reaching powers as a result of the provisions of the constitution. From the Constitution he derives the power to make appointments and removals, to make treaties with the consent of the Senate, to veto acts of the Congress, to call special sessions of the Congress, and to require the opinion in writing from the Heads of the various executive departments. The Constitution empowers him to be Commander-in-Chief of the army, navy and the airforce. He can grant reprieves and pardon to offenders. It is his duty to secure the faithful enforcement of the laws and to preserve, protect and defend the constitution of the United States.

The powers of the American President have also been enhanced by the various statutes passed by the Congress. In 1933, the President got discretionary powers, for reducing the gold content of the dollar and for issuing additional paper money. In 1941, the Lend-Lease Act was passed by the Congress, which authorized the President to supply ships, arms and amunitions etc. to the Allied countries.

The Presidents powers have also been enhanced by the judicial decisions of the Supreme Court. According to the decisions and interpretations made by the Supreme Court, the President can even grant pardon to the offenders, before they are convicted. Officials appointed by him on the advice and with the consent of the Senate can be removed by him unilaterally, without constituting the Senate. The President has also acquired some powers by usage.

## Executive Powers

The vast array of executive powers enjoyed by the President, make him the central figure in the American political system. There is no doubt that the American President is the most important and most powerful single figure in any democracy in the world to-day. The President has become sovery powerful that some people consider him as a threat to democratic government. There might not be any truth in this apprehension, but it can certainly be said without the fear of contradiction, that the controls over the aggrandisement of the executive authority built-in by the American constitution, are proving to be ineffective. In the words of Corwin: "Power of the purse is reduced by the Congress some what voluntarily in times of emergency exactly when expenditures are heaviest and the Presidential dominance is at its zenith. The Congress has a legislative power of indefinite scope and the further power to delegate power to the President. This attributes to the President on his own right an indefinite power to proclaim emergencies and to thereby appropriate an indefinite aggregate of powers in meeting them." But this does not mean that the American President has assumed dictatorial powers, although there is domination of the presidency in American political life. Theodor Roosevelt had asserted that it was the President's right to do anything that the needs of the nation demand unless such action is forbiden by the Constitution or the laws.

The President is the nation's chief executive. As per the provisions of the Constitution, it is the duty of the President "to take care that the law be faithfully executed". These laws refer to the federal laws passed by the Congress and these laws also include treaties which have the force of law. The laws passed by the State legislatures are executed by the governors and other authorities of the States concerned.

The President is empowered by the Constitution to make the appointments, such as the judges of the Supreme Court, members of the Cabinet, Under Secretaries, Assistant Secretaries, members of the diplomatic service, memebrs of all administrative bureaus, boards, commissions, officers of the armed forces, post masters, revenue collectors, customs officials and so many other high and minor officials. There are millions of civil officers and employees excluding the armed forces. These posts are divided into two categories such as the higher posts and the subordinate posts. The posts of the first category are filled up by the President with the advice and consent of the Senate. The President can fillup the posts in the second category either directly, if it is so provided by the Congress or these appointments may be made by the heads of departments or by the courts of law. The members of the Cabinet, Under Secretaries, and Assistant Secretaries, ambassadors, federal judges and various other high officials are included in the first category of posts. Presidential appointments in this category of posts are sent to the Senate, which may or may not confirm the appointments. The President can make nominations when the Senate is not in session, but all such nominations have to be confirmed when the Senate comes to session failing which the appintment would come to an end. However, fresh appointments may be given to such persons by the President again when the Senate goes out of session and such appointments are known as "Recess appointments". Normally the Presidents would not like to take recourse to this method as it is likely to enrage the Senate. It may be noted that despite the Senate's power of confirming the Presidential nominations, it gives a free hand to the President in choosing members of his cabinet. But in the matter of appointment of the judges of the Supreme Court, the Senate has become highly critical and several times it has rejected the Presidential nominations. The President, however, enjoys a freehand in the appointment of ambassadors, Ministers and Consuls in the diplomatic service.

In the matter of Presidential nominations, a convention has grown which is commonly known as "Senatorial Courtesy". This convention requires that, the President before making nominations of local officers (appointments to the states), such as a federal attorney , postmaster or collector of interal revenue in a particular state, should first consult the senators belonging to that State, provided they belong to the same political party as that of the President. If this convention is violated by the President, then out of courtesy generally the other Senators also vote against the confirmation of the Presidential nomination. It may be mentioned here that more than 95 percent of federal appointments do not require confirmation of the Senate. A portion of such appointmets is filled on the recommendations of the Congressmen of the districts concerned and a great portion are now appointed under the civil service rules.

The American Constitution provides that civil officers can be removed from service, if convicted of crimes like treason, bribery, other grave offences or misdemeanors. The constitution, is silent on the issue of removal of civil officers for incompetence or for the good of the service. However, in 1789 the Congress felt that the President could not be held responsible for the faithful execution of the laws, unless he was given power to punish and remove incompetent officers from service. In later years the Congress tried unsuccessfully to restrict this power of the President.

In 1867, the Congress passed the Tenure of Office Act, which provided that officials appointed with the Consent of the Senate, should continue to hold office unless and until their successors' appointments were confirmed by the Senate. This Bill was vetoed by President Andrew Johnson, but it was again passed by the Congress over the Presidential veto. The President declared it unconstitutional and a rift was started between the Congress and the President and the result was the unsuccessful impeachment of President Andrew Johnson in 1868. The Tenure of the Office Act was repealed by the Congress at a later date, but it insisted in 1876, that certain class of officials could not be removed from office without the advice and consent of the Senate. However, the attempt of the Congress to restrict the President's power of removal did not meet with success. In 19-20 President Wilson, removed a postmaster without the consent of the Senate and the Supreme Court held that the President as the nation's chief executive had the power to remove appointive officers and that this power could not be restricted by statutes.

In 1926, in the case of Meyers vs. United States, it was decided by the Supreme Court that the power of the President to remove federal officers was not subject to the advice and consent of the Senate. The Supreme Court, however, decided in 1935, that a member of an Administrative Board can be removed from service only on those grounds prescribed by law, and they cannot be removed on any other ground by the President. As regards to the present position pertaining to the power of removal, the President enjoys unlimited power of removal, except with respect to judges and regulatory commissioners, because the latter enjoy part judicial and part legislative powers. The judicial and the statutory limitations of the President's power of removal to certain extent have been able to reduce the evils of the Spoils system. However, still there are thousands of posts which can be filled by the President himself. The President thus enjoys vast powers of patronage, which add to his prestige and influence.

**Legislative Powers**

Inspite of the built-in conflict between the Congress and the President, in terms of the legislative powers as provided in the Constitution, the American President has emerged as a legislative leader. The absence of united leadership within the Congress and the increasing complexity of domestic and international problems provide sufficient scope for the development of Presidential leadership in legislative matters. Due to these factors, although the Constitution of the United States is based on the principle of separation of powers, the President enjoys substantial powers in the making of federal laws. The President has no power to summon meetings of the Congress except for special sessions and has no power to adjourn, prorogue or dissolve the Congress. He cannot take part in the proceedings of the Congress as he is not its member. He has also nopower to initiate any Bill in the Congress. Despite these fects, he exercises a lot of control in federal law-making.

The President has the power to call special sessions of the Congress and to recommend the passage of certain laws. After the Bills are passed by the Congress, they are sent to the President for his assent. The President may give his assent or may veto the Bills.

Article II, (3) of the Constitution provides: "He (President) shall from time to time give to the Congress information of the state of the union, and recommend to their consideration such measures as he shall judge necessary and expedient.." The President performs this constitutional role, by sending messages to the Congress at the beginning of each session. He recommends the need for certain legislation in these messages sent to the Congress. From time to time the Congress has passed many important Bills, basing on the Presidential recommendations. Declaration of state policies are also made by the Presidents through the messages sent to the Congress. The famous Monroe Doctrine was sent to the Congress through the Presidential message.

Washington and John Adams used to convey their messages to the Congress in person. Jefferson began to send his writen messages to Congress and this practice was followed till 1913, when Wilson delivered his message to Congress in person. After that the successive Presidents have used both the procedures. After the receipt of the Presidential messages in the Congress, recommending the need for certain legislation, these are referred to the appropriate committees of the Congress for the purpose of introducing legislation. The Presidential messages are also published in the newspapers and they give rise to a national debate on the policies of the government. The support of public opinion in favour of the Presidential policies facilitate the passage of legislation recommended by the President. The Congress has also got the power to reject the Presidential recommendations. When the President faces opposition from the congress to his recommendation, he tries to depend on popular support. He may also withhold patronage from Congressmen opposing him in the Congress.

It may be pointed out that the President is the leader of his political party and he can certainly count on the support of the Congressmen belonging to his party.

## The Veto Power of the President

The American President enjoys two kinds of veto powers: Suspensive veto and Pocket veto. Every Bill, after it is passed by both the Houses of the Congress, is presented to the President for his assent. After receiving the assent of the President the Bill becomes a law. However, the President has got the power of veto as given to him by the Constitution. According to this power, he can veto the Bills and return them unsigned with his objections within ten days's time, to the House where the Bills had originated. The Congress, however, can repass such Bills by a two-thirds majority and in such case, they become laws over the veto of the President.

It may be noted that although on hundreds of occasions the Presidents have used the veto power, only in very few cases, Congress has passed the Bills by two-thirds majority over the suspensive veto of the President. The President may neither give his assent to the Bill nor return it to the Congress and in this way after the lapse of the ten-day limit (excluding Sunday), the Bill shall become a law without the assent of the President.

The President may not either sign a Bill or return it to the Congress and if in the mean while the Congress is adjourned within the ten-day limit, the Bill does not become law. This kind of veto power is known as pocket veto of the President.

In case of the amendments to the Constitution which are passed by two-thirds majority are not presented to the President for his assent and are not subject to his veto. While the veto power has been freely used by some of the Presidents, others have exercised it with restraint.

### Emergencies and Presidential Powers

The American Presidents have always been given more powers during the emergencies to cope with the situation. for the first time during the period of the American Civil War, President Abraham Lincoln was granted extraordinary powers to maintain the unity and integrity of the nation. In 1917, President Wilson got such powers, when the United States entered in first World War. During the economic crisis in the U.S.A. in the 1930s, President Roosevelt who became the President in 1932 was granted discretionary authority by the Congress to deal with the economic crisis in an effective manner. President Roosevelt was also granted additional powers during the Second World War by several Congressional Acts. Most of these powers have not been withdrawn and the Presidents enjoy these powers even during the normal period.

### President's Powers Relating to Foreign Affairs

As far as the foreign relations of the U.S.A. are concerned, the President is all-in-all and these relations are carried on under his general direction and supervision. The President appoints members of the diplomatic service. He has also got the power to enter into treaties with the foreign countries, subject to the approval by the Senate by a two-thirds majority. Generally the Senate approves the treaties negotiated by the President but there are some occasions also when the Senate has refused ratification. The Senate refused to ratify the

Treaty of Versailles as a result of which America could not become the member of the League of Nation although it was one of its founder members. However, inorder to avoid the approval of the Senate, the President may adopt a new device. Instead of calling it a treaty, it may be named as "executive agreement", which does not require the approval of the Senate. The President has also got the power of granting recognition to other states. The U.S.S.R. was recognised by President Roosevelt in 1933.

### President as Commander-in-Chief of the Armed Forces

The American President is the Commander-in-Chief of the armed forces. When war breaks out he is empowered to take decisions as may be necessary to meet the requirements. The general direction of the national defence is under his control. The President can declare war only with the consent of both Houses of the Congress. However, as the Commander-in-Chief of the armed forces of the country, he has got the power to order for the mobilization of the army to any part of the world, and as such may create a situation, when Congress may have no alternative but to give its approval to the declaration of war.

### The Judicial Powers of the President

The American President also enjoys some judicial and quasi-judicial powers. He has got the powers to grant reprieves and pardons. This power of granting pardons relates to offences against the federal laws and not the State laws. However, the President cannot grant pardon in case of impeachment. The executive of a sentence can be stayed by the President by means of his power of reprieve. He can grant amnesty to a large number of offenders. The President exercises his power of granting pardon on the recommendations of the Attorney General.

### Limitations on the Presidential Authority

It is rightly said that the American President is a Collosus with feet of clay. Although he has got wide authority and powers, in the exercise of many of his powers, he is subject to certain limitations. He has no power to make laws on his own. He is bound by the decisions of the court and he is required to faithfully execute judicial decisions. He is forbidden to interfere with the governments of the states as long as they work within the framework of the constitution. He cannot appoint or remove members of Congress, the Governors of the States and local officials holding state or municipal office. The foreign policy followed by him is subject to the support of the Congress by means of legislation and funds. His treaty-making power is subject to the approval of the Senate. He cannot extend his term of office by even an hour. He cannot spend funds except in the specific manner and for particular programmes sanctioned and authorized by the Congress. If he is convicted of high crimes or misdemeanor, he can be removed from office by impeachment. The powers and influence of the President, in a system of checks and balances as provided in the American constitution, will largely depend on his personality and his power to maintain his independence.

**The Personality Factor**

It is noticed that the offices make the incumbents great, but it is equally true that some times the incumbents contribute to the greatness of the offices held by them. Despite the ever increasing dimension of Presidential authority, the effectiveness of his authority would depend upon his own personal qualities. In the American system of checks and balances and the commitment of the makers of the constitution to the doctrine of limited government, it is very difficult for a President to make his mark, if he is not a person endowed with great qualities of head and heart. The qualities of a great President have been enumerated by Laski. "He fixes his mind on great objectives. He is a safeguard against that banal dullness which makes democracy no more than a mass of private persons. The significance of a great President, therefore, liese not only in the measures he is able to carry out, but in the width of public interest he is able to vote. He gives to the democratic process a vividness and a reality which it lacks when a weak President is in office.... A President with ideas, has obviously supreme opportunities that no one can rival, while he is in office. The eyes of the whole nation are turned to him; whatever may be the voice it does not hear, his voice at least is certain to be heard. The very fact that he is President leads to the assumption that he will point to the direction in which the nation should move". As a matter of fact no other democratically elected functionary of the world can rival the powers of the American President. To a great extent, the destiny of the United States would depend on the imagination and initiative which the President is capable of showing. The effectiveness or otherwise of the government, depends on his keenness and initiative. "If he is anxious to do nothing, little can be done anywhere on the federal plane. If he is urgent about the programme he has in mind, he can be certain that public opinion will discuss little else. And even if he is defeated in his aims, the very fact that the discussion is wide spread, will mean politics that are vivid and attractice". The capacity of the President to maintain his independence from the influence of vested interest, will contribute to his effectiveness.

## American President Compared with British Prime Minister

Laski observed that the American President, is both more or less than the King; he is also both more or less than a Prime Minister. Like the British Monarch, the American President is the Head of the State and performs a large number of ceremonial functions. The President represents the prosperity and greatness of America and the unity of the American nation, just as the British Monarch is the symbol of the greatness and unity of the British nation. Both of them receive foreign ambassadors and foreign diplomats are accredited to them. But while the British Monarch is only a ceremonial Head, the American President is the real Head of the State. The British Monarch is hereditary; but the American President holds an elective office, while the British Monarch only reigns, the American President reigns as well as governs.

When the American President is compared with the British Prime Minister, we again find that, he is both more or less than him. We notice differences in the relative positions of the President and the Prime Minister as regards to the mode of their appointment. The American President is directly elected by the people and in a sense, he can be said to be his own Prime Minister. On the otherhand the British Prime Minister is appointed by the Monarch on the basis of the results of the general election.When a single party has got the majority, the leader of the party is chosen as the Prime Minister, but if no party has got majority, in the case the Monarch can play a vital role in the appointment of the Prime Minister.

The American President is both the real and the ceremonial Head of the State. In Great Britain, the Monarch is the titular head and the Prime Minister is the real Head of the executive. The American President is free from the control of the Congress and has no power to dissolve any House of the legislature. On the other hand, the British Prime Minister is the leader of the House of Commons and is subject to the control of the Parliament.

The American President has a fixed term of office for a period of four years. His office goes by the calendar. He cannot be removed from office except by means of impeachment which is extremely difficult. On the other hand although the British Prime Minister is elected for a period of five years he can be removed from office before the completion of his term by a vote of noconfidence. His office depends on the majority support in the House of Commons.

As far as the relationship with the Cabinet is concerned, the American President is the boss and the cabinet members are his subordinate officials. Although he may consult and discuss with them on various matters, yet his decision shall be final. He may rejected the recommendation of the entire cabinet and follow his own decision. But the British Prime Minister is not the boss; he is the colleague of the Cabinet members. He cannot ordinarily flout their opinion. He has to treat the cabinet Ministers on terms of equality and cannot treat them in a roughshod manner.

The American President overshadows the Prime Minister in a Parliamentary democracy. He has a secured office and for the effective exercise of his powers, he does not depend on the contingency of parliamentary majority. With majority support in both the Houses of the Congress, the President can almost exercise dictatorial authority. During the time of war or any emergency the President is able to take immediate decisions as was done by Roosevelt during the Second World War. But the British Prime Minister has to take the decision after consulting ther cabinet and knowing the mind of the House of Commons. It may be noted that while the British Prime Minister is only the Head of the government, the American President is both Head of the Government and the State.

## The President's Cabinet

The American President has a cabinet, but it is different from the cabinets provided in the countries having parliamentary system of government. The Congress was empowered by the American constitution, to create the various executive departments and define their powers and functions. The relation between the President and the Heads of the executive departments have also been defined by the constitution in the following words:

"The President may require the opinion in writing of the principal officer in each of the executive department". In 1789, in its first session, the Congress had established three executive departments–the State, treasury and war departments. Lateron, a postmaster general and an attorney general were provided in the same year and these two offices became regular departments only in 1829 and 1870 respectively. The other departments were created by the Congress at different times – the navy department in 1789, the interior department in 1849, agriculture department in 1889, commerce department in 1902, labour department in 1913. The departments of war, navy and airforce, were merged in one department of defence in 1947. The departments of health, education and welfare were also merged together. At present there are ten departments–State, Treasury, Defence, Justice, Post-Office, Interior, Agriculture, Commerce, Labour, and Health and Welfare.

The American Constitution does not provide for a cabinet and the Heads of the ten regular departments are known as the President's cabinet by custom alone. The American cabinet is called a cabinet by courtesy alone. It cannot be taken in the sense in which cabinet is understood in Great Britain. The President appoints these Heads of the ten departaments, with the consent of the Senate and the Senate never refuses consent in the appointment of the members of the Cabinet. Immediately after the election and assumption of office by the new President, he appoints his own cabinet members. As regards the appointment of his cabinet members, the President has absolute freedom. Generally the members of the Cabinet are selected by the President from his own political party but there have been exceptions also. If a Senator or a member of the House of Representative is selected by the President as the Member of his Cabinet, then he has to vacate his seat in the respective House. Generally these Heads of departments remain in office till the end of the President's term, but the President is free to remove any Member at any time. It is noticed that removals are rare and when a Member of the Cabinet does not pull on well with the President, he resigns and quietly goes out of the Cabinet. Thus Cabinet office in the United States is not looked upon as a career. In the words of Laski: "It is an interlude in career–leading towards no definite goal. Many of its members, after their term of office, retire into obscurity from which their elevation brought them". A particular Member of the Cabinet, after its first meeting said that: "I decided without much difficulty that it was not a particularly able group of men–Cabinets seldom are". Clinton Rossiter has observed that, "It is no longer a body upon which the President can rely for sage advice on great issues of State; it is not even, in its formal composition, a gathering of his most important and intimate associates".

In his attempt to revive the Cabinet, President Eisenhower, tried to give independent responsibility to the Members of the Cabinet in the capacity of Heads of Departments. A formal Cabinet Secretariat was instituted and he authorized cabinet level committees to deal with special problems. But even Eisenhower made use of the Cabinet only sparingly. He depended on the National Security Council in respect of Military and Foreign Policy questions. In reality the Presidents have their own method of working and they depend on other groups and agencies which perform the work, what a Cabinet might be supposed to do. This has reduced the importance of the Cabinet. In the words of Munro, "The Cabinet is not intended to be a representative body, or a professional group, or check upon the President. As a body, its members are, officially at any rate, the confidential advisers of the chief executive. But they are also the President's chief subordinates in performing his constitutional duty to see that the laws are faithfully executed".

**Functions of the American Cabinet**

The Amercan Cabinet is an advisory body to the President. The Members of the American Cabinet as Heads of their departments have various administrative duties to perform. From 1791, the Presidents have been summoning the Heads of Departments for consultation. The meetings of the Cabinet are held once in a week. The Cabinet only discusses those matters which are referred to it by the President. There are no rules of procedure and all matters are discussed informally and secrecy of the proceedings is maintained. Members do not make formal speeches. There is no comparison between the American cabinet and the British cabinet as the Members of the American Cabinet are not the colleagues of the President. They are called as the "members of the President's family". They are the advisers of the President and even this function rests upon custom alone and there is no legal or constitutional basis for it. The President is empowered to call special meetings of the Cabinet. The Cabinet is required to give advice only on such matters and this advice is not binding on him. Formal records of the discussions held in the Cabinet meetings are not kept. The Members of the Cabinet are not accountable to the Congress. They are not members of the Congress and cannot initiate legislation like the Members of the British Cabinet.

There is no collective responsibility in the American Cabinet. The Members of the Cabinet lack the representative Character, as they are nominated by the President. In the past there were some proposals to allow the Members of the Cabinet to sit in the Congress and initiate legislation, but these proposals were turned down by the

Congress. However, the Members of the Cabinet are required to give information to the Congress. They also appear before the various committees of Congress to defend their measures and politics.

The Members of the Cabinet are the Heads of their respective departments and have to perform their functions in that capacity. They are responsible to the President and work under his general direction. The Heads of the departments enjoy a fair amount of independence in performing their routine work and generally, the President does not interfere in their day-to-day work. As far as the departmental organisation is concerned, some of the departments have under-secretaries, and all the departments have assistant secretaries. Each department is divided into bureaus, divisions and other subordinate branches. The departments have defined functions, which are determined by law and executive orders. Departmental orders are issued by the Heads of departments. Appointments to the respective departments, are also made by the Heads, as provided by the Congress.

## The Vice-President

The Vice-President of the United States has got little actual power, but has got great potentialities. Some of the founding fathers of the American Constitution thought that this was an useless office, but history has proved the immense utility of this office. As per the provisions of the Constitution, in the event of a vacancy in the Presidential office due to removal, resignation or death, it is the Vice-President who has to succeed to this office. Vice-Presidents like Tyler, Fillmore, Andrew Jackson, Arthur, Theodore Roosevelt, Coolidge, Truman and Lyndon B. Johnson were made Presidents.

The Vice-President is elected along with the President in the same manner. Prior to the 12th Amendment of the American Constitution, the person getting the greatest number of votes, was to be President, provided this was also clear majority of all the electoral votes, and the persons getting the next highest number of votes was to be Vice-President. But as per the provisions obtaining to-day, the Presidential electors cast two votes–one for President and other for the Vice-Presidential candidate separately to avoid the complications. A candidate who secures absolute majority of votes is declared elected. In case no candidate secures an absolute majority of votes, the Senate elects one out of the two candidates securing the highest votes. The Vice-Presidential candidates are required to have the same qualifications as the Presidential candidates.

No person can become the President or the Vice-President of America, unless he is natural-born citizen of the United States, has completed 35 years of age and has resided in the United States for at least a period of 14 years. It is extremely difficult for a Roman Catholic or a non-believer in Christianity either to be sponsored as a Party candidate or to get himself elected to the exalted office of the President or the Vice-President.

Some conventions have developed pertaining to the election of the President and the Vice-President. As per the convention the President and the Vice-President should not belong to the same state. Parties while nominating their candidates for the two offices should keep in view the fact that both the candidates belong to different wings of the party.

The term of office of the Vice-President is same as that of the President.

## Functions of the Vice-President

(i) According to the American Constitution, the powers and duties of the President devolve upon the Vice-President in case of the removal of the President from office or on account of his death, resignation or inability to discharge the powers and duties of his office. There was no clear provision in the Constitution whether in such cases of assumption of the Presidential office, the Vice-President will also assume the title of President. However, Vice-President John Tyler was the first to fill a vacancy and he assumed the title of President and since then this custom is followed.
It may be pointed out that no President has so far resigned and none has been removed by impeachment although there was one case of unsuccessful impeachment against President Andrew Johnson. No President has also been removed from office due to inability to discharge the duties and powers.

(ii) The Vice-President of America is the ex-officio chairmen of the Senate–the upper House of the Congress. He has no voting power except the casting vote in case of a tie and has only perfunctory powers.

(iii) The Vice-Presidents were invited by some of the Presidents to attend the meetings of the Cabinet as a matter of courtesy. The Vice-Presidents may or may not accept this offer. President Roosevelt included Vice-President Henry Wallace in his cabinet. Vice-President Nixon was sent by President Eisenhower, on a tour of the Middle East, India and Pakistan.

The Vice-President's office is an insignificant office which is unique in its "lack of functions". Benjamin Franklin criticized the Vice–President as "His superfluous Highness". It was described by Wilson as "one of anomalous insignificance and curious uncertainty". People with outstanding talent and strength of character are not attracted to this office. Some suggestion have been made to transfer some of the ceremonial and other functions of the President to the Vice-President to increase the importance of this office. But nothing concrete has materialised till to-day.

# 5

# The Congress

The American Congress, which is the federal legislature is a bicameral legislataive body. The lower chamber is called the House of Representatives and the upper chamber is called the Senate. The Senate represents the States and the House of Representatives, represents the people of the United States. The American constitution has vested all the legislative powers in the Congress. The Congress also enjoys other powers in addition to its law-making powers. The Congress frames the policies of the nation and has got the power of impeachment. It has the power to amend the constitution with requisite majority support of the States and can also declare war by joint resolution. Through its power of control over the purse, it controls the government. The Congress also enjoys quasijudicial powers and can conduct investigations on various matters. It can also punish any person for contempt.

Inspite of all these powers the American Congress is not sovereign in the sense we call the British Parliament soveriegn. The Congress has got no original powers. Its powers are derived from the constitution. Thus it has got only delegated powers and functions under the limitation imposed upon it by the American constitution. A judge of the American Supreme Court has rightly observed that, "The constitution is the work or will of the people themselves, in their original sovereign, and unlimited capacity. Law is the work or will of the legislature in their derivative and subordinate capacity. The one is the work of the Creator, and the other of the Creature. The constitution fixes limits to the exercise of legislative auth-rity and prescribes the orbit within which it must move". The makers of the American constitution wanted to create a federal government of limited and divided powers. The basic powers were left to the people and the states. The rest of the powers were divided between the Congress, the

Presidency and the judicial branch. Thus there was no scope for either the supremacy or the sovereignty of the Congress.

The American Congress has got the power to make laws on any of the subjects granted to the federal government by the Constitution and is supreme within its own sphere of authority. The powers of the Congress can be enhanced by the amendment of the Constitution. The judicial decisions and interpretations made by the Supreme Court from time to time have also added to the powers of the Congress. In 1819, the doctrine of implied powers was accepted by the Supreme Court and the Congress has acquired many powers through this doctrine. Chief Justice Marshall who played a great role in the enunciation and the acceptance of this doctrine has explained it in the following words:

"This government is acknowledged by all to be one of enumerated powers. The principle that it can exercise only the powers granted to it is now universally admitted. But the question respecting the extent of the powers actually granted is perpectually arising and will probably continue to arise as long as our system shall exist.... The powers of government are limited and its powers are not to be transcended. But we think the sound construction of the constitution must allow to the national legislature that discretion with respect to the means by which the powers it confers are to be carried into execution, which enable that body to perform the high duties assigned to it in a manner most beneficial to the people. Let the end be legitimate, let it be within the scope of the constitution, and all means which are appropriate, which are plainly adopted to that end, which are not prohibited but consistent with the letter and spirit of the Constitution, are constitutional".

Due to this liberal interpretation of the Constitution the Congress has obtained various powers. The constitution has given the power to the Congress to "regulate Commerce with foreign nations and among the several states". As a result of liberal interpretation of the constitutional provision, from this power, Congress has got the right to regulate stock exchanges and the issue of securities. It has also got the power to control transportation of goods by rail, water, motor and air etc. It has also acquired the power to borrow money on the credit of the United States. As a result of the doctrine of implied powers it has got the right for the establishment and supervision of national banks, banking and credit institutions etc.

The Original Constitution granted 18 principal powers to the

Congress on which it could make laws. The important powers of the federal government are to conduct foreign affairs and make treaties with foreign countries, to coin money, to declare war, to raise and support armies and to maintain a navy and airforce, to regulate commerce with foreign countries and among the federating units, to admits new states into the federation and to establish post offices etc. There are also some concurrent powers which are exercised both by the state governments and the federal government. Powers like collecting taxes, borrowing money and the promotion of agriculture and education belong to the concurrent jurisdiction.

The states have the power to regulate commerce within the state, to make civil and criminal laws, to control the local government, to conduct elections etc. Both the federal and the state governments are prevented to pass bills of attainder, to enact ex post facto laws, to grant titles of nobility, to levy duties on exports etc.

The states are prohibited to make treaties, to coin money, to levy duties on imports, to deny any person the equal protection of the laws within their jurisdiction. The federal government is also prevented to deny the rights and privileges as given in the Bill of Rights (the first ten amendments), such as freedom of speech, or of worship, or of press or of assembly or of petition etc.

The Congress has got the most important power of lawmaking. It also has got administrative power pertaining to the administering and the enforcement of the laws passed by it. Through its control over the purse of the nation, it also exercises control over the executive. It is also the supervisory and the investigating body.

## The Senate

The American Senate is the most powerful second chamber in the world. It represents the federating units of the U.S.A. and consists of 100 members, having two senators from each State. Originally, the American Constitution had provided for the election of the Senators by their respective State legislatures. But in 1912, the 17th amendment of the constitution was adopted which provided that the senators were to be directly elected by voters of the respective states and not by the State legislatures. This amendment was a significant one as it gave representative character to the Senators and enhanced their status to a great extent.

As per the provisions of the constitution, a senator is elected for a period of six years, but one-third of the Senate's membership is renewed every two years. The Senate is a continuous body and the whole House is never dissolved. The senators can be reelected. After the election is over, the senators are required to take the oath of office.

A senator must have completed 30 years of age and must have been a citizen of the United States at least for nine years. At the time of election, he must be a resident of the State from which he is elected.

The Senate enjoys the right "to be the judge of the elections, returns, and qualifications of its members." On several occasions, the Senate did not permit its members to take the oath office, who in its opinion had used unfair means for winning the election.

The States of American have got equal right of representation in the Senate, irrespective of size and population. No State can be deprived of its equal representation to the Senate even by constitutional amendment against its will.

Immunities, generally granted to the members of the legislative bodies, are also enjoyed by the members of the Senate. The senators enjoy the freedom of speech in the House and they cannot be questioned or made accountable for the speech delivered by them. However, they can be punished by the Senate for unruly or disorderly behaviour by a two-thirds vote and can even be expelled from the Senate. They enjoy freedom from arrest while attending sessions, while going to attend the session or returning from the session, except for felony, treason or breach of peace. The Senate has been empowered to conduct investigations, through the investigating committees appointed by it.

As per the provisions of the American Constitution, the Vice-President is the chairman of the Senate. He has no power of voting, excepting a casting vote in the case of a tie and also has got no power to appoint the Committees of the House. A President pre-tempore is elected by the Senate in the absence of the Vice-President or when he takesup the responsibility of the office of the President of U.S.A. Other offices like the sergeant-at-arms, chaplain and clerks are also appointed by the Senate.

In addition to the regular sessions of the Senate, which are held each years, special sessions of the Senate are also called by the President, even when the lower house is not in session, for confirming treaties. There are certain functions like the trial of impeachments, confirmation of appointments made by the President and giving approval of the treaties negotiated by the President, which are the exclusive functions of the Senate.

The Senate follows very simple rules of procedure which are of a permanent nature. As per the accepted rules of procedure, every Bill is given three readings before it is passed. Before a Bill is referred to the appropriate committee, there are two formal readings of the Bill in the Senate. The third reading is an important stage when the Bill is considered in the Committee of the whole and amendments are moved. There are unlimited debates in the Senate and there is no time limit to the Speech of a Senator. The Senate, however, can restrict the time of the debates on any particular measure, by a two thirds vote. According to Rule 22 of the Senate Procedures one hour time limit can be imposed on the speech made by a Senator.

As a result of the freedom of debate in the Senate the pros and cons of all issues are fully discussed and even minorities get sufficient time to bring forward their criticisms etc. However, the system is not free from defects as it leads to filibustering or making of long and unending speeches for causing obstruction to certain legislative measures. It has got negative effective on the functioning of the Senate as many legislative measures are lost in this way.

Previously there were 33 standing committees in the Senate but at present there are 15 standing committees through which it does a large portion of its work. The Committees are–the committee on finance, appropriations] foreign relations, judiciary, armed services, interstate and foreign commerce etc. The various Senate Committees are selected at the beginning of each Congress. For the selection of the members of the standing committees, the proposals made by the Democratic and Republican caucuses are simply accepted by the Senate. The party caucus or conference is not an official committee of the Senate but a Committee of each political party. There is also a steering committee belonging to each political party in the Senate. The party having majority in the Senate usually has got more seats in the standing committees. The committee on committees assigns places to new senators on the various standing committees.

Although the Senate is the second chamber of the American Congress, it is not a secondary chamber like the British House of Lords. It enjoys co-equal powers with the House of Representatives and hence is the most powerful second chamber in the whole world.

### Functions of the Senate

The American Senate is a continuous body and has got immense legislative and executive powers. Its quasi-parmanent status and longer term have greatly contributed to its strength. The Senate is well organised and is a very compact body. Due to the small size in terms of its membership, it has emerged as a powerful deliberative body. There is no system of closure in the Senate and its rules of procedure are simple and permanent. The membes of the Senate are now directly elected and a part from being the representatives of their respective States, they also represent the people of the U.S.A. In view of these factors, the Senate enjoys immense executive powers.

## Legislative Powers of the Senate

The Senate enjoys co-equal legislative powers with the House of Representatives and thus is a co-ordinate branch of the Congress. Excepting the Money Bills in all other matters of law making, it enjoys equal powers with the House of Representatives. The American Constitution provides that, all Bills for raising revenue must originate in the House of Representatives. However, the Senate has got the right to propose amendments to the Revenue Bills. Sometimes these amendments have been very sweeping and they have considerably changed the Revenue Bill. The Senate has got the power to strike every thing from the Revenue Bills and initiate new revenue proposals through the process of proposing amendments. Thus it has got substantial powers in respect of the Money Bills also. On one occasion the Senate had proposed 847 amendments to a tariff measure submitted to it by the House of Representatives, it has acquired exclusive powers to originate such Bills through usage. However, no Revenue Bill or Appropriation Bill (both are terms as Money Bills) can be passed without the consent of the Senate.

Both Houses enjoy equal powers with respect to ordinary Bills. Such a Bill can be introduced either in the Senate or the House of Representatives. As a matter of fact more important measures are introduced in the Senate rather than the House of Representatives. No Bill can become law without the approval of the Senate.

The Senate has the power to undertake various investigations for the purpose of collecting data and statistics, which may be useful to it for framing legislation. This has made the Senate very powerful and has been responsible for increasing its influence.

On any legislative measure, if there is a disagreement between the two Houses of the Congress, a compromise is reached by referring the dispute to a Joint Conference Committee.

### Executive Powers of the Senate

The American Senate has also got very extensive executive powers. The American President has got the constitutional power of making the appointments to the high offices, but these appointments are subject to advice and consent of the Senate. The President is given a free hand in nominating members of his Cabinet and the members of the diplomatic service like ambassadors. The Senate is, however, critical about the nominations of the judges of the Supreme Court made by the President.

At the time of making federal appointments in the States, the President is required to consult individual Senators from the respective State, provided that they belong to his own political party. This is known as the custom of Senatorial courtesy, "Which has become a Liberum Veto". In case the President violates this custom, then the whole Senate becomes united to obstruct Presidential nominations. It has been rightly described that "the strength of the pack is wolf and the strength of the wolf is the pack. If suggestions of the Senators are ignored or if their objections to Presidential appointees are flouted, the Senate will frequently not approve the nomination". The President can make recess appointments, for which, the consent of the Senate is not necessary. The senate may turn down the appintment after it comes to session. The same peson may be reappointed after the session of the Senate is over. Thus the appointment can continue during the interval between two sessions of the Senate. No President would insist on giving recess appointment to the same person, when his appointment is repeatedly not confirmed by the Senate as this is likely to create bitterness between himself and the Senate.

In case of the appointment of the officers of the lower grade, whose appointment has been vested by Congress either in the President alone or the heads of departments or the courts of law, the consent of the Senate is not necessary.

### Treaty-making Power

This American Constitution has vested the power in the President to enter into treaties with foreign countries. But these treaties inorder to be valid must be ratified by a two-thirds majority of the Senate. The Presidents in most cases do not seek the advice of the Senate while conducting negotiations with the foreign countries. There are, however, cases when some Presidents maintained close touch with the leaders of the Senate (usually the Chairman of the Committee on foreign relations), When conducting negotiations for treaties. The Treaty of Versailles of 1919 which was negotiated by President Wilson, was rejected by the Senate as the President did not consult it prior to carrying out the negotiations. Usually most of the treaties are ratified by the Senate without amendments. However, prior to the rejection of the Treaty of Versailles, the Senate had also rejected some other important treaties. Through its power of ratification of treaties, the Senate exercises effective control over the Presidential policies in relation to the foreign countries. The treaties become law of the country as soon as they are ratified by the Senate.

## The Power of Impeachment

People in high offices, who are charged with treason, bribery or other severe crimes or misdemeanors, can be impeached by the Senate. The Senate has "the sole power to try all impeachments". The President, Vice-President and Civil officers can be impeached by the Senate as per the provisions of the consitution. The members of the Cabinet, judges of the federal courts and members of the diplomatic service are included in the category of civil officers. The charge of impeachment is brought by the House of Representatives and the Senate tries the case, sitting as a Court of impeachment. There is the necessary of two-thirds majority of the Senate for the conviction of a person on impeachment.

## The House of Representatives

The House of Representatives is the lower house of the American Congress and it consists of 437 members elected every second year. In the absence of specific Congressional legislation deciding the basis for the number of representatives to be elected from a State, it is being determined by Decennial Census. The House of Representatives represents the nation and not the States of America. Through constitutional amendment disqualification of voters on the ground of race, colour or sex, is forbidden. Thus as per the provisons of the constitution "the House of Representatives shall be composed of members chosen every second year by the people of the several states".

In the beginning there were 65 members in the House of Representatives, distributed among the thirteen states roughly according to population. Irrespective of the size of population, every state was, however, given one representative in the House. The qualifications of the voters for electing representatives to the House are to be determined by each state. According to the Constitution the "times, places and manner of holding elections for Senators and Representatives", were left in the hands of the respective State legislatures. Further, the constitution provided that "Congress may at any time by law make or alter such regulations, except as to the places of choosing Senators". American citizens who are qualified to vote at election of the State legislature are also qualified to vote for electing members to the House of Representatives. Theoretically the electorate consists of all citizens of both sexes over 21 yers of age (voting age in Georgia and Kentucky is 18 years, in Alaska 19 years and in Hawaii 20 years), but the franchise is still not universal. For the purpose of suffrage various requirements such as residence, registration and payment of taxes etc. are fixed by the States.

Due to increase in the number of states and the population of the country, the size of the House of Representatives was also increased and by the year 1911, there were 435 members. At present the size of the House if permanently fixed at 437 members. Approximately each member represents 3,50,000 people. After allotting one member to each of the States, the remaining seats are then divided among the several States according to population.

The House of Representatives has a tenure for two years and it cannot be dissolved earlier. Qualification have also been prescribed for the members of the House. He must be at least 25 years of age and also a citizen of the United States of seven years' standing. He should also be an inhabitant of the state from which he is elected. The constitution does not specify that a candidate must be a resident of the congressional district (electoral district), from which he seeks election. However, a local candidate is always preferred to an outsider as he is supposed to know the needs of the people better. Each state divides itself into as many congressional districts as it has to elect number of persons to the House of Representatives.

In this connection reference may be made to the old practice of "gerryman-during" in the United States. Through this practice of reorganising the congressional districts, the party in power tried to win more seats in election.

The respective States have their own laws for the nomination of the candidates for election to the House of Representatives. Nominations in two states are made by conventions of party delegates and the remaining States follow the practice of direct primaries. On the same day election is held throughout the country and the vote is by secret ballot. The House reserves the fight to judge "the elections, returns, and qualifications of its members". The House is the supreme authority to decide all disputes pertaining to the election. The House has the power to "punish its members for disorderly behaviour, and with the concurrence of two-thirds expel a member".

The members of the House of Representatives also enjoy the immunities which are enjoyed by the Senators. They enjoy freedom of speech in the House and for the speech made by him in the House, he cannot be questioned in any other place. The members cannot be arrested while attending sessions, in going to or returning from the sessions except for felony, treason and breach of peace.

There should be minimum one session of the House in a year which means that at least it must have two sessions within its life of two years. The members subscribe to an oath of office after their election to the House. The House elects its Speaker and also chooses its other officers such as, Sergeant-at-arms, chaplain and clerk etc.

The House has full power over its rules of procedure. In 1789 the first House adopted certain rules of procedure. The rules of the preceding House are re-adopted again and again with necessary changes. As a result of its long legislative experience, the House has developed numerous rules and precedents. The rules provide that a Bill should be given three readings before it is finally passed by the House. The rules of the House also impose certain limitations on the freedom of debate on any motion in the House. No person holding any office under the United States can be a member of either House of the Congress, during his continuance in office.

## The Speaker of the House of Representatives

The Speaker occupies a very important office and in fact, he is the central figure of the House. He is chosen by the House itself. The Speaker became very powerful during the 19th century and he was considered next to the President as far as powers were concerned. In the absence of a leader like the Prime Minister in a Parliamentary system, the Speaker acted as the leader of the majority party and became the master of legislation. In the words of Munro, the Speaker became, "a virtual dictator of legislation".

From time to time, there were protests against the dictatorial powers of the Speaker and there was a revolution against his powers in 1909-'11. This resulted in the substantial reduction of his powers. The Speaker lost his membership of the Committee on Rules–a very important committee. The House directly appointed the members of all the regular committees and this power of the Speaker was withdrawn. But even after the curtailment of his powers, the Speaker still remains a very important officer and a central figure of the House. The position of the Speaker has been nicely depicted by Finer in the following words:

"He still remains in intention and practice a party-man. He is still one of the very small knot of Congress leaders who treat with the President for passage of administrative measures. He is still consulted by and has great weight with his party, Steering Committee and the Floor leader of the majority party. He is still a major factor in deciding assignments to committees and the priority of business, because he is one of the most eminent, usually the most eminent, of his party; that indeed is why he was elected Speaker. Order and system in a House of 435 members there is bound to be, and the power of leadership must somewhere be lodged. Whilte, until 1910, it was concentrated in the Speaker and his friends by grace, it is now concentrated in the Speaker's friends and the Speaker. Leadership has been 'syndicated' or put into 'Commission', but the Speaker is still the predominant member of the Syndicate".

The Speaker is elected by the House itself at the beginning of each Congress. But it may be mentioned that he is a partyman and is selected by a caucus composed of members of the majority party. He continues to be a partyman even after the election is over and utilizes his powers and position for promoting the interst of his party.

## Powers of the Speaker

In the absence of legislative leadership of the Prime Minister as it is the practice in a parliamentary system, the Speaker of the House of Representatives became the leader of the House. The framers of the American Constitution, with a view to establish a system of checks and balances, had separated the executive and legislative branches of the government, leaving both Houses to work out their own plans of leadership. In the course of time the House grew in number and its legislative business was expanded. The responsibilities of the House rapidly increased due to the growth of population and developments in the spheres of science, technology and agriculture. The House found it difficult to adjust to the changing needs of the time. Thomas B. Reed, known as "Czar Reed" took the advantage of this situation and secured the adoption of rules which gave to the Speaker, virtual dictatorial powers over the House. In the words of Munro: "Beginning with Henry Clay, the Speaker gradually became the recognized leader of the majority party, hence of the House as a whole. He became the man on whom the majority dependend for getting its measure, safely through the maze of rules. More and more authority was absorbed into its hands until he became a virtual dictator of legislation."

The Speaker presides over the meetings of the House of Representatives. He conducts the proceedings of the House and recognises the members. As per the rules of the House, if two or more members rise, "The Speaker shall name the member who is first to speak". Through the effective exercise of this power, the Speaker is able to control the course of debate in the House. It may however, be mentioned that this power to recognize members has been greatly reduced by the rules and precedents of the House.

The Speaker maintains order and decorum in the House. He has the power to call members to order. The members must address the chair respectfully and must obey the Speaker's rulings. If any member creates disturbance or shows disorderly conduct, the Speaker may either suspend business or instruct the sergeant-at-arms to quiet any disorder in the House. But the Speaker has no power to censure, expel or punish a member as is usually done by the Speaker of the British House of Commons. In America, these powers are exercised by the House.

The Speaker has the authority to interpret and apply the rules of the House. The Speaker, if he so desires may participate in the discussions of the House and in such a case, he calls some member to take the chair temporarily. He enjoys the rights and privileges of the other members of the House and has a vote. Each political party has also its floor leader in the House, who is elected by the party caucus, at the beginning of every Congress. The floor leaders play a significant role in the House.

## The Speaker's Position

The Speaker continues to occupy an important position, despite the Revolt of 1910 which reduced his powers. After the Revolt, Speaker Joseph G. Cannon has described the position of the Speaker in the following words: "The Speaker does not believe, and always has believed, that this is a government through parties and that parties can act only through majorities. The Speaker has always believed in and bowed to the majority in convention, in caucus, and in legislative hall and to-day profoundly believes that to act otherwise is to disorganize parties, i.e., to prevent coherent action in any legislative body, is to make impossible the reflection of the wishes of the people in statutes and in laws."

## Comparison with the British Speaker

The British Speaker and the American Speaker, despite the similarity of designation, greatly differ from each other in terms of their powers and position.

(i) The Speaker is unanimously elected in Great Britain. He is no doubt a partyman, but the opposition is consulted, before his name is proposed. His name is dropped, if opposition objects. On the other hand in the United States, the election of the Speaker is a contested one. The Speaker invariably is the nominee of the majority party, but the minority party does put its candidate and voting taken place. The is no question of unanimous acceptance of the Speaker as it happens in the United Kingdom.

(ii) The Speaker is returned unopposed from his constituency in Great Britain, as many times as he desires to be returned. Thus it is said that he who once becomes the Speaker, he becomes the Speaker for all times, provided he has a mind for that. But in America, the Speaker has to fight hard to get himself reelected to the House of Representatives. Even if he is reelected, there is no guarantee, that he would again become the Speaker.

(iii) The British Speaker becomes a non-party man immediately after his election to that office. He cuts off all his connections with the party conferences and does not associate himself with party resolutions. But the American Speaker is openly identified with his political party and as leader of his party in the House of Representatives, he tries to defend the party's interest. Thus while the British Speaker is non-partisan, the American Speaker is out and out a party-man.

(iv) The British Speaker is impartial and judicious in his decisions. He gives fair rulings according to the precedents of the House. On the other hand the American Speaker lacks fairness and objectivity as he uses the power of his office to promote his party's interests.

(v) The rulings given by the American Speaker are not final and the House of Representatives may overrule the interpretation by a majority vote. On the other hand, the ruling of the British Speaker is final and is never challenged by the House of Commons.

(vi) The British Speaker does not take part in the debates and never votes except when there is a tie. But the American Speaker takes active part in debates and participates in the proceedings as a member of the House. He has also got the right to cast his vote.

(vii) The American Speaker is comparatively weaker than his counterpart in England in relation to the appointment of the Chairment of Standing Committees. While the British Speaker appoints the Chairmen of the Standing Committees from Chairmen's panel consisting of persons nominated by the selection committee, this power has been taken away from the hands of the American Speaker in April, 1911.

(viii) Due to his political neutrality and impartiality the British Speaker enjoys the confidence of the whole House and is respected by one and all. But the American Speaker does not enjoy the same prestige and respect because of his partisan attitude. The British Speaker is not a leader but an umpire. His office is regarded as an office of great honour and prestige. But the American Speaker identifies himself with his political party and becomes a party leader. Hence he does not enjoy the same prestige and honour like the British counterpart.

(ix) The American Speaker acts as the leader of the House. But in the U.K. this role is performed in the House of Commons by the Prime Minister.

### Functions of the House of Representatives

The House performs legislative functions. Bills can be introduced in the House on any topic that falls within the jurisdiction of the federal government. While ordinary Bills can be introduced in any House of the Congress, all Bills for raising revenue (Money Bills), must originate in the House of Representatives. The House has also acquired the right to originate Appropriation Bills by usage, eventhough the Constitution did not give this power exclusively to the House of Representatives. Thus through its control over the purse of the nation, the House can exercise control over the executive. The President needs the consent of the House along with the Senate to declare war. It has the power to initiate cases of impeachment before the Senate.

### House of Representatives Compared with the Senate

Although the House of Representatives is the lower chamber

and the Senate is the upper chamber, it would be misleading to think that the House of Representatives is more powerful than the Senate. The American Senate is more powerful than the House of Representatives and occupies the most enviable position among the second chambers of the world. While in most of the countries of the world the upper chamber is comparatively less powerful than the lower chamber and in the course of time their powers have decreased, in America it is not only more powerful, but also it has gained in power and prestige. Prof. Lindsay Rogers, aptly observes that the American Senate is "the most remarkable invention of modern times". It was regarded as the sole effective federal chamber by Prof. Laski. In the opinion of F.J. Haskin, "There are things which the President and the Senate may do without the House of Representatives and the things which the House and the Senate may do without the assent of the President yet the House and the President can do comparatively little without the assent of the Senate".

There are several causes for the superior strength and prestige of the American Senate. Some of the causes are discussed below:

***(1) Small size and long tenure***

The Senate consists of 100 members as against the unwieldly size of the House of Representatives consisting of 437 members. This small membership has made the Senate a more compact and efficient body. Due its unwieldly size the debates in the House of Representatives are not of such high standard as those in the Senate. Further while the Senators are elected for a period of six years, members of the House of Representatives are elected for a term of two years. The long tenure gives ample scope to the Senators to acquire more experience, develop parlimentary skill nad make greater impact upon the nation. The members of the House of Representatives are always worried about their elections and due to their short tenure are not in a position to make any impact upon the nation. It is a fact that more ambitious and outstanding political personalities are attracted towards the senate rather than the House of Representatives.

***(ii) Greater freedom of speech***

Greater freedom of speech is employed by the Senators in comparison to the members of the House of Representatives. In the Senate the rules of procedure are relatively simple and members get ample time to discuss verious issues. This is possible because of the small size of the Senate. Due to this power the senate has become the most effective forum for ventilating the grievances of the people. A Senator "gives a vivid reality to political democracy in the United States which no other institution as fully or so gladly supplies". As a result of the freedom of speech and the presence of more talented and experienced political personalities in the Senate its debates are of a high standard and they are given wide publicity by the press. On the contrary discussions in the House of Representatives do not inspire much interest and get less coverage in the national papers.

### *(iii) Direct election of the Senators*

In most of the democratic countries of the world where the lower chamber claims superiority over the upper chamber, it is based on the fact that its members are directly elected, whereas the members of the upper are either hereditary or indirectly elected. In the U.S.A. as the Senators are also directly elected like the members of the House of Representatives, the House of Representatives cannot have the claim to superiority on this ground. Thus the Senate is equally a popular chamber like the House of Representatives. Moreover, when a member of the House of Representatives, represents only his constituency, the Senator represents his state. In the American federal setup where the states are the indestructible units of the indestructible union, the Senators, as the representatives of the states in the Congress enjoy a prestigious position.

### *(iv) Solidarity of the Senate*

Members of the Senate have unity and solidarity, irrespective of party affiliations. Whenever there is any attack on the rights and privileges of one senator, the entire senate becomes united to fight against that. Due to this it has not allowed any President to violate the rule of senatorial courtesy. This sense of solidarity which the Senators have guarded jealously, has been responsible to make the Senate the most powerful second chamber in the world. There is no such unity among the members of the House of Representatives.

### *(v) Control over the Executive*

In countries where there is parliamentary system of government, the lower house becomes more powerful due to its control over the executive. But in the U.S.A. there is Presidential form of government and the executive is not responsible to the House of Representatives, which is the lower chamber. There is no direct accountability of the executive to the legislature and whatever control the legislature exercises over the executive, it is being done by the Senate. Due to this power of control over the executive, the Senate has acquired a position of precedence over the House of Representatives.

### *(vi) Senate's equal legislative and Financial powers*

In other democratic countries the second chambers have comparatively less share in law-making and financial matters. This gives a periority of position to the lower house. The British House of Common and the Indian Lok Sabha play predominent role in comparison to the House of Lords and the Rajya Sabha, respectively. But in America the House of Representatives and the Senate have co-equal powers in law-making and financial matters. The British House of Common can override the veto of the Lords by passing a Bill twice in two consecutive sessions. In India on the event of a difference of opinion, between the two houses concerning the passage of a Bill, a joint session of the two houses is called to settle the problem, where the Lok Sabha has an advantage over the Rajya Sabha on account of its larger membership. But in the U.S.A. in the Joint Committee constituted for settling disagreement between the two houses consists of equal members from both the houses, in which the Senators play a leading role due to their wide legislative experience and longer term of office.

In the financial matters, although the constitution gives some priority to the House of Representatives by providing that money bills can originate only in that house, in ultimate analysis this becomes meaningless as the Senate can make amendments to the extent of making it a new bill. According to Murrey, "the Senate has founded a way of doing what the constitution did not intend to do it". Thus the American Senate does not have a secondary position in respect to the legislative and financial matters. On the contrary, the Senate has a dominant role in law-making.

### *(vii) Special powers of the Senate*

The American Senate enjoys certain special powers which are not exercised by any other second chamber of the world. Presidential appointments are subject to the approval of the Senate. Without the approval of the Senate, no treaty negotiated by the President can be valid. The Senate plays a vital role in administration through its power of approving Presidential nominations. The President has to keep the Senate informed about important developments in administration. Through its power of ratification of treaties negotiated by the President, the Senate exercises great influence on American foreign policy.

The Senate is empowered by the constitution to elect its/chairman and the Vice-President of the U.S. in case the electoral college does not come up with the election of the President and the Vice-President.

***(viii) Senate as a court of trial***

The constitution gives the power of impeaching the President, Vice-President and all other important civil and political officers for treason, bribery, misdemeavor and other crimes. The charges are framed by the House of Representatives by two-thirds majority and the Senate can convict the person by two-thirds majority. An impeached officer has to be ipso facto removed from his office.

All these powers have made the Senate, the most powerful second chamber in the world and have give it a rare eminence denied to the House of Representatives. In the words of Bryce, the Senate is the "centre of gravity in the government, an authority to check and correct, on the one hand, the democratic recklessness of the House, and, on the other the monarchical ambition of the President".

**Committees of the House of Representatives**

Due to the absence of legislative leadership of the Council of Ministers as is the case in a parlimantary system of government, the Committees of the American Congress play a prominent role in the legislative process. In America the Committees initiate legislation, whereas in Great Britain this work is being done by the Ministers. Most of the work of the House of Representatives is done through its various standing committees. There are at present 19 standing committees of the House viz., the committee on rules, ways and means, appropriations, judiciary, interstate and foreign commerce, armed services, public works, post offices and civil services, banking and currency, education and labour, agriculture etc.

After the receipt of the Presidential message in the American Congress, the various standing committees introduce legislation based on the message. The standing committees are technically elected by the House, but the actual selection is made by both parties holding a caucus or conference, when a new House meets. Each political party through its party caucus selects a member of its own members for the varius committees. The Republican caucus appoints a "Committee on Committees", which assigns the Republican members to the various standing committees.

The Democratic caucus selects its members for the committee on ways and means and the members of this committee assign Democratic members to the various standing committees. Majority of seats in the standing committees and the post of the chairman go to the majority party in the House of Representatives. The House of Representatives honours the selection of members made to the various standing committees by the party caucuses. For the purpose of investigating into certain matters, the House of Representatives also appoints certain committees. Sometimes special or select committees are also created for dealing with particular problems. The House has the power to appoint a conference committee. The Joint Committee of Conference of both the Houses meets for solving disputes between the two Houses.

The Committee of the whole house is an important committee which is constituted for discussing all revenue and appropriation Bills. When the House mets as the Committee of the whole, then the Speaker does not preside over the House.

The Committee on rules is also a very important committee of the House. This Committee has 14 members and has got the power to draft a Bill and introduce it in the House.

**Process of Law-Making in the Congress**

The Presidential system of government in America which is based on the principle of separation of powers does not provide for the participation of the American President and his Cabinet directly in the process of law making. Government measures may be introduced in the Congress through a friendly Senator or a member of the House of Representatives, who at the time of introducing the measure may announce that the government desires to have such a measure passed. Such measures are generally drafted by the government or Bills can be drafted by the Congressmen by taking the help of the legislative reference service. Bills or resolutions may be introduced by congressmen at their own initiative or at the instance of some individuals or organisations. In every session of the Congress large number of Bills are introduced which represent the interests of different groups, individuals and organisations. Munro has aptly described that, "It is merely a play upon words to say that Bills 'Originate' in Congress.

The real initiative in law-making belongs to militant organisations in every corner of the land–organisations of farmers and workers, organisations of manufacturers and merchants, and a multitude of organisations, whose main function is to promote this or that novelty in legislation".

All the Bills and resolutions carry serial numbers. The first reading of the Bill is formal and is deemed to have been over when its title is printed in the Journal and Congressional Record. These measures are then referred to the appropriate standing committees. Opportunity is given to the people who want to speak for and against the Bill and even paid attorneys appear to argue either in support or against the Bill. The Committee comes to known about the merits and demerits of the Bill after hearing the arguments on both sides. The Committee is all powerful in respect of reporting on the Bill. It may report back without any change, may amend the Bill of change the Bill entirely and may putup a new Bill. When the Bill has a favourable report from the Committee, then it is sent to the House where it is set upon one of the three calendars for a second reading. The Committees make favourable reportts on about 20 per cent of the Bills, and the remaining Bills are not at all reported as they are not considered essential. This leads to the 'Pigeon-holing' of the Bills. There is however, no guarantee that a Bill with a favourable report will be passed by the Congress. It can only be said that such Bills have a good chance of passage.

Measures reported to the House by the Committees go to the respective calendars. Measures relating to revenue, appropriation and public property go to the union calendar, which are considered by the Committee of the whole House for their second reading. All other public Bills go to the House calendar, which for their second reading are considered by the House itself. Bills of non-public character go to the calendar of the committee of the whole–commonly known as the private calendar. Then there are two other calendars known as the consent calendar and the discharge calendars, to which Bills may be transferred from the Union and House calendars. On the first and third Mondays of each month, some of the non-controversial Bills which are referred to the consent calendar, are passed without any debate, amendment or without a second and third reading.

In case of a discharge calendar, the House can take a Bill from the standing committee for its own consideration. A discharge motion requires the signatures of half of the House membership and generally relates to a Bill on which the Committee has not reported for thirty days. Thus the procedure becomes rigid and difficult.

It may be mentioned that special days are allotted for consideration of Bills the first and third Mondays of each month for the consent calendar, the second and fourth Mondays for discharge motions, the first and third Tuesdays for private calendar. Nearly half a dozen standing committees including the committee on appropriations and the committee on ways and means have certain right over others for introducing their Bills. However, on certain days, this right can be exercised only by a two-thirds vote, which is not normally available. With the help of a simple majority, special orders may be issued by the rules committee. With the help of such orders restricting the time on debates, the majority party is enabled to expedite the passage of its important measures. There are also calendar Wednesdays when the unprivileged public Bills are considered. By a unanimous or a two-thirds vote or by a special order from the rules committee, the House may allot any day or all the days for consideration of the Bills of the privileged committees.

Before a Bill is finally passed by the House of Representatives, it is given three readings. The first reading is a nominal one and it is supposed to be over, when the title of the Bill is printed in the Journal and Congressional Record. The second reading is very important, as usually amendments are offered at this stage. The third reading is formal and in fact the whole Bill is never read at this stage, except the title of the Bill. However, a fall discussion on the Bill can be demanded, if the Bill is strongly opposed in the House. Under such circumstances, a further debate takes place in the third reading and additional amendments may also be offered. The Bill is sent to the Senate with the signature of the Speaker, after its final passage by the House of Representatives.

When a Bill comes to the Senate from the House of Representatives, it has got several alternatives. It may pass the Bill without any change, or with some amendments. It is also free to totally reject the Bill. The Senate Committees are free either to report or not to report on the measures. The Bills are killed, if the committees do not report back on the Bills to the Senate. When Bills are passed by the Senate in amendment form they are sent back to the House of Representatives for its acceptance in the amended form. If the House does not agree to the amendements, the Bill is referred to a joint conference committee of both the Houses for coming to an agreement.

The Bill is sent to the President for his aproval, after it is passed by both the Houses. The Bill may be signed by the President, in which case it becomes an Act. However, the President may keep it without signing for a period of ten days, when automatically it becomes a law without his signature. A Bill has to be again repassed by two-thirds majority in both the Houses of the Congress to override Presidential veto. However, if a Bill is sent to the President for his signaute and is not signed and if Congress is adjourned within the ten-day limit, the Bill is lost by the application of 'Pocket veto'. Amendments to the constitution, after having been passed by two-thirds majority, are not presented to the President for his assent.

**Financial Procedure**

As per the provisions of the constitutions, all Revenue Bills in the United States must originate in the House of Representatives. In all other matters, each House of Congress has a wide initiative in finance. The President of America is responsible for making a budget and proposing it to the Congress. But the Congress has the final power to do what it likes with the Presidential proposals.

The Budget and Accounting Act of 1921 governs the financial procedure prevalent to-day in the United States. Before the Act came into effect, all the estimates were submitted to the Secretary of the Treasury, who in turn transmitted them to the Speaker alongwith his estimates for revenue. Then these Bills were considered by the appropriate committees in detail and after going through the details, these appropriation Bills were submitted to the House of Representatives. Under this system, the heads of departments and bureaus as well as lobbyists put pressure upon the committees for increasing appropriations. The system could not work satisfactarily, as under such circumstances, it was not possible to maintain economy. The necessity of economy was felt during the First World War (1914-1918), as there was considerable increase in the expenditure. To overcome this difficulty, the Congress passed an Act in 1920, which provided for a regular national budget system. President Wilson, vetoed this Act, on account of some of its objectionable features. These featurs were deleted and the Act was readopted by the Congress as the Budget and Accounting Act of 1921.

As per the provisions of the Act two separate agencies are set up–the general accounting office under the Comptroller General and the Bureau of the Budget under a Director of the Budget. Regular auditing of the accounts of all the offices is being done by the general accounting office. This office maintains its independence and impartiality. The Bureau of the Budget also had more or less independent status although it was nominally under the control of the Treasury Department. But in 1939, the President of America became the supreme controlling authority of the Bureau of the Budget and the Director of the Bureau is appointed by him and is responsible to him alone.

Each department, board, bureau, commission etc., prepares estimates for the next fiscal year. Then these are submitted to the Director of the Budget. It is the duty of the Director to examine and revise the estimates in consultation with the departments and other officials. After proper scrutiny these Estimates are combined together and the document is known as the budget. It needs the approval of the President for its printing and submission to the House of Representatives. Thus it is clear that at present the executive in America is responsible for the planning of the budget.

The Committee on appropriations looks after the appropriation side of the budget and the Committee on ways and means looks after the revenue side. These measures are then placed before the House of Representatives by these committees after studying and discussing the various appropriations and tax measures. Proposals for supplementary appropriations do not go to the Bureau of the Budget. These are sent directly to the various committees and if they report favourably, they are sent to the Committee on appropriation for approval.

The House of Representatives discusses the appropriation Bill in Committee of the whole and the Bill is given three readings before it is finally passed. The House reserves the right to make alterations in the Bill, but generally major changes are not made.

The appropriation Bill goes to the Senate after it is passed by the House of Representatives. The Bill is discussed by the Committee on appropriations, after which it is reported by the committee to the whole Senate. The Senate may pass the Bill in the original form in which it has been passed by the House of Representatives or may pass it with amendments and in the latter case the Bill is again returned to the House for concurrence. If the House does not accept the amendments made by the Senate, then the Bill is referred to a Joint Conference Committee of both the Houses. This Committee tries to bring a compromise between the two Houses and the Bill is finally passed by both the Houses and sent to the President for his approval. Normally the President approves the appropriation Bill. He might not approve of some items in the Bill, but he is not allowed to make piece-meal objections. He can however, veto the whole budget, in which case the various departments would have no funds for a considerable period and the whole administration would be paralysed. This has weakened the veto power of the President in respect of the appropriation Bill.

The executive and legislative organs have joint responsibility in approval of the budget. The Director of the Budget has the initiative in recommending appropriations. The President gives approval to such appropriations. It may be mentioned that the Congress has also the power either to reject or approve such appropriations. Thus the appropriations cannot be passed without the co-operation between the executive and legislative branches of the government.

It is however, interesting to note that the Secretary of the Treasury in America is not responsible for preparing the budget. This is being done by the Director of the Budget. But in almost all the democratic countries of the world, preparation of the budget is the responsibility of the Finance Minister.

It may be mentioned that although the Secretary of the Treasury has no initiative in financial matters, he exercises great influence in the matter of raising revenue and spending of money. The Treasury Department is a very important department in the U.S.A. The collection of revenue is in the hands of the Secretary of the Treasury and he gets it done through the bureau of internal revenue and the customs services. The custody of the public funds and paying of all Bills of expenditure, which have been properly authorized, are vested in the Treasury Department. It also supervises the currency, control of the mint and the coining of money etc.

# 6

# Party System and Pressure Politics

The American Constitution did not provide for political parties. But it is not possible to think of a democratic system without political parties and political parties have emerged for the smooth functioning of the American political system. The political parties play a very important role in America. The parties take part in the election of the President, Vice-President, Senators, Members of the House of Representatives and the State Legislatures and local bodies.

In the initial state of the development of the party system there were the Federalists, who believed in strong federal government and there were Anti-Federalists who were opposed to giving more powers to the federal government. Then there were the Federalists and the Republicans. At present the Democratic party and the Republican party are the two major political parties of America. Some other parties like the Socialist party, Communist party and Prohibition party etc., also exist in America, but they have only marginal influence in the political process of the country.

We do not notice any fundamental difference in the principles and programmes of the two major political parties. In the words of Bryce: "The two parties are like two empty bottles, each denoting the kind of liquor it contains". Finer has aptly put it that: "America has only one party, the Republican-cum-Democratic, divided into two nearly equal halves by habit, the contest for office, the Republican being one-half and the Democratic the other half of the party".

The political power in America has been shared by two parties and the presidency has gone to either of them. Although several times third parties did set up their candidates for the Presidential office, no third party ever got the chance to enter the White House. It has been rightly said that, "Third parties in American national politics have played the role of innovators of policy not of holders of office". At present the two major parties are the Democratic party and Republican party. The Democratic party came into existence during Washington's administration, under the leadership of Jefferson. It was known by various names such as, Anti-Federalist, Republican. Democratic Republican and finally Democratic. This party has survived under very difficult circumstances. The Federalist party led by Hamilton was rechristened as the Republic party. It passed under the names of Federalist, National Republican, whig and finally the Republican.

## Party Organization

In accordance with the principle of popular sovereignty, in America, at least theoretically, the authority of the party organization starts at the base. But in actual practice the leaders and the party elite have the power of initiative. The party caucus, the party convention, the Direct Primary and Nominating petition are the four devices which are followed by a party in America for the nomination of the candidates. Since 1830 the undemocratic party caucus has been replaced by nominating conventions. Now there are National conventions for the selection of Presidential and Vice-Presidential candidates and state-wide conventions are used for nominating state offices. But in the course of time due to lack of interest on the part of the people in selecting delegates to these conventions, these bodies were dominated by corrupt bosses. Due to this, with some exceptions, they were replaced by the Direct Primary, Open Primary, and Closed Primary. As per the new plan, the members of each party vote by secret ballot for those whom they desire as their candidates in the general election. Thus the primary elections are held as a prelude to the general elections and the party nomination is determined by the results of these primaries. The party committees which select candidates for the Primaries, play an important role. Regular election authorities conduct the election by all Primaries which are regulated by comprehensive laws. Finally, there is the method of Nominating Petition which has to be signed by a number of qualified voters. But this method is not applicable to the two major parties which have to nominate their candidates either by convention or Direct Primary. Nomination by petition is confined to independents or minor third parties. However, this method is extensively used in non-partisan local elections.

## Party Programmes

In the U.S.A. the party programme is drawn up as a resolution by a committee of the National Convention. It is subsequently presented before the general body of the convention for adoption. Congressional investigations are made to collect data about the socio-economic problems and issues. Each party tries to exploit the weakness of the other inorder to appeal to the matter, in projecting alternative policies and programmes. The party platforms very often become the forum for carrying out election propaganda. Maximum use is made of newspapers, radio and television to popularized party programme which is "a mixture of policy and methodology". In the U.S.A. the election campaign is more prolonged than in Great Britain or the Continental countries. Each party makes the effort to reach the people directly inorder to elist the support of maximum number of voters.

## Impact of Law on the Parties

Although the constitution of the United States did not make any mention to the political parties and they were considered as private organisation similar to Trade Unions, free to organise as they liked and spend any amount of money in the elections, to-day most of their activities are regulated by laws. Laws even regulate the amount and sources of contribution and the amount of expenditure of the party at the time of election. Laws define the organisation and the nature of political parties. The requirements to get party nominees on the ballot are also specified by law. The composition and powers of party committees and the methods for nominating party candidates are prescribed by law. Thus the parties have now become quasi-official agencies of the government. It was rightly observed by a U.S.A. federal court that, "The party may, indeed, have been a mere private aggregation of individuals in the early days of the Republic, but with the passage of years, political parties have become in effect state institutions, governmental agencies through which sovereign power is exercised by the people".

## Party Constitution

The rigorous discipline of the British political parties is not found in the American political parties. The American parties are not as centralised as the British parties. American political parties are manned by professionals and work for the achievement of strictly proffesional ends. Each party has its organisation at the national, state and local levels. Each party has got its National organization which consists of a National Committee, the Senatorial Campaign Committee.

It is the duty of the National Committee to raise funds for the party, supervise the work of the party, keep up the tempo of publicity and party propaganda and to conduct the Presidential campaign. The Senatorial Campaign Committee of the Republicans has got seven members nominated by the Chairman of the Republican Conference in the Senate, where as the Democratic party's Senatorial Campaign Committees are generally engaged in carrying out compaigns and raising and distributing funds for that purpose. The Congressional Campaign Committees of both the Republican and Democratic parties aid the campaigns of party nominees for the House of Representatives. Nominations to the Congressional Campaign Committees of both the parties are made by state party delegations in the House and are ratified by the party caucus.

Parties in America have also got their state organizations for the purpose of capturing state and local offices as well as participating in national contests. For managing local party and maintaining grassroot contacts, each party has a County Committee in every county. American parties have also City Committees in important urban centres for managing the city affairs of the party.

The Precinct Committee forms the base of the party and this one-man committee performs the routine function of maintaining the party's contacts with the voters. He is an employee of the County or City Committee and works as an official agent of the party organization.

In the U.S.A. there is continuous party activity only at the state level but not the national level as it is a Presidential type of government and elections take place as power the provisions of the Constitution. Elections take place more frequently in parlimentary type of governments than in the presidential systems and party professionals in America remain comparatively ineffective and inactive during the intervals between the elections.

## Pressure Politics in the U.S.A.

Pressure groups play an important role in the American political system. They constitute the core of political influence. They have become an integral part of the governmental machinery. Prof. V.O. Key is of the opinion that, "Prominent place must be given to the activities of private organisations if one is to understand the American Political System because these associations constitute links of communication between citizens and the governments". It is now increasingly recognised in America that pressure groups are not only a part of governmental process, but also they are indispensable for the success and effectiveness of any political system. Their essential role in democratic politics cannot be disputed. When a group of people have certain shared attributes, share certain common attitudes and make claims on other groups and on the political process with a view to realise their aims that arise out of their interests and attitudes, they constitute a pressure group. Pressure groups pursue their own particular interest, but to avoid public criticism, they try to present their particularistic interests and particularistic attitudes in the form of general interests and general attitudes. It is interesting to note that they present their view of the general interest in such a manner that their own particular interests are promoted.

In the U.S.A., the pressure groups employ agents, known as "lobbyists" to keep in close contact with government agencies for the purpose of influencing legislation and administration in favour of the group interests. They also spend vast amounts of money for winning the supports of public opinion for their aims and objectives. They hire the services of public relations experts to influence the mass media like press, radio and television, inorder to build up goodwill for their objectives.

In the past the pressure groups were considered dangerous for the healthy functioning of the democratic system of government. In the words of Frederich, "they were held up to scorn both by muck-rackers and by sane students of politics. They were the sinister force growing at the foundations of modern democracy, of representative government, and the world 'lobby' supposedly comprehended a whole congerics of abuses, corruption, fraud, and the like". But now these groups are considered as inevitable and as a healthy factor for the smooth working of the political system. In the modern times these groups have become highly complex and have acquired their own status. They are able to influence the process of law-making to a considerable extent and have become a legislature behind a legislature. Professor Finer rightly describes them as "the anonymous empire". In the U.S.A., several factors like the continental size of the country, the absence of responsible government for undertaking legislative initiative, the vagueness of party programmes and the amorphous character of the Congress, have been responsible to increase the influence of the Pressure groups. Since the Congress is the law-making body, people who have a stake in congressional legislation feel the vital need for influencing individual members and committees of the Congress.

There are a wide variety of Pressure groups in the U.S.A. There is the Chamber of Commerce which looks after the large number business interest of its members. The American Federation of labour, the Rail-road Brotherhoods, and the United Mine Workers and the Congress of Industrial Organizations are some of the Organizations of labour which try to protect the interests of the working class. The American Medical Association (A.M.A.), the American Bar Association and the National Education Association are some of the Professional associations which take active part in politics and influence legislation both at the state and national levels. There are also religious organization like the National Council of Churches (Protestant) which take great interest on legislative matters. Women's organizations such as the league of Women voters, the American Association of University Women or the Business and Professional Women are all active in influencing legislation in their favour. There are also local organizations like the Community Improvement Associations which demand civic amenities in the form of street lighting, police patrolling, sanitation, drainage and other facilities. Civil clubs such as the Rotary, Lions, Civitan and Kiwanis sponsor many projects for promoting the general interest of the people and try to mobilize public opinion in support of their projects. These groups also have considerable influence in the political process of the U.S.A. Thus in America the Pressure groups constitute a powerful political force. In the words of Professor Laski, "There is a real sense in which these pressure groups despite their seeming incoherence are a kind of Congress behind the Congress whose authority must not be minimised. They can do a great deal for a member of the House, not least for the unimportant or the new member. They can help him with his speeches. They can organise for him a publicity back home or in his stage which he himself might not so easily secure. They can see that he meets important people, not least upon important occasions. And since the lobbyists have usually the closest relations both with the great press agencies and the remarkable corps of special correspondents which the great metropolitan newspapers maintain in Washington, they can, project a leader into a national figure. At the least, if he is co-operative they can make his constituents feel that their representative in the House is something more than the local boy who has made good. If he wins the supports of the right lobbyist at the right time, that may will be a decisive factor in his political career".

In America the Pressure groups try to influence the nominations of members to the Congress and their elections. After the elections are over, these Pressure groups maintain their pressure on the members of the Congress and the government officials. They carry on continuous propaganda for influencing public opinion in their favour both at the national and the state level. Although the Pressure groups are extra-constitutional bodies, in terms of their tremendous influence over the process of law-making, they are viewed as the third chamber of the legislature.

# 7

# The Federal Judiciary

For the satisfactory working of a federal system, there is the necessity of an effective and indepenent judiciary. A federal constitution provides for the distribution of powers between the federal government and the federating units. Thus always there is the probability of transgression of jurisdiction either on the part of the federal or state governments which may lead to conflict and dissensions. Hence, there should be an independent and impartial judiciary to decide the disputes and settle controversies regarding powers and jurisdiction of the respective governments. In a federal state the judiciary plays the role of interpreting the constitution and giving decisions in the disputes and controversies between the federal government and the states or between the states themselves.

Article III of the American constitution provides for a Supreme Court: "The Judicial power of the United States shall be vested in one Supreme Court, and such inferior courts as the Congress may from time to time ordain and establish". The Congress was given the power to take necessary steps for the organization of the Supreme Court and the establishment of other Federal Courts. The jurisdiction of the Federal Courts has been defined by Article III of the Constitution in the following words:

"The judicial power shall extent to all cases, in law and equity, arising under this constitution, the laws of the United States, and treaties made, or which shall be made, under their authority; to all cases affecting ambassadors, other public ministers, and consuls; to all cases of admiralty and maritime jurisdiction; to controversies to which the United States shall be a party; to controversies between two or more states; between a State and citizens of another state; between citizens of different states; between citizens of the same state claiming lands under grants of different states, and between a state or the citizens thereof, and foreign states, citizens, or subjects".

Thus the above mentioned constitutional provision makes it clear that the judicial powers of the Supreme Court shall extend to cases arising under the constitution, laws and treaties made by the United States, cases affecting diplomatic immunity of the ambassadors, public ministers and consuls, cases arising under the Admiralty Law as distinct from common law and cases of controversies between the states etc.

The Federal courts are forbidden to take cognizance of any suit brought against a state "by citizens of another state or by citizens or subjects of any foreign state". As per the eleventh amendment adopted in 1798, all such suits can be filed only in State Courts and that too with the consent of the state legislature. However, the Federal Government of the United States, or any other state of the union, or any foreign state can sue a state in the Federal Courts of America. The American Federal Courts have jurisdiction over controversies between citizens or subjects of foreign states and American citizens, and between the citizens of various states of the Union.

The Federal Courts administer statutory law, common law, equity, admiralty and maritime law. The American common law is based upon the principles and procedure of English common law. It may be noted that over the years, judicial decision and statutes of the Congress have greatly altered the common laws. The procedure of equity, which came from England is simple and it relates to several classes of civil cases only. The American constitution and statutes enacted by the Congress, determine the criminal jurisdiction of the Federal Courts. The Federal Courts mainly deal with civil cases, although they are sometimes required to deal with other cases also.

**The Supreme Court**

The judicial power of the United States is vested in the Supreme Court, which is the highest court of the country. In the words of Dr. Finer: "Such a court (Supreme Court), with such functions is the most original, the most distinctively American contribution to political science to be found in the constitution. It is even more. It is the cement which has fixed firm the whole federal structure".

The American Supreme Court has played a very vital role in developing the sense of unity and cohesiveness and strengthening the Federal Government of the United States. In this direction the role played by Chief Justice Marshall, who was a federalist and became the Chief Justice in 1801, has been universally acknowledged as a remarkable achievement. By his doctrine of implied powers, he gave a large number of powers to the Federal Government, which the original framers of the constitution had probably never contemplated. Without this remarkable achievement of Chief Justice Marshall, the United States would have continued as a loose confederation despite the federal constitution of April 30, 1789. In the words of Lord Bryce: "No other man did half so much either to develop the constitution by expounding it, or to secure for the judiciary its rightful place in the government as the living voice of the constitution. No one vindicted more strenuously the duty of the court to establish the authority of the fundamental law of the land, no one abstained more scrupulously from trespassing on the field of executive administration or political controversy. The administration and respect which he and his colleagues won the court remain in bulwork; the traditions which were formed under him have continued in general to guide the action and elevate the sentiments of their successors". Federalism might have failed in the United States in the absence of such a distinguished person who was responsible for transforming the federal structure devised in the 18th century to satisfy the requirements of a small population of 13 states living in pastoral cum-agricultural age, into a dynamic one, suitable to meet the requirements of a highly industrialised country consisting of 50 states to-day.

## Organisation of the Court

The Supreme Court of America stands at the apex of the judicial pyramid. It is the creation of the constitution, whereas the other federal courts have been created by the Congress. The number of judges of the Supreme Court has not been fixed by the constitution. The Congress has got the power either to increase or decrease the number of the judges of the Supreme Court. In the beginning it consisted of a Chief Justice and five associates. The membership of the Supreme Court was reduced to five in 1800; increased to seven in 1807; increased to nine in 1837 and ten in 1863; reduced to seven in 1866; and in 1869 it was fixed at nine. At present, the Supreme Court consists of the Chief Justice and eight associate judges.

These judges are appointed by the President with the consent of the Senate. No qualification has been prescribed for the judge of the Supreme Court. The President is free to appoint any person as judge, for whom senatorial confirmation can be obtained. However, there is an established tradition of selecting men of high prestige and outstanding ability as judge of the Supreme Court.

**Tenure**

The judges of the American Supreme Court hold office during good behaviour. They can only be removed by impeachment. A judge may retire on reaching the age of 70 years or at any time thereafter. In case he has served on the Bench for the years, then he can retire with full salary. A judge may also retire at the age of sixty five years with fifteen years of service, and receive full pay for life. The life tenure of the judges of the American Supreme Court has been subjected to criticism. It is argued that this practice is not only undemocratic but also it strikes at the roots of efficiency. On the otherhand security of tenure in terms of life appointment is defended on the ground that it would promote and protect integrity of the judges and will be conducive to sound performance. It may be observed that over the long years since its inception, the Supreme Court has been able to maintain its competence, and prestige at a very high level and has won the confidence of the whole nation. As it has been already mentioned, a judge of the Supreme Court cannot be removed except by impeachment. It may be remembered that impeachments are very rare. There has been only one case of unsuccessful impeachment against a judge of the Supreme Court.

The constitution guarantees that the salary and other privileges of the judges shall not be altered to their disadvantage during the term of their office.

**Sessions**

The sessions of the Supreme Court begin in October and end in June. It holds one regular session every year from October to June. Special sessions may be called by the Chief Justice when the Court is adjourned, but there must be urgent and important reason for such purpose.

The presence of six judges is necessary to constitute a quorum.

The Chief Justice presides at all sessions and announces its orders. He is the executive officer of the Court. The hearings of the Courts are conducted on Tuesday, Wednesday, Thursday and Friday. On Saturday, the judges consult among themselves and register their opinions. Judgements are delivered in public on Monday. At the time of deciding any case all the judges sit together and there are no benches. Decisions may either be unanimous or divided and in the latter case, the majority and dissenting opinions are usually recorded Judges who agree with the majority decision but have different reasons for the same, wirte their concurrent opinions separately. The decisions of the Supreme Court are published in the United States Reports.

## Jurisdiction of the Court

The Jurisdiction of the Supreme Court of America can be classified into two categories: Original and appellate. Cases can be taken to the Supreme Court by original suit or by appeal. The original jurisdiction of the Supreme Court is limited by the constitution to specified cases such as ambassadors, public ministers and consuls. It also extends to all such cases in which a state is a party. There are limited number of cases which come to the Supreme Court in its original jurisdiction.

The appellate jurisdiction of the Supreme Court extends to a large number of cases. In accordance with this power of the court, appeals may be taken from the decisions of the lower federal courts and the State Courts. However, all the cases cannot be taken in appeal to the Supreme Court. An appeal can be made to the Supreme Court under certain conditions. Cases from the highest state courts can be directly taken in appeal to the Supreme Court and the lower federal courts do not come into picture in this respect. In this connection, it may be mentioned that although the Supreme Court hears appeals from the federal courts.

The American Supreme Court does not act as an advisory body as is the case with the Indian Supreme Court. It had declined to give any adivce to President Wilson when he asked for its opinion on a proposed treaty. The Supreme Court has never given advisory judicial opinion on hyopthetical questions. It also does not give judgement upon purely political questions.

## Judicial Review

The power of judicial review is the most important power of the American Supreme Court. In accordance with this provision the Supreme Court has the power to determine whether a law passed by the Congress or any state legislature or any provision in any state constitution or any other public regulation, having the force of law, is in consonance with the constitution. If it is violative of the provisions of the constitution, the Supreme Court can declare it as unconstitutional and thus invalid. Hence in determining the constitutionality of any legislation, the court is not concerned of any legislation, the court is not concerned with the wisdom, experience or policy of legislation. Chief Justice Marshall explains it in the following words: "It neither approves nor condemns any legislative policy. Its delicate and difficult office is to ascertain and declare whether the legislation is in accordance with, or in contravention of, the provisions of the constitution; and having done that its duty ends". Whenever any provision of law, executive order, interpretation or decree is challenged in the Supreme Court, it interpretes the constitution to determine the constitutionality of the challenged provision. This basic power of the court to interpret the constitution and determine the constitutionality of the challenged provision or a statute is called the power of Judicial review. This power has made the Amercain Supreme Court, the most powerful judicial organisation of the world. In the words of Munro: "The most distinctive attribute of the Supreme Court is its power of judicial review. This is the power to determine whether a law passed by Congress, or any provision of a state constitution or any law enacted by a state legislature, or any other public regulation professedly having the force of law is in consonance with the constitution of the United States". Thus the Supreme Court has got the power to declare a law passed by the Congress as unconstitutional. This power to declare the laws repugment to the constitution as unconstitutional is also enjoyed by the lower federal courts, but appeals against such decisions can be taken to the Supreme Court. In all such matters of declaring a federal law or state law or any other regulation as ultra-vires, the American Supreme Court enjoys the final authority.

The judicial supremacy of the American Supreme Court has become an accepted fact of the American political system. The Congress has also accepted the supremacy of the court over the laws passed by it. The State constitutions and the laws passed by the state legislatures are also subject to the power of judicial review of the American Supreme Court. If any state law or constitution is in conflict with the national constitution, the Supreme Court shall declare it as unconstitutional or ultravires. The Supreme Court has played a very vital role in this sphere. The liberal interpretation of the constitution by the Supreme Court, has considerably helped in the development of the constitution and in the increase of the powers of the federal government. It has helped in settling the conflicts of jurisdiction between the legislative and executive organs of the government, between the states interse and between the states and the federal government. The rights, liberties and privileges of the individual are also protected by the Supreme Court against any encroachment. In the words of Munro: "The development of the Supreme Court into a final arbiter of constitutional disputes is one of America's most important contributions to the science of government". Supreme Court's power of judicial review has proved very useful. In the past this power was not exercised by any court but now such power is being enjoyed in varying degrees by the courts in Australia and India.

Declaring the intention of the founding fathers of the American constitution, President Jefferson had said that they designed to establish three independent departments of government and not to give the judiciary the right to review the acts of the Congress and the President. But it may be stated that majority of the members of the Philadelphia convention favoured judicial review. Alexander Hamilton was of the view that the Supreme Court should have the power to set aside Congressional legislation. He wanted independent judiciary as "an excellent barrier to the encroachments and oppressions of the representative body".

In 1803, in the case of Marbury vs Madison, the American Supreme Court for the first time faced the issue of judicial review. In this famous case Chief Justice Marshall gave the verdict that the constitution is the Supreme law of the land and therefore must be paramount to any statute in conflict with it. The Supreme Court is the final authority to interpret the constitution and to preserve and protect it. Thus it is required under the constitution, that any congressional statute, which violates the constitution, which is the fundamental law of the country should be declared ultra-vires by the court. The principle of judicial review was firstly established after this judgement of the Supreme Court. This power of the Supreme Court to invalidate congressional laws and other provisions is no longer questioned. It is being accepted as a part of the American constitution.

The American Supreme Court has earned wide popularity for its independence and impartiality. It has never mixed up judicial questions with political questions. It has refused to become a party to any political issue, by declining to give advisory opinion on such issues. Irrespectives of their political alligiance prior to appointment after their appointment as judges of the Supreme Court, they do not remain as democrats or Republicans and become non-partisan in their attitudes and approaches. They also give up their business connections, if any. This is highly essential to maintain their impartiality and independence.

**Criticism of Judicial Review**

The power of judicial review of the American Supreme Court has been subjected to searching criticism. By the exercise of this power, the Supreme Court has become not only the third chamber of legislation, but also the super legislature. A law can be declared unconstitutional if five out of the nine judges give such a verdict, eventhough the other four judges do not consider it unconstitutional. Thus the fate of any Congressional legislation or any other provision is being determined by the majority of one and this means that the action of one single judge can a set aside the laws passed by the Congress and also signed by the President. This practice is being considered as arbitrary and undemocratic. There has been a demand from several quarters for the termination of this undemocratic practice. It may however be pointed out that very few laws passed by the Congress have been declared unconstitutional by a slander majority of only one and in most cases laws which are declared unconstitutional or ultravires, have the support of overwhelming majority of the judges of the Supreme Court. Some suggestions were offered in the past, that law should be declared unconstitutional only by a two-thirds decision or by unanimous decision of the judges.

It has also been argued that the American Supreme Court has become the citadel of reactionary forces and vested interests. On several occasions, its decisions have stood in the way of social progress. Some of the American Presidents like Jefferson, Jackson, Lincoln and Franklin D. Roosevelt have also criticised the power of judicial review of the American Supreme Court as undemocratic and arbitrary. During the time of President Abraham Lincoln, the congressional legislation abolishing slavery, was declared as unconstitutional by the Supreme Court. Lincoln's victory in the civil war could only set aside this unpopular decison of the Supreme Court and slavery was abolished by adopting the thirteenth amendment to the constitution in 1865.

In the past, some proposals were made to take away this power from the hands of the Supreme Court. It was also proposed that to counteract the power of judicial review of the Supreme Court, the American Congress may be given the power to repass a bill by two-thirds votes, which has been declared as unconstitutional by the court. During the recent times, the Supreme Court also declared, President

Roosevelt's New Deal legislation, as unconstitutional. President Roosevelt was so much annoyed with the Supreme Court that in 1937, he secured the introduction in the Congress, a court reorganization bill to reform the Supreme Court. It was the purpose of this Bill to raise the number of judges from nine to fifteen inorder to neutralise the resistance of the more conservative element in the judiciary. But this Bill was rejected by the Congress.

By and large, the American opinion is in favour of the Supreme Court. The Americans are eager to maintain its independence and impartiality. They are convinced that the Supreme Court with its powers of final control over the President and the Congress, is indispensable to their political system. They are not prepared to increase the powers of either the President or the Congress at the cost of the Supreme Court. It may also be remembered that the Supreme Court has played an important role in strengthening the federal government. By his Doctrine of Implied powers, Chief Justice Marshall, who was a federalist, greatly helped in increasing the powers of the federal government. But for judicial review, writes Munro, "The American Constitutional system would have become a hydra-headed monstrosity of forty-eight (now fifty) rival sovereign States. In a country having separation of powers and a political system in which the executive is independent of legislative control and the legislature cannot be dissolved earlier than the expiry of its term, the power of judicial review constitutes the ultimate safeguard of individual liberty".

# The Constitution of Switzerland

1

# Evolution of the Swiss Constitution

There are linguistic, religion and racial diversities in Switzerland. Inspite of such diversities, Switzerland has very successfully withstood the test of time and has been able to maintain itself as the oldest democracy of the world. The economic and political forces have to some extent succeeded in changing the forms of democracy in Switzerland, but the spirit of democracy of the Swiss people has remained unaltered. Switzerland has also continued to be the oldest continuous Republic of the world.

The various diversities which are noticed in Switzerland may be properly understood, if we study the process of constitutional development in that country. Before the Confederation was formed, there were several sovereign states in Switzerland which were not tied up by any co-ordinating central authority. These states were known as cantons.

On August 1, 1291 the cantons of Uri, Schwyz and Unterwalden entered into a perpetual league of friendship for common defence against external aggression. There were eight members in the league by 1335 and by the year 1513, the membership had gone upto thirteen. However, till 1798, the number of cantons comprising the federation was not increased. These thirteen cantons formed a loose confederation. The central government was conspicuous by its absence. The common central organ was known as the Diet, in which all the cantons, (which were sovereign) were equally represented. The decisions of the Diet did not have the binding effect and any Canton was free to obey it or not to obey it.

In 1798, armies of the French Revolution invaded the Swiss territory and Switzerland came under French Occupation. France enforced a new constitution in Switzerland as a result of which the "one and indivisible" Helvetic Republic was established. Switzerland was divided into 18 cantons and a highly centralized form of government was established, under the influence of France. Uniformity in administration and legislation was provided throughout the country and the cantons were deprived of their local autonomy. Switzerland became a protectorate of France. A unitary constitution was imposed on it by the French government.

The new constitution did not suit the Swiss genius and there soon grew resentment against it. Consequently in 1803 Napoleon, through the Act of Mediation was obliged to grant back to a great extent the autonomy Switzerland enjoyed before 1798, i.e., before its invasion by France. However, after the fall of Napoleon, a new Federal Constitution was provided by the Diet for Switzerland. This was known as the Federal Pact of 1815, and was endorsed by the Congress of Vienna. Due to this reactionary federal constitution the central government became extremely weak and the cantons had become sovereign states. The number of cantons was then 22.

In 1830, there was a liberal revolution in Paris. The Swiss people also started an agitation and the reactionary governments in the cantons fell one after another. The aristocratic and the oligarchic political culture of the Swiss cantons were gradually destroyed and democracy started taking deep roots in the Swiss soil. Thus under the changed circumstances the new governments of the Cantons, decided to amend the Pact of 1815, so as to facilitate the emergence of a strong federal government. But these liberal reforms were vehemently opposed by some of the Catholic cantons. These cantons organised themselves into a separate alliance known as the 'Sonderbund'.

A civil war broke out in Switzerland in 1847 in which the 'radicals' and the 'federalists' came to a direct clash. The league of Seven Catholic cantons–'Sonderbund', threatened to seccede from the confederation. But these cantons were quickly defeated. As a result of this a new federal constitution was drafted and adopted in 1848 by the people by a constitutional referendum. It was approved by the majority both of the cantons and the people. Thus from a loose confederation, Switzerland emerged as a Federation. The cantons were no doubt allowed to retain certain vital powers in their own sphere, but were deprived of their right to secede, to make war, or such other matters of common federal interests.

The Swiss Constitution of 1848 was totally revised in 1874. This revised constitution with the several amendments, which forms the constitutional laws of Switzerland till to-day, was again a victory for the forces in favour of a strong federation. As a result of this new constitution the position of the centre over the cantons was further consolidated. In the words of Arnold J. Zwicher, it "augmented the powers of the central government and laid the legal foundations for the present legal and constitutional system of Switzerland". At present the Swiss Confederation comparises 25 cantons–19 full cantons and 6 half cantons.

Although German, French and Italian are the three official languages of Switzerland and on the ground of religion the people are divided into the Protestants and the Catholics, Switzerland is a Nation. In the words of Munro: "the Swiss form a thoroughly coherent nation. They have behind them a tradition of self-government extending back six hundred years or more". Lord Bryce has correctly observed that the Swiss are "not only a united people, but one of the united and certainly the most patriotic among the people of Europe".

## Characteristic Features of the Constitution

In the community of world constitutions, the Swiss constitution forms a class by itself. It presents the successful model of direct democracy. It provides for a political structure, which is a harmonious combination of both the Presidential and the Parliamentary models and the vices of neither. In the Swiss democracy, the individual is given the maximum freedom to think, express and assert himself, without the fetters of party control. In no other political system of the world democracy and democratic institutions are valued so highly as they are being done in Switzerland.

Some of the important features of the Swiss constitution are discussed below:

### *(i) A Written and Rigid Constitution*

Switzerland has a written constitution. It was adopted in 1848 and was drastically revised in 1874. There have been more than fifty amendments to the constitution so far. There are 123 articles and five clauses under Transitory Provisions. From the point of its comprehensiveness, it stands midway between the American and the Indian constitutions. In size it is one-fourth of the Indian constitution and twice as long as the constitution of the U.S.A. Despite the written nature of the constitution, it has also given rise to several conventions. For example, the naturalization of foreigners is done by the cantons, though the constitution leaves this to the Confederation. The election of the Presidents and Vice-Presidents of the two Houses of the Federal Assembly takes place every year instead of after every session as provided in the constitution. The cantons of Bern, Zurich and Vaud are always represented on the Federal council and there cannot be more than five councillors from the German cantons.

Switzerland has a rigid constitution. The revision of the Constitution may be done either by the two Houses of the Federal Assembly with compulsory referendum or by a direct popular demand viz., initiative by 50,000 qualified voters. The amendment is declared adopted if approved of by the majority of Swiss citizens taking part in the vote and by the majority of the cantons.

### *(ii) The Unique Parliamentary Pattern*

The Swiss constitution is at once parliamentary and presidential. There is no nominal head like the British King or the Indian President. The federal council, which is the chief executive of the country is at once the nominal and the real executive. It resembles the American President he is at once the king and his own Prime Minister. This makes it nearer to the Presidential model than the parliamentary model.

Switzerland has a plural executive consisting of seven members, known as the Federal council. All the members of the Federal Council are equal in status and power and the Presidentship of the Council goes by rotation. There is no Prime Minister of the British or the Indian type.

The Federal Council has no power to dominate over the Federal Assembly and its subordination to the federal legislature is real unlike the British system where in reality the Council of Ministers dominate the Parliament with the support of party majority.

However, it may be noted that the Council of Ministers or the Federal Council in Switzerland enjoy the fixed term of office for a period of four years and does not serve in the pleasure of the legislature. While the accountability of the Federal Council to the legislature makes it parliamentary its fixed tenure of office makes it presidential.

It may also be mentioned that like the British and the Indian systems, there is no political homogenity of the Federal Council. Members are taken from different political parties and they are allowed to speak out their minds publicly in the interests of the nation, even if it amounts to opposing their own cabinet colleagues. Thus the Swiss constitution provides for a unique system of government which is a queer combination of the parliamentary and presidential models.

***(iii) The Plural Executive***

There is a plural executive in Switzerland, known as the Federal Council. It consists of seven members. Although the councillors are not members of the Federal Assembly, they can introduce Bills and take part in the debates and deliberations. They are elected by the Federal Assembly for a period of four years and cannot be removed from office prior to the completion of their term. The Federal Council acts more or less as a Cabinet. There is a queer combination of the parliamentary and the presidential principles in the organisation and functioning of the Swiss Federal Executive.

***(iv) Secularism***

There is no State religion in Switzerland and hence it is a secular state. The Swiss constitution grants freedom of conscience and religious worship to every citizen.

***(v) Federalism***

Switzerland is described as a confederation by the Constitution, but in practice it is a federal republic. It consists of 22 cantons (19 full cantons and 6 half cantons) and has a federal structure. There is a Federal Assembly, Federal Council and the Federal Tribunal or the Federal Judiciary. Powers are divided between the federal government and the cantons. The powers of the federal government have been specified by the constitution and the residuary powers belong to the cantons. There are also certain concurrent powers, which are exercised by both the federal government and the cantons.

***(vi) Direct Democracy***

Switzerland is an unique example of a true democracy. There is provision for direct legislation. The devices of referendum and initiative are very important. Referendum is compulsory for constitutional amendments and optional for other laws. Initiative is permitted for constitutional amendments only. As far as the cantons are concerned, referendum is universal in all the state except five cantons, where the system of 'the Lands gemeinde' (direct democracy), which is much older than the devices of referendum and initiative, is in practice. The adult male citizens used to assemble in the annual open air meeting and decide on various matters–such as election of officials, amendment of the constitution, voting on bills and the adoption of the budget etc. Women did not enjoy the right to vote in Switzerland till 1971 when right to vote was granted to them by a constitutional provision. Prior to this many attempts were made in Switzerland to grant the right to vote to women without any success.

*(vii) The Federal Tribunal*

The federal judiciary in Switzerland is known as the Federal Tribunal. It has got limited power of judicial review. The laws passed by the Federal Assembly cannot be declared unconstitutional by it. However, if a law passed by the legislature of any canton is the conflict with the federal constitution, then it can be declared as unconstitutional by the Federal Tribunal. Thus in Switzerland the supremacy of the federal constitution has been established.

*(viii) Swiss Neutrality*

Switzerland is a neutral state and it tries to maintain its neutrality steadfastly. For this purpose it did not take part in the First World War and the Second World War. Inorder to maintain her neutrality, it has also not sought the membership of the U.N.

*(ix) Dual Citizenship*

The Swiss constitution provides for dual citizenship. Each citizen is a citizen of a canton and also of Switzerland. This kind of dual citizenship is also followed in the U.S.A. on the contrary, the Indian constitution provides for single citizenship.

*(x) Bill of Rights*

There is no separate Bill of Rights in the Swiss Constitution. But the Swiss citizens enjoy civil, political and economic rights and these rights are mentioned in the various articles of the constitution. Civil rights like right to freedom of conscience and religious worship, right of education, freedom of the press, freedom of marriage, and the protection of the national languages are enjoyed by the Swiss citizens. However, certain limitations may be imposed on these rights in the national interest. Then certain political rights are granted such as the right to vote and contest in the elections. Every Swiss citizen having voting right can be elected to the Federal Assembly, Federal Council and the right to equality before the law are granted to the Swiss citizens. A sentence of death is not pronounced for a political offence. The economic rights include freedom of trade and commerce throughout the country, insurance for accident, sickness and old age and invalidity etc. All these are justiciable rights.

# 2

# Direct Democracy in Switzerland

The practice of direct democracy in Switzerland has not only strengthened the democratic principle of the sovereignty of the people in the true sense of the term but has also made it practicable. In the words of Lord Bryce: "Nothing in Swiss arrangement is more instructive to the student of democracy for it opens a window into the soul of the multitude. Their thoughts and feelings are seen directly and not refracted through the medium of elected bodies".

The two important devices of direct legislation–referendum and initiative–have their origin in Switzerland. These institutions of direct legislation have been followed by some other countries from Switzerland. The practice of direct democracy in Switzerland has been highly appreciated by many scholars and constitutional experts. In the words of Munro, Switzerland is "one of the oldest, smallest, and best of the world's democracies. With its plural executive, its unique interpretation of the principle of ministerial responsibility, and its free use of direct legislation, the Helvetic republic has illumined both the science and art of the government". Lord Bryce has also praised the unique Swiss institutions in the following words: "It contains a greater variety of institutions based on democratic principles than any other country.... democracy is there more truly democratic than any other country in the world".

In Switzerland there is indirect democracy together with the institutions of direct democracy. Direct legislation is unequalled as an instrument of practical instruction in politics. The institutions of referendum, initiative, recall, plebiscite and primary assemblies are the institutions of direct democracy. In some of the Swiss cantons primary assemblies of all adult citizens, known as 'Landsgemeinde' exist, while in the other cantons, the institutions of referendum and initiative are in operation. Recall and plebiscite are generally not resorted to in Switzerland.

### Landsgemeinde

It is the most picturesque and fascinating of all political institutions in Switzerland. In five cantons of Switzerland this institution of direct democracy is in operation. A Landsgemeinde is a political assembly which meets annually in the open air.

The annually elected Landamman presides over the meeting of the Landsgemeinde. The entire adult population of the canton has the right to participate in the deliberations and to exercise his right to vote. This peoples' assembly is the sovereign authority and the political power of the community rests in this body. It enacts laws and ratifies those which have been previously passed by the executive council, which is elected by it. It passes resolutions and settles current questions pertaining to finance and public works. It elects the executive council and many other important officers including the judges. Although the powers of the landsgemeinde vary from canton to canton, they have some general powers such as, revision of the constitution, passing ordinary legislative measures, taxation, alienation of public property, franchise grants, creation of new offices and fixation of their salaries and elections of the executive and judicial officials of the community. Thus the system of Landsgemeinde represents the purest form of democracy in Switzerland. In the words of Llyod, "The sovereign power of the people is directly exercised in all the critical acts of the government by the full assembly of citizens forming the largest and most conspicuous example of what Roussean and certain other philosophers regard as the only democracy.

### The Referendum and Initiative

Referendum is the reference of an enacted measure by the legislature to the people for approval. On the other hand initiative is a positive action by which a given number of electors may propose on enactment either by the people or by the legislature. If such a measure is approved by the required majority it becomes, a law. Thus a referendum may be compared to a shield with which the people ward off undesirable legislation and the initiative is compared to a sword with which it cuts the way for enactment of its own ideas into laws.

In Switzerland there are three devices of direct legislation such as, the compulsory constitutional referendum, the constitutional initiative and optional legislative referendum. The compulsory constitutional referendum is used for amendments of the federal constitution. Any amendment to the federal constitution, after it is passed by the Federal Assembly has to be referred to the people, for expressing their views on the proposed amendment to the fundamental law of their country. The constitutional amendment can be adopted, only if it has been approved of by majority of the voters taking part in the referendum and by a majority of the cantons.

Constitutional initiative is the device through which amendments are propsed to the constitution by the people. An amendment to the constitution can be initiated by 50,000 voters. The proposed amendment may be in the form of a general recommendation or a fully drafted Bill. If the amendment is approved by majority of the voters and majority of the cantons, it becomes adopted.

The optional legislative referendum is used for ordinary law-making and in respect of international treaties concluded for more than 15 years or for an indefinite period. Eight cantons or 30,000 voters can make a petition for a referendum on a Bill passed by the Federal Legislature, before its enactment. Thus the electorate has the power of veto even in matters of ordinary legislation, passed by the Federal Assembly. Thus in Switzerland the will of the people is supreme and a legislature with its transient majority is not allowed to rule roughshod over the people as it happens in other democratic countries. In such countries people elect their representatives who constitute the legislative bodies for a fixed period of time. Although in theory the people have the supreme authority, in actual practice the legislature exercises all powers, often, with little regard for the wishes of the people.

## Referendum and Initiative in the Cantons

Referendum is compulsory in all cantons in respect of amendments to their constitutions. For ordinary laws, it is compulsory in some cantons and optional in others. At present, there is the provision of referendum in all cantons except three. It is applicable to constitutions and ordinary laws alike. The method of initiative may be used, for proposing changes not only in the constitutional laws, but also in ordinary laws. In those cantons where the 'Landsgemeinde' system of direct democracy is followed, there is no room far any kind of referendum.

## Factors Responsible for the Success of Direct Democracy in Switzerland

The factors which have contributed to the success of direct

democracy in Switzerland are numerous. Some of the important factors are discussed below:

***(i) Character of the Swiss People***

The Swiss people are great advocates of political moderation. They exercise the rights of referendum and initiative with balance and discretion. The political moderation, the simple and frugal habits and examplary good sense of the Swiss people are chief among the several factors which contribute to the success of direct democracy. If the Swiss people would have held extreme views in matters relating to the principles and policies of the government, then the Swiss system would have become unworkable.

***(ii) Neutrality of the Country***

Switzerland has been permanently neutralised by international law and hence it is free from the complications of a foreign policy in the interest of which a country has to maintain a certain amount of secrecy in its policies and activities. Secrecy in a country's dealings is a living contradiction of the system of referendum which insists on open discussion of all important public issues, before they are either accepted public issues, before they are either accepted or rejected. It can thus be concluded that without neutrality, direct democracy would not have been possible in Switzerland.

***(iii) Small size of the Country***

Switzerland is a small country and in some cantons, the size of the population is very much limited. Due to this small size of the population, it is possible on their part to debate and discuse issues which are referred to popular vote, without much cost in terms of time and money. It is extremely difficult to practise democracy in a big country as it would involve huge expenditure and it may degenerate into a corrupt device.

***(v) System of Education***

The Swiss educational system which teaches the citizen the immense importance of his duties and creates the required political awareness in him, helps the successful working of direct democracy in Switzerland. The Swiss citizens are made aware that the rights and the duties are correlated and one cannot enjoy the rights in the true sense of the term without a proper performance of his duties. Thus the right to vote is accepted by the Swiss citizen as a sacred trust. Due to this they never shirk their political responsibility and give sound decisions in a majority of the cases.

## An Evaluation

For a better evaluation of the institutions of direct democracy which are functioning in Switzerland, they may be compared with similar institutions which are working in some of the American states.

It may be noted that the adoption of the practices of referendum and initiative in Switzerland, was inspired by the consideration of democratic theory and not due to any discontent with the working of representative legislatures as was the case with the American states who introduced such measures because of their dissatisfaction with the conduct of the representative bodies. There were glaring legislative abuses in the American institutions and hence there was the demand for the introduction of the devices of direct democracy. This difference in attitude is a basic difference which is responsible for certain differences in their working. In Switzerland more emphasis is given to referendum than to initiative, because they wish more to approve than to check and direct their law-makers. On the contrary in America, there is emphasis on initiative rather than referendum, as they have no faith in their representatives and want to direct them. In America, even the direct democratic practice of initiative is abused as the Agents of political associations try to purchase signature or forge them, in favour of proposals initiated by them.

In some of the American states with direct democratic institutions, the practice to recall representatives and elected officials prevails. This is desired to act as a check on the malfunctioning and the indifference of the representatives after their election. There is no practice of recall in Switzerland.

Thus it can be argued that for the success of direct democracy certain basic conditions are essential and it cannot function efficiently only through extraneous constitutional arrangements.

# 3

# The Federal Assembly

The Swiss federal legislature is known as the Federal Assembly, which consists of two chambers – the Council of States (upper chamber) and the National Council (lower chamber). There is the principle of equality of Cantons in the organisation of the Council of States, like the representation of the American states in the Senate. The membership of the National Council is based on population.

According to the Swiss constitution the supreme authority of the State is vested in the Federal Assembly, subject to the rights reserved to the people and the Cantons. William Rappard in his famous book, 'The Government of Switzerland', observes that: "Not only does the federal legislature legislate in legislative as well as in constitutional matters, but it also elects the members both of the executive and of the judiciary and its decisions are subject neither to an executive veto nor to any judicial review. It is in truth supreme as long as it retains the confidence and performs the will of the electorate".

## The Council of States

It consists of 44 members. Each full canton is represented by two members and each half canton is represented by one member. In this respect the Swiss Council of States resembles the Senate of the U.S.A. and Australia. The method of electing the members and their qualifications are not determined by the Swiss Constitution. These are left to the discretion of the Cantons and there is obviously no uniformity in such rules. Members to the Council of States are elected in some cantons by the people and in others they are elected by the Cantonal legislatures. Their terms of office vary from one to four years. A three-year term however, is gradually accepted by most of the cantons. The cantons are at liberty to recall any of their representatives and nominate others in their place. The Council elects its own President and Vice-President. In accordance with a convention, the Vice-President of one session, normally becomes the President for the next year.

## The National Council

This House consists of 187 members and has a term for 4 years. It is the popular House and is constituted through proportional representation. As per the constitution there must be one Deputy for each 24,000 people and thus the strength of the House varies from census to census. It continues for the fixed term of four years and cannot be dissolved earlier by the executive. The executive in Switzerland also has a fixed term and it cannot be removed from office by the legislature as is the practice in Great Britain. Election takes place after every 4 years on the last Sunday in October. The term of the National Council was originally fixed at three years, but since 1931, it has been fixed at four years. Such of the cantons including the half-cantons, which have population less than 24,000, also elect one member each for the National Council and thus there is no proportional representation in such cases. Every Swiss citizen who has completed the age of 20 years is entitled to vote and all citizens qualified to vote are entitled to election to the National Council, unless they are clergymen. Previously there was only Manhood suffrage but now women suffrage has been introduced. The National Council holds two regular sessions a year and also holds special sessions, if required.

## Organisation of the Federal Assembly

There are similar organisations for both the Council of States and the National Council. As per the provisions of the Constitution, a President and a Vice-President are to be elected, at every session, for each House. These official are not eligible for re-election, at the expiry of their term of office. However, on the basis of the growth of a convention, the President and the Vice-President of both the Houses are elected for one year and not for every session as provided by the Constitution. The Presidents of both the Houses are merely chairmen and do not have the powers and privileges enjoyed by the British Speaker. The posts of the Presiding officers are rotated among the different parties in the lower House and among the cantons in the upper House. At the time of the election of members of the Federal Council and the Federal Tribunal, the Presiding officers vote as ordinary members, but in case of a tie in the House, they have a casting vote.

The presiding officers do not get any salary, but they occupy positions of great honour and eminence. This honour is generally conferred on old and senior members.

The Council of States and the National Council have separate sessions, but they meet in joint sessions also when (i) members of the Federal Council, the Chancellor, the judges of the Federal Tribunal, the Commander-in-chief and other high officials are to be elected; (ii) there is a conflict of jurisdiction between the federal and some other authority and (iii) the grant of pardon is to be discussed. The President of the National Council presides over the joint sessions of both the Houses.

## Power of the Federal Assembly

The two Houses of the Federal Assembly have co-equal powers in respect of all matters of legislative authority including the Money Bills. No Bill can be enacted unless it has been passed by both the Houses. It is a matter of interest that deadlocks between the two Houses are rare, as in actual practice the Council of States is inclined to making concessions. This aspect of the Swiss legislators is highly appreciated by Lord Bryce. In his opinion the average member in the Swiss legislature, "is solid, shrewd, unemotional, or at any rate indisposed to reveal his emotions. He takes a practical commonsense and what may be called a middle class business view of questions. As a result of these qualities of the Swiss legislators, the National Assembly has been the most business like legislative body in the world, doing its work quietly and thinking of little else. There are few set debates and still fewer set speeches. Rhetoric is almost unknown. Speakers are not interrupted and rarely applanded".

The powers of the federal assembly extend into every field of government subject to the rights reserved to the people and to the Cantons. As long as it enjoys the confidence of the people the Swiss federal legislature is all powerful. The Judiciary in Switzerland has no power of veto or judicial review to declare the laws passed by it as unconstitutional or invalid. Thus it has got supreme power to legislate on all federal subjects, enacts the budget and levies taxes are provided for in the constitution.

## Legislative powers

Th: Federal Assembly has legislative, executive, administrative and judicial powers. It can pass laws and legislate ordinances on all matters which are granted to it by the Federal constitution. Treaties and Constitutional Amendments are subject to the approval of the Federal Assembly. The annual budget is also passed by it. Within 90 days of the passage of a Bill, 30,000 voters or 8 cantons can make a petition for referendum, provided the Bill is not declared urgent. As per the provisions of the Constitution, Constitutional amendments must be approved by a majority of voters in a majority of Cantons. Neither the federal executive nor the federal judiciary have any power of veto, over the laws passed by the Federal Assembly.

**Executive Powers**

The Federal Assembly has also important executive and administrative powers. The members of the Federal Council and the Federal Tribunal are elected by the Federal Assembly. It also elects the Chancellor and the Commander-in-Chief of the Army in case of war. It has the power to declare war and conclude place, to make alliances and treaties with foreign countries. It guarantees Cantonal Constitutions and takes measures to ensure external safety and the preservance of independence and neutrality of Switzerland. It supervises the functions of the federal Civil Service.

**Judicial Powers**

Prior to the revised Constitution of 1874, the Federal Assembly enjoyed several judicial powers. But now these powers have been curtailed to a great extent and have been transferred to the Federal Tribunal. However, the Federal Assembly still enjoys some judicial powers like the examination and settlement of petitions against administrative decisions of the Federal Council, settlements of conflicts of power between federal authorities, proclamation of amnesties, pardoning of offences against the federal laws, and receiving annual reports of the working of the Federal Tribunal.

**Limitation of the Powers of the Federal Assembly**

It may be pointed out that the members of the Federal Council are not the members of the Federal Assembly and are not responsible to it as is the practice in other parliamentary systems. They cannot be removed from office by passing a vote of no-confidence against them. The Federal Assembly has also become weak, due to the introduction of the system of proportional representation. Then the device of referendum has also weakened its position, as the electorate has the power to reject laws passed by it. Rappard rightly observes that: "To-day inspite of all the constitutional prerogatives of the Federal Assembly, the lead has clearly passed to the Federal Council. The People, however, through the federal initiative and referendum, have gained an appreciable part of the real legislative power lost by their representatives".

## The Process of Law-making in Switzerland

In Switzerland, as far as law-making is concerned, both the Houses of the Federal Assembly have absolutely co-equal powers. Every Bill is introduced simultaneously in both the Houses. This is different from the practice in other countries. The ordinary Bills are introduced in any one of the Houses, and is sent to the other House, only after it is passed by the House in which it was originally introduced. Any member of the Council of States or the National Council may introduce a Bill. However, most of the important Bills are introduced by the Federal Council. Either House may also, by a resolution request the Federal Council to prepare a Bill on some specified subject. The legislative committees which have representatives from the various political parties, do a great deal of legislative work in both the Houses.

There is similar type of committee system in both the Houses. A reporter is appointed to make a report on the Bill to the House concerned, after a decision is made by the Committee. For important Bills, two reporters may be appointed to report in the German and the French language. In case of controversial Bills, two more reports may be appointed to report the majority view and minority view. Generally the committees neither reject nor drastically amend the Bills, which are introduced by the Federal Council. When there is a difference of opinion between the two Houses on any Bill, a conference committee is appointed consisting of members from both the Houses, to come to a compromise. If there is difference of opinion even at this stage, then further discussion on the Bill is given up. But differences of opinion between the two Houses are rare as the Swiss Council of States takes a cooperative and progressive stand on most of the issues. In the words of Munro, "Unlike most upper chambers,...has not acquired a reputation for conservation. No one ever speaks of the Swiss Council of States as a citadel of reaction or a brake upon the wheels of progress".

# 4

# The Federal Council

The executive powers of the Swiss confederation are vested in a Federal Council consisting of seven members Thus there is a plural or collegiate executive in Switzerland. In most of the other democratic countries, there is a single executive who may be called as the King. Emperor, President, Chairman or may be called by any other title. The framers of the Swiss Constitution followed the American model based on the Congress, but as far as the executive was concerned, they did not provide for an elected President of the American type. Inspite of their awareness that a single executive has the inherent advantage of unity, efficiency, continuity and promptness of action, they did not provide for such a system as they were afraid that it might develop autocratic or monarchical tendencies. The founding fathers of the Swiss Constitution provided for a plural executive because the system was working successfully in the cantons.

## Organisation of the Federal Council

The members of the Federal Council are elected by the two chambers of the Federal Assembly in a joint session, shortly after the election of the new National Council. The members hold office for four years (until 1931, it was 3 years), unless the National Council is dissolved earlier. There is a total removal of the Federal Council, after every renewal of the National Council. Any Swiss citizen eligible for the membership of the National Council, is eligible to become a member of the Federal Council, subject to the condition that there can be only one member in the Federal Council belonging to the same canton. There is no bar to the re-election of the members of the Federal Council and usually they are returned. There have been Councillors who held office as long as 32 years. But due to development of conventions not more than five of the seven Councillors can belong to the German speaking cantons. According to another convention the largest German speaking cantons–Berne and Surich; the largest French speaking Canton–Vaud, must always be represented in the Federal Council According to a new convention the Italian speaking Canton, Ticino is also represented in the Federal Council. Although there is no constitutional restriction on electing members to the Federal Council, from out-side the ranks of the Federal Assembly, in actual practice the councillors are chosen from among the members of the Federal Assembly. They have to resign from their membership of the Federal Assembly after they are elected to the Federal Council and special elections are held to fill their vacancies. Members of the Federal Council are prevented from holding any other office or engaging themselves in any other profession. The members of the Federal Council can take part in the deliberations of both the Houses of the Federal Assembly, but they are not members of either House.

### The Chairman and the Vice-Chairman

The Chairman and the Vice-Chairman of the Federal Council are elected by the Federal Assembly. The Chairman of the Federal Council is the President of the Swiss Confederation during his year of office. The Vice-Chairman is the Vice-President of the Confederation. The President and Vice-President are not eligible for re-election immediately after retirement. By custom the Vice-President of one year is the President of next year and accordingly the office passes by rotation among the members of the Council. The President of the Council is at once the replica of the British Prime Minister and the British King–the two offices being combined together. In terms of his authority he is closer to the British King than the Prime Minister. He has no special power or authority. He is the totlar head of the state and performs only ceremonial functions. He presides over the meetings of the Federal Council and exercises a casting vote in case of a tie. He is both head of the state and the government and represents his country on occasions of ceremony. He does not enjoy any special privileges. He has no authority over his colleagues and has no role in their selection. In the words of Munro: "His legal powers are virtually the same as those of the other councillors although he sits at the head of the table". It is a fact that most Swiss citizens can recall the names of the majority of the councillors, but they are not likely to recall the name of the President for the current year. The Vice-President presides, when the President is absent.

## The Unique Position of the Swiss Executive

The Swiss Federal Council combines in itself the elements of the American and the Biritish executive and marks a difference from both the executives. The members of the Federal Council are not members of the Federal Assembly and are not accountable to it, but they can take part in the deliberations in both the Houses of the Federal legislature. The members of the American Cabinet like the Swiss Councillors are also not members of the Congress, but they do not have the power to take part in the debates of the Congress. The members of the British and the Indian Cabinet are members of the Parliament and are answerable to their respective legislatures. Thus while enjoying the privilege of participation in the debates of the legislature like their British and Indian Counterparts, the Swiss Councillors are free from accountability to the legislature like their American counterparts. The members of the Federal Council of Switzerland enjoy fix tenure of office and cannot be removed from office by the legislature by passing a vote of no-confidence. The relation between the Federal Assembly and the Federal Council have been aptly described Lord Bryce in the following words: "Legally the servant of the legislature, it exerts in practice almost as much authority as do English and more than do some French Cabinets. It is a guide as well as an instrument, and often suggests as well as drafts measures". This has been elaborated by Rappard as follows: "The influence of the Federal Council on the Federal Assembly is.... actually more rather than less decisive than that which the British Cabinet exercises on the House of Commons". And again in the words of Munro: "The executive branch of the government in Switzerland guides the legislative branch as effectively as in Great Britain, perhaps even more so". Thus the Federal Council of Switzerland consists of some of the unique features taken from the American and the British models which contribute to its stability and effectiveness.

## Functions of the Federal Council

### *Executive Functions:*

The Federal Council of Switzerland has executive, legislative and judicial functions. Article 95 of the constitution states–"The supreme directing and executive authority of the Confederation is exercised by a Federal Council composed of seven members". It has multifarious functions like conducting the foreign affairs, executing the laws and the judgements of the Federal Tribunal, controlling the armed forces etc. It appoints all federal officers other than those chosen by the Federal Assembly and the Federal Tribunal

It guarantees the enforcement of cantonal constitutions, examines the treaties of the Cantons between themselves or with the foreign countries and gives its approval there to if it thinks fit. Guaranteeing the external security of Switzerland and the maintenance of its independence and neutrality is the responsibility of the Federal Council. It maintains tranquility and order in Switzerland. The work of all the officials and servants of the confederation is supervised by the Federal Council. It renders accounts of receipts and expenditure to the Federal Assembly and prepared the federal budget. After the approval of the federal budget is approved by the Federal Assembly, the Federal Council looks after the collection of revenues and supervises all expenditures. It submits its report regarding its activities in both foreign and internal affairs, to the Federal Assembly.

***Legislative Functions***

The Federal Council also has equally impressive legislative functions. The council introduces all most all the important legislative measures in both the Houses of the Federal Assembly. The Federal Assembly may also request the Council to prapare Bills on specific matters in compliance with the resolutions adopted by it. Opinion of the Federal Council is also sought on Bills submitted by the private members, before they are taken up by the Federal Assembly for discussion. In the words of Munro: "This does not mean that the members of the Federal Council have a veto upon legislation. They sometimes present, at the request of the chambers, Bills that do not meet their approval, and Bills of this type have occasionally been passed. The Federal Council or Council of Ministers, in a word, is expected to participate actively in the law-making process but not to feel hurt if its advice is disregarded."

***Judicial Powers:***

The Federal Council also exercises some judicial and quasi-judicial powers. Previously it used to decide disputes on constitutional law and also served as the chief administrative court of the Confederation. It present this power of deciding constitutional controversies has been entrusted to the jurisdiction of the Federal Tribunal (Federal Court), of Switzerland. The Federal Tribunal also acts as the administrative court and hears complaints against the public authorities. However, the Federal Council, has still some jurisdiction in cases falling under administrative law.

## The Federal Chancery

The Federal Council has both collective and individual functions. It has regular meetings under the chairmanship of the President. It has secret sessions and its proceedings are not published. The decisions are taken by majority vote and the quorum of the meeting is fixed at four members.

A Federal Chancery was established as per the Constitutional amendment of 1931. The Chancery acts as the secretariat of the Federal Assembly and the Federal Council. The Chancellor is elected by the Federal Assembly and he also acts as the head of the Civil Service of Switzerland. The Federal Council exercises the power of special supervision on the activities of the Federal Chancery.

# 5

# The Federal Tribunal

The Federal Tribunal, established by the Swiss Constitution of 1848 had very limited powers and was subordinate to the Federal Assembly and the Federal Council. But this position was changed by the Constitution of 1874 and larger powers were given to the Federal Court for the administration of justice in federal matters.

## Organisation

The Federal Tribunal is the only federal court in Switzerland. As per the constitution, the Federal Assembly determines the nature of organisation, number of judges, the term of office and emoluments etc. The appointment of the judges of the Federal Tribunal is made by the Federal Assembly, after paying due regard to the representation of the three official languages. Any Swiss citizen who is eligible for election to the National Council is also eligible for the Federal Tribunal. At the time of the election of the members of the Federal Tribunal, priority is given to their legal qualifications. In the beginning there were 9 judges in the Federal Tribunal, but with the extension of its jurisdiction, the number of judges has been increased to 26. There are eleven substitute judges also. The judges are elected for a period of six years by the Federal Assembly. Usually they are re-elected as long as they are willing to serve. A President and Vice-President of the Federal Tribunal are also elected by the Federal Assembly for a term of two years and they are not eligible for re-election immediately.

## Jurisdiction on Powers

The jurisdiction of the Federal Tribunal extends to civil, criminal, administrative and constitutional cases. The Federal Tribunal sits in 3 sections.

### Civil Jurisdiction

As a civil court, it has original jurisdiction in all cases of controversies arising between the Confederation and the Cantons, between the Cantons; between the Confederation on the one part and corporations or private individuals on the other, where the latter are plaintiffs and the dispute involves a sum of at least 4,000 francs and between Cantons on the one part and corporations on private individuals on the other, where either party so demands and the dispute involves a sum of at least 4,000 francs. The Federal Tribunal has also appellate jurisdiction in all civil cases comming up from the Cantonal Courts of final appeal, where the amount under dispute is at least 4,000 francs.

### Criminal Jurisdiction

The Federal Tribunal with the assistance of a jury, has extensive powers of trying cases of high treason against the Confederation, revolt, and violence against the federal authorities, crime and offences against international law, crimes and political offences which are the cause of disorders necessitating armed federal intervention and charges against officials, appointed by a federal authority when brought before the Tribunal by that authority.

### Constitutional Jurisdiction

In constitutional cases the Federal Tribunal has got original jurisdiction in all cases of conflict between the Confederation and Cantons, or between Cantons complaining about the violation of constitutional rights of citizens and complaints by the individuals inrespect of violation of treaties.

In 1914, there was a constitutional amendment, proposing the establishment of a Federal Court of administrative justice. But in 1925, the Federal Assembly decided that the Federal Tribunal should also act as the administrative court.

The Federal Tribunal upholds the Federal Constitution and the federal laws as against the Cantonal Constitutions and laws. It can declare a Cantonal law as unconstitutional, if it is in conflict with the federal constitution, the Cantonal constitution and the federal laws. The Tribunal must uphold the Cantonal constitution as against the Cantonal laws, or administrative acts when trying the cases of violation of individual rights.

The Tribunal has got only limited right of judicial review. It has no power to invalidate a federal law on the ground that it is violative of the federal constitution. It is laid down in the constitution, "that the Federal Tribunal shall administer the laws, as passed by the Federal Assembly". The federal constitution is interpreted by the Federal Assembly and not by the Federal Tribunal. However, a proposal was mooted in 1939, to grant the power of judicial review to the Federal Tribunal in respect of federal laws, but it was rejected by a large majority. The citizens thought that such a power of the Tribunal would not only constitute a challenge to democracy, but also to their own sovereignty as manifested through the devices of legislative referendum and initiative. Thus the methods of Direct Democracy which are in force in Switzerland have imposed considerable restrictions on the power of judicial review of the Federal Tribunal.

# The Constitution of the People's Republic of China

# 1

# Introduction

In the context of China one should keep in mind, what Napoleon had once said about it: "There lies a sleeping giant. Let it sleep, for when he wakes, he will shake the world". This prophetic statement came true and the People's Republic of China has now emerged as one of the most powerful countries, which poses a danger to world peace and the territorial integrity of its neighbours. It has emerged as a major Asian power and the Communist party has made a total consolidation of the political and military powers in its hands. It conquered Tibet in 1959 in total disregard for world public opinion and 1962, attacked the northern frontiers of India to teach her a lesson for giving political asylum to Dalai Lama the emigree ruler of Tibet. The 'Hindi-Chini Bhai Bhai' euphoria which preceeded the pre-Nineteen hundred sixty two period of relationship got a rude shock and India's eyes were opened to the gravity of the situation.

The Kuomintang Government was driven from the mainland to the island of Taiwan. The Communist Party of China tried to build its own socio-political and economic system based on its own theory of socialism and posed a severe challenge to Moscow's claims of ideological infallibility and ominiscience. It refused to become a Soviet satellite and insisted on ideological differences with Russia. Taking advantage of the deteriorating relations between Moscow and Peking, the U.S.A. made attempts to come closer to China so as to build up international pressure on the Soviet Union. Now there is also an attempt from the side of Soviet Union to have better relations with China and to solve the existing misunderstanding between them. Due to all these facts the Chinese political system has attracted the attention of the scholars and students of political science and its appraisal and analysis has become a matter of general interest.

A brief account of the development of the Chinese political

system is given below:

There was no Central Government in China prior to 1949 and it was never united. The Republic was established on October 10, 1911 with Dr. Sun Yet Sin as the President. Provisional Governmental institutions were established. Elections under this system were held in 1912-13 in which Kuomintang headed by Dr. Sun Yat Sen, got majority in both House of the Parliament. But the War Lords refused to obey the authority of the Central Government.

The parliament was soon dissolved by Yuan Shih-Kai who assumed dictatorial powers. After the death of Yuan in 1913, the Provisional Government and constitution as proclaimed by Dr. Sun were restored again. But there could be no constitutional progress as the War Lords and the military general again refused to obey the central authority. People lost confidence in Western democratic institutions.

The task of framing a permanent constitution for the country was never takeup seriously. Between 1913 and 1928, until the time the Kuomintang could stabilize its position, there came into existence as many of as six constitutions, but none could function smoothly. The failure to provide a permanent constitution for the country, developed authoritarian tendencies in the Kuomintang and was responsible for its decay.

## Constitutional Structure under the Kuomintang Administration

There were five branches of administration, such as, Executive, Legislative, Judicial, Examination and Control. The officials were all members of the Kuomintang and were to be supervised by the Political Council of the Central Executive Committee of the Kuomintang.

There was an element of authoritarianism in the administration. Political activities other than that of the Kuomintang were not allowed. This was necessary because the central authority was threatened.

The Chairman of the State Council was the Chief of the State. The Provincial and local offices functioned under the direct supervision of the Central Government in theory, but in practice they were controlled by the Kuomintang.

In 1931, the National Government was established on a more solid constitutional basis. A provisional constitution was proclaimed, which curtailed the powers of the Chairman of the State Council. There was no provision for the amendment and interpretation of the constitution. There was the monopoly of the Central Executive Committee and the Chairman–the boss of the Kuomintang exercised all powers.

In 1937, the Japanese attack forged unity between the National Government and the Communists, who were fighting against the autocratic regime of the Kuomintang. The failure of the Kuomintang to resist the Japanese attack, started a movement in the country for a united front with the Communists. On this issue, the army of Chiang Kaishek was divided and he was forced to agree for forming a united front with the Communists. But this could not last longer and civil war started in China.

Before the civil war, attempts were made by the American representative Mr. Marshall, to call a national conference of all major political parties to decide the future political setup of the country. This move was supported by the Communist Party in the beginning. The Kuomintang agreed reluctantly to this proposal.

A multiparty political consultative conference met and agreed to convene a National Assembly in May, 1946. It also proposed the formation of an Interim Coalition Government and ereorganisation of the army. The Conference also appointed a Committee to draft a constitution to be submitted to the National Assembly, which it did. But in the meanwhile the truce between Kuomintang and Communists expired and civil war started again. This resulted in the victory of the Communist Party. In 1949, the People's Republic was established and a provisional constitution known as common programme was proclaimed.

The provisional constitution was replaced by another constitution in 1954. It may be noted that this constitution was also not contemplated to be a final document on the form of government. Thus a new Constitution was adopted on March 5, 1978 by the fifth National People's Congress of the People's Republic of China. It aims at making China a great and powerful country.

# 2

# Main Features of the Constitution (1954)

The Constitution of the People's Republic of China is based on the principles of Marxism-Leninism as applied to China. Emphasis is given upon the clear objective of building a socialist state, free from all kinds of inequalities and exploitations. Like any other Communist Constitution, it is more of a manifesto than a Constitution. The main features are discussed below.

### *(i) A Brief Document*

It is a simple and brief document consisting of only 106 articles. Its language is simple and lucid and can be understood by the working masses. This constitution was drafted by the Central People's Government Council, appointed on January 13, 1953, under the Chairmanship of Mao Tse-tung. The Constitution lays down in detail the political, economic and social objectives of the socialist regime. Article 4 of the constitution, refers to the determination of the People's Republic to ensure the gradual abolition of the systems of exploitation and the building of a socialist society. Highlighting the objectives of the Constitution Clyde says: "The constitution of 1954 is an important political manifesto announcing the basic principles of state power, military organisation, economic, cultural and educational policy and foreign policy".

### *(ii) Constitution for Transitional Period*

The framers of the Chinese constitution knew that under the Communist system it was bound to make rapid progress and in the course of time the constitution would become outdated. Then there would be the necessity of a new constitution to meet the requirements of the people. The preamble of the constitution says: "From the founding of the People's Republic of China to the attainment of a socialist society is a period of transition". The 1954 Constitution was expected to continue for 20 years during which period China expected to attain her socialistic goal.

***(iii) Socialistic Goal***

It lays down that during the period of transition the fundamental task of the State is, step by step to accomplish the socialist transformation of agriculture, handicrafts and capitalist industry and commerce. The determination of the Chinese people to build a socialist system was manifested through the constitution. It is laid down in Article 6, that the state owned economy is socialist economy owned by the whole people. The state is led by an alliance of the working class and the peasants.

***(iv) Democratic State***

According to Art. 1, the People's Republic of China is a "People's democratic state and all powers belong to the people". The working class has not monopolised all state power. It has entered into an alliance with the peasants and forged a broad people's democratic front with all classes, groups and organisations, under the leadership of the Communist Party of China. It emphasises that as it is a state of the people, the people must safeguard the state against the attack of the imperialists and other enemies. According to the constitution the "State must rely on the masses of the people, constantly maintain close contacts with them, Need their opinions and accept their supervisions".

***(v) Charter of Rights***

The state must protect, the peasant ownership of land and other means of production and the property of the co-operatives. It has to abolish the ownership of capitalist property. Citizens will have right to lawful income and right to inherit private property. Chapter III of the Constitution grants the rights to the citizens and imposes duties on them. It guarantees the most important right to work and right to rest and leisure. The rights are enjoyed by all Chinese citizens, irrespective of any differences of caste, creed, colour or sex. The constitution lays down that, "It is the honourable duty of the citizens to perform military service according to law".

***(vi) Parliamentary Government***

The constitution made provision for a responsible government.

The government is responsible to the highest organ of state power– the National People's Congress. The National People's Congress is a unicameral legislature, which meets once every year. It elects the Standing Committee, its Chairman, Vice-Chairman and other members. The National People's Congress elects the Chairman of the Chinese Republic. He is the Chief Executive of the State and has the power to appoint and dismiss the Premier of the State Council and other members. He exercises arbitrary powers.

The State Council is the highest administrative organ of state power. It is responsible to the National People's Congress, and when it is not in session, to its Standing Committee. There is thus a three-tier system; the Legislature, the Executive and the Administrative with the two latter organs responsible to the former.

***(vii) A Unitary State***

The Chinese constitution provides for a unitary state. Article 3 of the Constitution of 1954 states that, "The People's Republic of China is a single multinational state. All nationalities are equal. Discrimination against or oppression of any nationalities are prohibited. Regional autonomy applies where people or national minorities live in communities. National autonomous areas, are inalienable parts of the People's Republic of China". The Chinese national minorities do not possess the right of secession. The Chinese constitutions claim of guaranteeing regional autonomy to the national minorities is more theoretical than real. There is too much centralized authority and ruthless enforcement of the social, economic and political reforms sponsored by the Communist party. The subjugation of Tibet in 1959, and the brutal suppression of the culture, religion and heritage of the Tibetans is the evidence of the hollowness of Maoist's claim of assuring regional autonomy to the National minorities and the existence of excessive centralized control. In Chine the power is completely centralized in the National People's Congress, which guides and supervises Provincial People's Congress. The Provincial People's Congresses, guide and supervise the county Congresses, which in their turn guide and supervise the town People's Congress. It is noteworthy that every Congress is subject to the supervisory and over-ruling power of the Congress above it. The National People's Congress is the all-powerful authority in China.

As far as administration is concerned, the State Council is the all-powerful organ of administrative power which is supervised by

National People's Congress. The State Council supervises the local councils and has the power to remove them. The local councils are subject to guidance and supervision of local people's Congresses at corresponding level of which they are creations. They are also subject to the guidance and supervision of local councils at the next higher level. Finally, all the units are subject to the co-ordinating guidance of the State Council itself.

***(viii) Democratic Centralism in the Communist Party***

The Communist Party of China is characterised by the principle of democratic centralism. There is the democratic principle of election of all the leading party organs at all levels. The party congresses at each level in the hierarchy. At the highest level, National Party Congress elects the Central Committee. The elected party committees are accountable to their respective party congresses. They are required to submit reports regarding their work, to their respective congresses at regular intervals. Individual party members have the right to differ from the party decisions and directives and communicate their opinion directly to the Central Committee, bypassing other party levels. However, the practical exercise of this right is a rare possibility.

Party centralism is manifested from the fact that the individual is subordinate to the organisation, the minority is sub-ordinate to the majority, the lower level is sub-ordinate to the higher level and the entire party is sub-ordinate to the Central Committee. In comparison to the democratic aspect, the aspect of centralism is more prominent and the party forms a "pyramid with orders being transmitted from the apex down to the lowest levels for execution and information concerning how policy is being implemented, sent back up the party chain of command". The Communist Party insists on unquestionable loyalty of the members and the lower bodies to the directives from higher party authorities.

Thus it is evident that in the Chinese Political System, there is greater emphasis on centralism than on democracy. In the opinion of Ogg and Zink, "It is different to believe that democratic centralism embodies as much of democracy as of centralism". The Chinese argue that without an element of centralism it is not possible to achieve rapid economic growth and eradicate social disparities. For speedy progress and development, democracy has to be blended with centralism.

***(ix) Duties of Citizens***

The Constitution of China is a unique document, as it has not only provided for certain fundamental rights like the American and the Indian Constitution, but also gives a list of duties which are to be performed by the citizens. Whereas in other democratic countries, the emphasis is on the rights of the citizen to the extent of minimising or ignoring the importance of duties, in the Chinese constitution, duties are considered equally important like the rights. As a matter of fact the constitution gives more emphasis on the duties than on the rights of the citizen. According to Article 100, the "citizens of the People's Republic of China must abide by the Constitution and the law, uphold discipline at work, keep public order, and respect social ethics". Among the important duties of the citizen, the duty to regard work as a matter of honour, occupies the prime of place. It is the duty of the citizen to respect and protect public property, to pay taxes according to law, to defend homeland and to perform military service. The performance of these duties by the citizens was necessary inorder to create the conditions suitable for the full enjoyment of their rights.

***(x) Chinese People's Political Consultative Conference***

The Constitution has made provision for a democratic united front. All the democratic parties, groups and classes take part in this united front, under the leadership of the Communist Party of China. This front is called Chinese People's Political Consultative Conference (CPPCC). The Preamble of the Constitution state that, "In the Course of the great struggle to establish the People's Republic of China, the people of our country forged a broad people's democratic united front, composed of all democratic classes, democratic parties and groups, and popular organisations, led by the Communist Party of China. This people's democratic united front will continue to play its part in mobilizing and rallying the whole people in a common struggle to fulfil the fundamental task of the state during transition and to oppose enemies within and without". The CPPCC met for the first time in September 1949 and proclaimed the establishment of the People's Republic of China. It also adopted the common programme as incorporated in the provisional constitution. It lost its purpose after the establishment of National People's Congress. However, this body still continues and plays its role in forging alliance between workers and peasants.

# 3

# The Structure of the State Under the New Constitution

The new Constitution of China was adopted on March 5, 1978. Like the earlier constitution, the new Constitution also lays emphasis on the building of a socialist society and continuance of the Revolution under the dictatorship of the proletariat. It gives priority to taking forward the three great revolutionary movements of class struggle, the struggle for production and scientific experiment. The purpose of this new constitution was to make China a great and powerful socialist country equipped with modern agriculture, science and technology and highly developed system of national defence.

The new constitution does not radically differ from the old constitution. However, the new Constitution has abolished the two institutions of the Chairman of the People's Republic of China–to which there was a special reference in the old constitution, as well as the Chinese People's Political Consultation Conference (CPPCC). The Chairman of the Standing Committee of the People's Congress has been accorded the status of a formal Head of the State as was the case in Soviet Russia under the Stalin Constitution. Constitutional recognition has also been given to the Communist Party and it is accorded a supreme position. Its Chairman has been made the head of the armed forces. Although the new Chinese constitution has many similarities with the Soviet constitution, it does not follow it too rigidly. There are similarities between the National People's Conference of China and the Supreme Soviet of the U.S.S.R. The Standing Committee of the N.P.C. is analogous to the presidium of Soviet Union. Both the constitutional systems are characterised by democratic centralism. In both the countries the Communist party occupies the supreme position. In democratic countries of the world no such constitutional recognition is given to the parties.

The structure of the state provided by the new constitution is discussed below:

## National People's Congress (Articles 20-23)

It is the highest and supreme organ of state power. It is the parliament where the people's representatives sit and deliberate on state policy. According to the Constitution this is the final authority in matters of making law in accordance with the provisions of the constitution.

### Its Composition

The number of deputies to the Congress and the manner of their election are to be prescribed by electoral law. The deputies are elected by the People's Congresses of the provinces, autonomous regions and municipalities directly under the Central Government and by the People's Liberation Army. They are elected by secret ballot after democratic consultation. All citizens who have attained the age of 18 have the right to vote and be elected irrespective of nationality, race, occupation, six, religion, education, property, social origin, residence or status. Every voter is entitled to one vote. Landlords, counter revolutionaries, have been deprived of political rights and insane persons have been denied the right to vote. At present there are about 3000 deputies in the National People's Congress.

### Term of Office

It is elected for a period of 4 years and two months before the expiry of the term of office the Standing Committee of the N.P.C. must carry to completion the election of deputies. Under exceptional conditions, if the election cannot be held in proper time, the life of the N.P.C. can be extended until the next first session i.e., for one more year, as the N.P.C. meets only once every year.

The meetings of the N.P.C. are convened by the Standing Committee of the N.P.C. once every year. But if 1/5 of the deputies so desire, the session can be convened at any time. The N.P.C. elects a Presidium to conduct its sessions.

### Powers and Functions

It is an all powerful body at least in theory and enjoys unlimited powers. Its functions are varied and wide and can divided into two categories : (a) General or policy-making functions and (b) Procedural functions.

(a) *General of Policy-making Functions:* It has the power to amend the Constitution and enact the laws of the People's Republic of China. It takes final decision about the economic plans of the country. It approves the state budget and the financial report presented by the State Council. It ratifies treaties with foreign countries and takes decision on questions of war and peace.

(b) *Procedural Functions:* It decides on the choice of the Premier of the State Council upon the recommendations of the Central Committee of the Communist Party of China. On the recommendations of the Premier of the State Council, it appoints the other members of the Council. It elects the President of the Supreme People's Court and the Chief Procurator of the Supreme People's Procuratorate. It decides on the choice of members of the Council of National Defence. It exercises such other functions and powers as the National People's Congress deems necessary.

While having the sole authority to elect or appoint the members of the above said institutions, the N.P.C. has the right to remove from office the following: (a) the members of the state council, (b) the President of the Supreme People's Court, and (c) the Chief Procurator of the Supreme People's Procuratorate.

## The Standing Committee of the N.P.C.

It is the most important organ of the N.P.C. and is elected at the first session of the new N.P.C. by the deputies for a term of 4 years. It is composed of the Chairman, the Vice-Chairman, the Secretary General and the Members. There were 65 members in the previous Standing Committee. The N.P.C. is empowered to recall the members of the Standing Committee. As a matter of fact, although it has all-embracing and vast powers, it meets once a year and it is not possible for this unwieldly body to perform all these functions. Thus what is a legal truth is a political untruth. Most of the functions of the N.P.C. are performed by the Standing Committee which is a smaller and more effective body. However, in reality both the Congress and its Standing Committee dance to the tune of the Communist Party and its top leaders who are all-in-all in the Chinese political system.

The Standing Committee remains in session continuously and functions as the supreme authority of state power when the N.P.C. is not in session. During this period it performs all the functions which are constitutionally vested in the N.P.C. It is a permanent body of the N.P.C. and has supreme control over all the organs of administrative power. The State Council (Council of Ministers) is responsible to the Standing Committee. It is through the Standing Committee that the Ministers are responsible to the N.P.C.

### The Functions of the Standing Committee

*Functions with regard to the N.P.C.*: It conducts the elections to the N.P.C. and convenes its sessions at intervals, provided by the Constitution or if a demand to that extent is made by 1/5th of the deputies of the N.P.C.

*Legislative Function* :- It interprets the laws and adopts decrees when the N.P.C. is not in session.

*Relations with the State Council*: The State Council headed by the Premier, is the administrative wing of the Chinese state. The state Council is responsible to the Standing Committee for all its actions. The Standing Committee has the power to remove the Premier, the Vice-Premier and the other members of the State Council, when the N.P.C. is not in session.

*International Relations and Emergencies*: The Standing Committee appoints and recalls the diplomatic representatives to the foreign countries. It ratifies treaties with foreign countries and decides the questions of war and peace, when the N.P.C. is not in session. It can declare the promulgation of Martial law and can order general or partial mobilisation.

*Other Functions*: It supervises the functions of the Supreme Court and the supreme People's Procuratorate. It has the power to annue decisions and orders of the State Council which contravene the Constitution, laws or decrees. It can annue or revise the decisions of any provincial governmental authority, or Autonomous Regions and Municipalities, directly under the control of the Central authority.

The Standing Committee exercises its functions until the next N.P.C. elects a new Standing Committee. It is responsible to the N.P.C. which has the power to recall any member of the Standing Committee.

### Committees of the N.P.C.

The National People's Congress appoints various Committees for the discussion of various legislative proposals, before the final decision is taken. The following are the important commiitees of the N.P.C.–Nationalities Committee, Bill Committee, Budget Committee,

Credentials Committee and other necessary committees. These committees function under the supervision of the Standing Committee when the N.P.C. is not in session. According to the Constitution all the organs of state power, must submit all informations to these Committees, whenever required.

### Privileges of Deputies

The Deputies of the National People's Congress enjoy parliamentary privileges as enjoyed by members of parliament in other countries. They cannot be arrested without the prior permission of the N.P.C. or its Standing Committee when the N.P.C. is not in session. Deputies have the right to express their views and to address questions to the State Council or to the Ministries and Commissions, which are bound to answer.

The deputies are under the control of the units which elect them and can be recalled, if wanting in performance of their assigned duties. This has ensured people's participation in the affairs of the state.

### The State Council

The State Council is the highest administrative organ of the state. According to Article 30, "The State Council is the Central People's Government and the executive organ of the highest organ of state power".

*Composition:* It is composed of Premier, Vice-Premiers, Ministers, Heads of Commissions and the Secretary General. The Prime Minister is appointed by the N.P.C. on the recommendations of the Central Committee of the Communist Party. The rest of the members are appointed by the N.P.C., on the recommendations of the Premier. The appointment of the members of the State Council, as a whole must be approved by the N.P.C. which is also the removing authority.

### Power and Functions

It formulates administrative measures, issues decisions and orders and looks to their implementation in accordance with the constitution, laws and decrees. The State Council submits bills to the N.P.C. and the Standing Committee of the N.P.C. for appropriate legislation and enactment of laws.

The State Council co-ordinates and leads the work of Ministers, Commissions and the local administrative organs.

It executes the economic plans and provisions of the budget. It controls foreign and domestic trade. It directs educational, cultural and public health works. It is responsible for the conduct of external affairs. It guides the organisation and building up of defence forces. It protects the interests of the state, maintains public order, safeguards the rights of citizens and administers affairs concerning Chinese residents abroad. It appoints and removes administrative personnel. It exercises such other functions as vested on it by the N.P.C. or the Standing Committee of the N.P.C.

The Prime Minister directs the works of the State Council and presides over its meetings. The Ministers and other Heads of Commissions direct the work of their respective departments inaccordance with the laws and decrees of the country. The Ministry is a large body consisting of about 40 to 45 members. There is a cabinet type of body consisting of the Premier, the Vice-Premiers and the Heads of the Commissions. The State Council is accountable to the N.P.C. and when the N.P.C. is not in session, it is accountable to the Standing Committee. The Cabinet meets frequently and takes decisions on vital questions of administration. The Cabinet cannot override either the N.P.C. or its Standing Committee. The N.P.C. can direct the dissolution of the State Council. Thus the tenure of the State Council depends on the backing of majority in the N.P.C. or the Standing Committee of the N.P.C.

From the foregoing analysis of the powers and functions of the State Council it is evident that both in theory and fact it performs significant functions and exercises powers like a Cabinet in any parliamentary form of government. The State Council as a whole is a very large body and it does not meet very frequently. However, the Premier and the Vice-Premiers who head the various administrative departments, constitute a Cabinet like body and meet quite frequently. They wield the real authority in the country. But despite all the powers given to it by the constitution, the Council of Ministers or its Premier, play only a second fiddle to the Chairman of the Communist Party. The Premier is a nominee of the Chairman of the party and is bound to remain loyal to him. The Premier in China cannot dominate over his cabinet colleagues, in the way a Prime Minister does in U.K. or India. Under the peculiar Chinese situations, it is the Communist Party which is all powerful and all other organs of state power, irrespective of their constitutional position and powers, have to run the errands of the party and its Chairman.

# 4

# The Communist Party of China

The Communist Party plays a predominant role in the Chinese political system and it runs a parallel government. Policies framed at the level of the party are implemented by the government as groups of party members occupy top-ranking places in the government. The organic character of the government also facilitates strong party control. Then there is the practice of democratic centralism which means that the minority should obey the majority, the lower party bodies should obey the higher party bodies and all party bodies should obey the controlling body of the party. It is rightly observed by Bernett that, "The Communist Party is the ultimate political authority and the source of all decision making on the mainland China today".

The party emerged in China in 1921 and had a very horrible beginning. Its membership was limited and the Party suffered from many defects due to the lapses of its leaders. It was virtually on the brink of extinction in 1935. At this time Mao appeared on the horizon of the Party. The war with Japan and the failure of the Chinese government provided the Party with an excellent opportunity to gain popularity and strength. By the end of the Second World War, over one million Chinese had accepted its membership. In the post-war period the attempt to form a coalition government of KMT and the Communist Party failed and civil war started in China, which lasted from 1945–1949. Till his death in September 1976, Mao Tse-tung, became the supreme master of China and exercised unquestioned authority over all the organs of state power.

In China no body dared to challenge the despotic authority of Mao Tse-tung. All the other organs of state power were reduced to a subordinate position and could never think of exercising their Constitutional powers without the consent of this huge collosus. He was the main exponent of Marxism and Leninism in China. He was the chief theoretician of the Communist Party and the principal organiser and the sole interpreter of Marxian theory, inaccordance with the requirements and the genius of China. These interpretations have been described as the 'thought of Mao'.Maoism differs from Marxism and Leninism on many vital and fundamental points. He did not follow the principles and strategy of the Soviest Communist leaders and tried to maintain the independent identity of China even in the ideological sphere. This resulted in a split in the Communist camp.

## Democratic Centralism in the Party

The Chinese Communist Party follows the principle of democratic centralism which signifies centralism on the basis of democracy and democracy under centralised guidance. The democratic element is evident from the fact that the leading bodies of the party at all levels are elected. The National Party Congress elects the Central Committee and the local party congresses, elect their respective Local Party Committees. The Central Committee and the Local Party Committees are responsible to their respective party Congress to which they report on their work. All leading bodies of the party are required to pay constant heed to the views of their local organisations and the rank and file of party members.

Centralism is evident from the fact that when there is a party conference a representative of the higher party bodies is present and he acts like a party whip. He indicates the line of discussion and points out what they are supposed to discuss. He may participate in the discussion and usually sums up the proceedings at the end of the meeting. He is required to send a report to the Party body, he represents in the Conference.

The party is the central nervous system of the entire body politic, providing direction and purpose to every organisation. It co-ordinates many diverse activities and accomplishes its work, by placing a hoast of members throughout the government. These individuals serve as catalytic agents, imparting momentum, guiding and goading the government bureaucracy.

But the party insists in maintaining its separate organisation, distinct from the governmental organisation.

All questions of national character, requiring uniform decision for the whole country are dealt with by the Central Party organisation so as to contribute to the centralism and unity of the party. All questions of local character are left to the local party organisations. But the ultimate control is vested in the party centre and the principle is that, "decisions taken by lower organisations must not run counter to those made by higher organisations". In all matters of controversy, the decisions of the higher party organisations are final.

**The National Party Congress**

According to the Party's constitution, the National Party Congress is "the highest leading body of the party". Its work is to hear and examine reports of central party organs, to determine the party's mass line and policy, to revise the Party Constitution and to elect the Central Committee. Nominally all powers belong to this body, but actually all powers have been delegated to the Central Committee, which can postpone the convening of the Congress indefinitely. The Congress is not convened as long as the party leaders have not finalised, the party line for the approval of the Congress. There was no Party Congress session from 1945 to 1956. The National Party Congress is a rubber stamp organisation, convened as a sop to 'Party democracy'. Due to its huge size fruitful debate and positive policymaking cannot be carried out in its meetings.

**The Central Committee**

According to the Constitution it is responsible for major policy formulation and execution. Its task is defined as one of directing the entire work of the party, representing it in relation to the other parties and organisation, setting up and directing new party organs and supervising and allocating party cadres.

The Constitution of the Party provides for two plenary sessions per year for the Central Committee, but that depends on the convenience of the Polit Bureau. Just as the Central Committee acts for the Party National Congress, when it is not in session, as also the Polit Bureau acts for the Central Committee when it is not in session. The short session and the vast size of the Central Committee make it unfit and unwieldy as a policy-making body.

Though the Central Committee as a whole has become unimportant, as a policy-making body, many of its members are responsible for execution of policy at lower party and governmental levels.

The membership of the Central Committee is drawn roughly in equal proportions from four major groups: (i) Central Party Organisations, (ii) Provincial Party Organisations, (iii) Central and

Provincial Governmental Organisations, and (iv) The Armed Forces.

The Constitution of the party defines the relation of the Central Committee with the mass organisations and armed forces. The Central Committee is charged with guiding, "the work of the central state organs and people's organisations of a national character through leading party members' groups within them". This is accomplished by the elections of four smaller executive agencies consisting of the members of the Central Committee. The Central Control Commission (one of these four agencies), has no policy making power. Central Polit Bureau, the Standing Committee of the Central Polit Bureau and the Central Secretariat, constitute the central core of the policy formulation and policy implementation machinery in Communist China.

### The Central Political Bureau

It exercises all the powers of the Central Committee, when that body is not in session. It consists of 26 persons, out of which 20 are voting members and 6 are non-voting members or alternates. Mao Tse-tung had a special position in the Polit Bureau. If he was committed to any official policy, invariably that was supported by all. In case he had no commitments, he took the opinion of the other members. Decisions are taken by consensus.

### Standing Committee of the Polit Bureau

It was not there before 1956. The Secretariat attended to the daily work of the Central Committee according to the decisions of the Polit Bureau. Composed of 5 top-ranking members of the Polit Bureau, the Secretariat became an inner cabinet, lending a final degree of centralisation and exclusiveness to party policy-making. In 1956 this was formally identified as a Standing Committee. Major policy-shifts are referred to the Polit-Bureau. Meetings are informal and a discussion among members may become a meeting. As long as Mao Tse-tung was there he played a predominant role in the meetings. His genius and personal factors brought him preeminance. He followed the principle of liquidation of his enemies in the beginning. Subsequently he followed the policy of reindoctrination and rehabilitation. He made new contributions to the Communist theory.

### The Party Secretariat

It was created in 1956 and it operaters under the direction of the

Polit Bureau and its Standing Committee, in attending to the day-to-day wrok of the Central Committee. Supervision and co-ordination of policy rather than formulation of policy, is its primary responsibility. But due to its political stature, it is able to enforce its decisions on party personnel, responsible for carrying out party directives. The Secretary General of the Party directs the activities of the Secretariat and is a member of three important Central organs–Polit Bureau, Standing Committee and Secretariat.

## Central Organs of the Party

*Organisation Department:* It is in charge of party organisation, recruitment of party personnel and the maintenance of discipline in the party.

*The Propaganda Department:* It remains busy with indoctrinating the party members, civilians and army personnel. It gives wide publicity to the party line and the ideological orientations of the party from time to time.

*Social Affairs Department:* It investigates into the loyalty and the security of the members of the party. It controls the Ministry of Public Security of the government. The General Political Department deals with Army loyalty.

*United Front Department:* It deals with the puppet political parties in China and maintains contact with the overseas Chinese.

*Rural Work Department and Industrial Work Department:* The Rural Work Department deals with farm labourers, agriculture and agricultural production as well as the implementation of party policy with respect to agriculture. The Industrial Work Department deals with the establishment of heavy and small scale industries and the implementation of party policy in industries.

*Finance and Trade Department:* This is a new department. Previously these works were done by provincial departmants. It maintains liaison with party committees dealing with finance, trade, taxation, banking and distribution of food materials.

*Communications Work Department:* This has replaced the Party's older departments in the Ministry of Railways, Communications, Posts and Tele-communications.

*Liaison Department:* This department maintains contact with Communist parties in other countries of the world. This department is not publicly identified and most of its work is done secretly.

*Provincial Departments:* There are Provincial Department at the

Provincial level to deal with matters of local concern. Besides the regular departments, there are committees under guidance of the Secretariat, like the Women's Work Committee.

## The Party and the Government

There are party groups in every government office. They work in two ways: (i) Analyse party policy in the office and (ii) Send reports to higher party organisations. The higher party organisation sends new directives, if necessary, and directs the higher government office about the requirements of the lower office. Thus the party controls the entire administrative apparatus of the government. The party has both intensive and extensive control over the government and it is difficult to say where it begins or ends. There is neither legal nor constitutional limit to the party's control over the government. The party has the power to issue directions to the various administrative units. The party's control over the government is being ensured, by the necessary cadre support, through which the governmental policies are implemented. The mischief of the bureaucracy is reduced. As all the important executive positions are held by party leaders, the hiatus between party and the government is greatly reduced. The party has also very effective control over the army and other defence forces. Mao started the Cultural Revolution with the support of the armed forces and purged the party and the government of the forces enimical to him and his ideological shift. It may also be pointed out that in China, the judicial organ of the state also works as an extension of the party. Shen Yu-dai has rightly observed that: "The Chinese Communist Party's complete control over the government is perhaps the most amazing phenomenon in modern totalitarian politics."

# The Constitution of Japan

# 1

# Development of Japan's Constitution

## Introduction

Japan consists of four main islands–Honshu, Kyushu, Hokkaido and Shikaku and is situated to the East of Asia. It is often called the 'England of the East" and has many similarities with that country. Both England and Japan are groups of islands and just as England is separated from Europe by sea, so is Japan separated from Asia. Both the countries followed a policy of isolation for a considerable period of time and both the countries were transformed into highly industrialised societies after the Industrial Revolution. They have deep faith in democracy despite the continuance of Monarchy, as a legacy of past history and tradition.

Japan has a total area of 14, 27, 266 square miles, which is roughly one-eighth of India and Honshu is the largest island. Flourishing big cities like Tokyo, Ngoya, Yakoshama, Kyoto and Koh are situated in this island. Japan is a very beautiful country which is resplendent with the glorious colours and contours of nature.

It has mountain terrain and has about 250 mountains of the height of more than 2,000 metres. Kyoto is the biggest plain near the city of Tokyo and is very thickly populated. The two other plains are Nanti and Kynkei. The most fertile lands of Japan are situated in these plains. Japan has no great river vallies and most of its rivers are short and swift. Although the terrain makes it impossible to use the rivers for the purpose of navigation, the rivers of Japan are a vital source of hydro-electric power.

Fish is the main diet of the Japanese people and fishing plays an important role in the Japanese economy. Fish is available in plenty near the sea coast line and about 20 per cent of the population of Japan is engaged in fishery.

Japan has thick green forests which play a significant role in the

Japanese economy. Most part of the mountains terrain is covered by forests and wood for building and fuel purposes as well as synthetic fibre is obtained from these forests.

Due to its peculiar geographic location Japan is earthquake prone and there are about 1500 earthquakes of different intensities during the year. It abounds in coal mines, but the emphasis is on hydro-electric power as the coal mines are not located in the industrial areas. There are also big copper mines and gold and silver are found in the South-Western part of Kyushu. Since 1900, the petroleum resource of Japan has been considerably enhanced. Besides these, zinc, tin, iron, sulphur and lead are also available in Japan which enrich its industrial potential. However, Japan is not self sufficient in iron and large quantities of iron ore are imported from India and many other countries.

Japan is a highly industrialised country and depends on foreign trade for its affluent economy. Despite its industrialisation, a large segment of the people of Japan depend upon agriculture. There is intensive cultivation in Japan as the cultivable land area is less and rice constitutes the main crop. Through scientific methods of cultivation and the use of high-yielding variety of seed, attempts are made to grow crops which ripen soon and often two to three crops are grown. Sericulture is also very popular in Japan.

The Arians belonging to the Caucasic stock, were the first settlers on the Japanese islands, but they were later replaced by the Mongoloids. Japan established its relationship with Korea in the third and fourth century. Japan is greatly indebted to Korea and China for the development of its art of weaving, tanning, handicrafts, metal work, painting and education. In the sixth century Buddhism reached Japan through China and Korea and the Japanese customs, traditions and life style are greatly influenced by Buddhism even till to-day despite its modernization and industrialization. A segment of the Japanese people also follows Shintoism, which believes in ancestor worship. Christians are also in a sizable number in Japan and have contributed to the Westernization of the people. The Japanese people enjoy religious freedom and are free to profess their own religion.

Japan is to-day one of the most affluent countries of the world and has reached the highest stage of industrialisation and modernization. But despite its modernization and industrialization, the Japanese people have great love for their ancient culture and traditions and they have very carefully preseved these traditional values. They are God-fearing and fatalist and sincerely believe that their country is created by God.

The strength and unity of Japan depend to a large extent upon its common language, common culture and a common way of living. Although there are people of different racial stocks such as the Mongoloid, Caucasic and Negroid, there is no racial conflict in Japan and all are guided by a strong sense of nationalism. The Japanese are extremely nationalistic and are prepared to make any sacrifice for their country.

In the Russo-Japanese War of 1905, Japan defeated Russia, the mighty European power, and destroyed the commonly accepted myth that the Europeans are superior to the other people of the world. The victory of Japan in the Russo-Japanese War of 1905, was also a great landmark in the history of feedom struggle in India as it provided tremendous inspiration to the Indian people to fight for their freedom. The people of India were freed from their pessimism and defeatism and thought that if the Japanese could defeat the so-called invincible European Power Russia, they could also defeat the British power in India and destroy British imperialism. Thus since 1905, in addition to other internal factors, the Japanese example inspired the Indian Extremists to launch their uncompromising battle for the freedom of the country.

Japan fought on the side of Germany during the Second World War and defeated by the Allied Powers. The Japanese attack against the American Fleet at Pearl Harbour, provoked the U.S.A. to drop atom bombs at Hiroshima and Nagasaki, the two Japanese cities, which were totally devastated. There was wanton destruction of human life and property and the pollution of the environment in an unprecedented scale. It was a severe shock to the conscience of the world and the American action was subjected to criticism. Despite its defeat in the War, the bravery and courage of the Japanese people was unprecedented and the speed with which the war-shattered economy of Japan was reconstructed is a glorious testimony of the dedication and commitment of its people.

## Development of the Constitution

The constitutional history of Japan can be divided into three periods–Prefeudal age, Feudal age and the post-Feudal age. There is a common belief that the empire of Japan was founded by Emperor Jimmo in 660 B.C. and his dynasty continues to exercise unbroken dynastic rule till the present day. In the ancient time there was patriarchal rule and the Emperor ruled like a father over the family. Although in theory the Emperor was the sole owner of all property and lands, he distributed the lands for cultivation among different families of the cultivators and exercised his powers through the tribal chieftains. Thus the exercise of royal power was decentralised and this arrangement continued till 645 A.D.

Then started the second period in the constitutional history of Japan which continued upto 1185 A.D. Feudalism became deeply entrenched in Japan during this period. Since the 5th Century A.D. Japan came under the strong influence of the Chinese cultivation and this led to the gradual establishment of the centralised bureaucracy. The Emperor withdrew the powers previously exercised by the feudal lords and began to rule like a despot. He exercised direct political power over the people and become the source of all power and authority both temporal and spiritual. He was greatly influenced by Confucianism and Shintoism in the enlargement of his powers, prestige and honour. As sovereign ruler of the country he become the highest priest of the nation and the Chief Commander of the military services. The Fujimara dynastry played a key role in the politics and the administrative of the country during this period.

The third phase is characterised by the decline in the powers of the Emperor and the usurpation of the powers by the bureaucracy which exercised all powers in the name of the Emperor. It led to the increase in the powers of the members of the Fujimara dynasty, who held the highest offices in the State. Some other factors like the increase in the number of manors and the birth of the 'Samurai' class also contributed to the decline in the powers of the Emperor. The royal revenue was substantially decreased and the administration became extremely corrupt and ineffective. Due to the loosening of the central control over the provinces, there was chaos and confusion and the life and property of people were endangered. The feudal lords became very powerful and they maintained their own private armies. With the dissatisfied aristocrats taking up the banner of revolt against the misrule of Fujimara administrators and joining the 'Samurai' class, a new class of people emerged into prominence. The leaders belonged to the Taira and Minamoto races and there was a feud among these two races for supremacy of power. In this conflict the Minamoto race established its supremacy by defeating the Taira race, and Yorimoto, the head of the Minamoto race assumed the title of 'Shogun'. Peace was established after a century of civil feuds. But this arrangement could not continue for a longer period and power passed into the hands of military leaders.

The influence of this military regime which continued for long seven centuries, left its deep imprint on the customs, traditions, ideas and the institutions of the Japanese people. In theory the Shogun was the centre of all power and authority, but in reality he exercised his powers with the help of powerful feudal lords. There was a civil war in the later part of the 16th Century between the feudal lords and Tokygawa Iyeyashu won a decisive victory in the year 1600 and assumed the title 'Shogun' in 1603. The Tokygawa regime continued till 1867 and in that year the last Tokygawa Shogun resigned. The Emperor assumed all powers and reestablished his authority in Japan.

**Salient Features of the Meiji Constitution**

Significant developments took place during the Meiji rule in Japan. It became involved in the Sino-Japanese war of 1894-95 and after ten years it was again involved in the Russo-Japanese War of 1904-05. In this war Japan was victorious. Victory in the wars led Japan to rejoin South Sakhalin and acquire Formosa and Korea.

Since 1874, there was demand in Japan from different quarters for contitutional reforms. The Senate created in 1874 as a deliberative body, without the power to legislate, did not satisfy the aspirations of the people. In 1877 there was an agitation for a new Constitution and consequently in 1878, more concessions were given to the people to pacify the popular demands. Representative assemblies were set up in 1880, elected on the basis of limited franchise. This was also far short of popular expectations in the sphere of constitutional reforms. In 1887, the government finally assured the people in the name of the Emperor, that the parliament will be convened in 1890 and a new constitution would be granted.

Prince Ito was sent abroad to study the various constitutions and after his return, he was appointed as the Chairman of the Bureau for Investigation of Constitutional Systems. Prince Ito was influenced by the German Constitution and he recommended the restoration of the nobility as preliminary step to the formation of the Upper Chamber of the Japanese Parliament. The Cabinet was also modelled on the German pattern and Ito was made the Prime Minister.

The draft Constitution was ready by 1888 and it was presented to the newly created Privy Council for ratification. After its ratification by the Privy Council with some minor changes, the constitution was granted by Emperor Meiji to the people of Japan on February 11, 1889.

The salient features of this Constitution known as the Meiji Constitution are discussed below:

### *(i) Written and Brief*

The Meiji Constitution was a written Constitution and it was very brief about half as long as that of the American Constitution. There were 76 Articles and these were divided into seven parts. The Constitution was brief because many items like the House of Peers, Finance, Elections and succession to the throne were covered by group of organic laws promulgated soon after the declaration of the Constitution. It was also the intention of the makers of the Constitution to make it as brief as possible. The Constitution was also written in a very simple language understandable even by the common man.

### *(ii) Imperial Government*

The power and authority of the Emperor were duly emphasised by the Constitution in the very first Article which provided that: "The empire of Japan shall be reigned over and governed by a line of emperors unbroken for ages eternal". The powers of the Emperor were enumerated in Articles 1 to 17. The Emperor was the source of all authority and all the laws were sanctioned by him. The sessions of the Diet were called by him and he had the power to dissolve the lower House. As head of the Executive he appointed all the officers and was the Supreme Commander of the army and navy with power to declare war. Conclude peace and make treaties with foreign countries. He had the power to issue ordinances to meet urgent and grave situations. Despite these vast powers, Meiji Constitution reigned but did not rule. He had to exercise his powers in consultation with the Ministers and the Privy Council.

### *(iii) Fundamental Rights*

The Rights and duties of the Japanese people are enumerated in Articles 18 to 32 and are incorporated in the second chapter of the constitution. The Japanese citizen enjoy the right against arbitrary imprisonment, and detentions. Nobody can be punished except according to the procedure of law. The Constitution guarantees right to property and the freedom of religion. The rights to form associations and hold public meetings and freedom of speech and expression are also guaranteed by the Constitution.

But most of these rights were hedged by several restrictions and limitations as Article 20 provided that the people could enjoy these rights "subject to the restrictions placed by law". There was neither the provision for the writ of Habeas Corpus nor the Judicial Review of the Courts. Thus in reality the fundamental rights were very much restricted.

The Constitution also emphasised several duties of the citizen and the two important duties were–the duty to pay taxes and the duty to undergo military training.

### *(iv) Organisation of the Diet*

The Constitution provided for a bicameral legislature–the House of Peers and the House of Representatives were the two chambers of the Diet. There were 400 members in the House of Peers, who belonged to the noble and higher ranks of the society. The House of Representatives consisted of 450 members elected directly by the people for four years. The House of Peers had a 7 years tenure. Only males had the right to vote and the voting age was fixed at twenty-five. A voter was also required to be a tax-payer, paying at least 15 yen annually in direct taxes.

There was one annual meeting of the Diet and the duration of the session was fixed at 3 months. The Diet was subordinate to the executive as it did not have any control either over the executive or the passing of the budget. The government work was mostly done through decrease rather than through Acts.

### *(v) Privy Council*

The Privy Council was to act as an extra institution between the Cabinet and the Emperor and as per Article 56 it was required to deliberate upon important matters of the State. Its strength was about 26 members and usually they were big businessmen, diplomats, generals, admirals and other men of distinction. The Ministers were the ex-officio members of the Privy Council. The members of the Council enjoyed life tenure and it was required to approve the emergency decrees, the declaration of war and peace. On matters relating to the throne and the royal family the Emperor was given advice by the Privy Council. The Privy Council was superior to the Cabinet as in case of disagreement between the two, the Emperor accepted the advice of the Council.

### *(iv) The Cabinet*

There was no specific reference to the Cabinet in the Meiji Constitution. It was only provided that the Ministers shall give advice to the Emperor on various matters concerning the administration of the State and shall be responsible for it. However, the Cabinet came into existence in 1885, alongwith the formation of the government. The Emperor appointed the Prime Minister on the advice of the Privy Council and it was not obligatory to appoint the leader of the majority party. But the practice of appointing the leader of the majority party as Prime Minister, started in 1920 due to the development of party system in Japan. The other Ministers were appointed by the Emperor on the advice of the Prime Minister. The Ministers were not necessarily the members of the Diet. The Cabinet had one meeting per week. The Ministers gave advice to the Emperor and were responsible to him. The Emperor could remove any Minister for inefficiency or for other reasons. The House of Representatives had no power to drive out the Cabinet by a vote of no confidence as it is done in other parliamentary systems.

***(vii) Rigid Constitutions***

The Meiji Constitution was rigid in nature and a proposal for amendment could be submitted to the Diet only by an imperial order. Two-thirds of the total number of members were required to be present for opening the discussions on amendment and no amendment could be passed unless a majority of not less than two-thirds of the members present voted in support of it. As the Emperor was the sole author of the Constitution, he had the right to intimate the amendments. But strangely enough, no amendment was made to the Constitution and it was replaced by a new Constitution in 1946.

# 2

# Salient Features of the Shova Constitution of Japan

The Meiji Constitution which came into force in November 1890 continued upto May 1947. The defeat of Japan in the Second World War, necessitated the making of a new constitution. The Allies after occupying Japan, appointed General Mac Arthur as the Supreme Commander with the responsibility to prevent the future emergence of Japan as a menance to world peace and the establishment of a responsible government. Gen. Mac Arthur abolished the control of the army over the administration and stopped military education in the schocls. Prime Minister Shidehra was asked by Gen. Mac Arthur to prepare a new Constitution in the place of the Meiji Constitution. A Constitution Committee was constituted with Matsumoto Joji as its Chairman. The Constitution prepared by Dr. Joji was not acceptable to Gen. Mac Arthur and hence he asked the Government Section of his headquarters to quickly prepare a Constitution. The draft Constitution was forced upon Japan by Gen. Mac Arthur and the Emperor issued the decree. The draft Constitution was passed by both the houses of the Diet on October 7, 1946 and it was assented by Emperor Hirohito on 3rd November. The Constitution known as the Shova Constitution came into force on May 3, 1947.

The following are the main features of the new Constitution.

### *(i) Sovereignty of the People*

Unlike the Meiji Constitution which was gifted by the Emperor to the people of the new Constitution sovereignty is vested in the people. The 1947 Constitution expressly declared that it was the act of the Japanese people and the Emperor was the symbol of the State and derived his powers and position from the will of the people. According to the new Constitution the Emperor is specifically forbidden to exercise "power related to the government". He however, can perform certain "acts of State".

### *(ii) Written and Rigid Constitution*

The Constitution of 1947 consists of 11 Chapters and 103 Articles. The Western influence is very much evident in the Constitution as it was the handiwork of Gen. Mac Arthur. The Meiji Constitution was inspired by the German and the Prussian institutions. But the new Constitution was inspired by the American, British and other Western Constitutions.

It is also a rigid Constitution. The procedure of amendment of the Constitution is different. Amendment can be initiated by the Diet, through a concurring vote of two-thirds or more of all members of each house. After it is passed by the Diet, it will be submitted for the ratification of the people. It shall become an integral part of the Constitution only after such ratification. Previously in the Meiji Constitution the power of initiation of amendment was vested with the Emperor.

### *(iii) Renunciation of War*

The new Constitution declares the commitment of Japan to internation peace and the renunciation of war. It is specifically provided that Japan shall not go to war for the settlement of its international disputes. It was decided that Japan will not maintain land, sea and air forces, which could be used to intimidate other nations. But Japan's right to use force for its own defence and security was recognised by Gen. Mac Arthur, who was the chief architect of the new Constitution.

### *(iv) Limited Monarchy*

Under the new Constitution, the Emperor became the symbol of the State and the unity of the people. Under the earlier Constitution he was the source of all authority and power. But under the new Constitution the Emperor became a Constitutional head. He was required to perform all his acts on behalf of the people and with the advice and approval of the Cabinet. The expenses of the royal household were to be met from the annual Diet appropriations. He is required to perform his acts according to parliamentary conventions. The Japanese Emperor reigns but does not rule like his British counterpart.

### *(v) Parliamentary Government*

The British pattern of parliamentary government is established by the new Constitution. The Diet is the sole law making body. It is the highest organ of the State. The Prime Minister and his Cabinet colleagues are responsible to the Diet. If a vote of censure is passed against the Cabinet by the House of Representatives, then the Cabinet has to resign or make an appeal to the nation. Under the Meiji Constitution the Prime Minister alongwith his Cabinet was responsible to the Emperor and not to the Diet.

### *(vi) Unitary Government*

The New Constitution provides for a unitary system and the provinces draw their power from the Centre. This kind of devolution of authority has been made for efficiency in administration and the powers of the provinces may be changed at any time by the Centre. The Diet is the only law making body for the whole country and the provinces do not enjoy and such power. Thus in Japan there is centralisation of power like the British political system.

### *(vii) Bicameral System*

The Diet which is the highest law making body has two chambers, such as, the House of Councillors, which is the upper chamber and the House of Representatives--the lower chamber. There are 250 members in the House of Councillors, elected for six years; one half of whom retire after every three years. The House of Representatives consists of 486 members, who are elected for four years. Although the Money Bills cannot be introduced in the House of Councillors, it has got the power to alter or reject these Bills. However, supremacy in legislative matters rests with the House of Representatives as in case of any deadlock between the two houses, if a bill is passed by the House of Representatives by a two-thirds majority for the second time, it will become an Act.

### *(viii) Fundamental Rights*

The various fundamental rights of the Japanese people are enumerated in Chapter III of the new Constitution. These rights are declared as "eternal and inviolate". The Japanese people were also granted certain fundamental rights under the Meiji Constitution, but these rights could not be enforced as no court had the power of judicial review. An Act or decree of the Emperor could not be declared unconstitutional, when it specifically violated the fundamental rights. But the new constitution not only elaborately defines the fundamental rights, but also the judiciary is given power to protect these rights.

Important rights such as right to equality before law, abolition of discrimination, right to franchise, right to freedom of religion, press, right to education, right to assemble etc. are incorporated in 31 Articles in this Chapter.

***(ix) Duties of the Citizen***

The Japanese citizen is also required to perform three important duties:

(i) The obligation to provide education to all boys and girls under their protection;
(ii) the duty to work; and
(iii) the duty to pay taxes.

***(x) Independence of Judiciary***

The new Constitution was based upon certain Judicial reforms introduced by the Allied authorities after the Second World War. Article 76 provided the powers of the Supreme Court of Japan. Establishment of administrative tribunals was prohibited. It was provided that no executive organ shall exercise and judicial power. The Supreme Court is made independent of both the executive and the legislature. The judges can only be removed by inpeachment. This power was taken away from the hands of the executive. If any law, decree or ordinance violates the spirit of the Constitution, it can be declared as unconstitutional by the Supreme Court. Thus the Japanese Supreme Court enjoys the power of judicial review like the American Supreme Court. The Supreme Court did not enjoy the power of judicial review under the Meiji Constitution.

***(xi) Adult Suffrage***

There is provision for adult suffrage under the new Constitution. There was no adult suffrage under the Meiji Constitution and the voting right was only exercised by men of 25 years of age or above provided they paid at least 10 Yen annually in direct taxes. The new Constitution grants voting rights to all men and women who have completed 20 years of age and the property qualification has been abolished. Now women enjoy equal rights with men.

***(xii) Supreme Law***

Article 90 provides that "This Constitution shall be the supreme law of the nation and no law, ordinance, imperial rescript or other act of government or part thereof, contrary to the provisions hereof, shall have legal force of validity". Article 97 provides that there shall be no violation of the fundamental rights guaranteed by the Constitution to the citizens.

Article 99 categorically stipulates that the Emperor, the Regent, the Ministers of the State, the members of the Diet, Judges and all other public officials have the obligation to respect and uphold the Constitution.

# 3

# Fundamental Rights

The fundamental rights are declared "eternal and inviolable" by the new Constitution of Japan. The judiciary is given power to protect the fundamental rights. The Japanese fundamental rights are more eleborate and definite than the American Bill of Rights. They highlight the liberal and democratic aspects of the Japanese Constitution.

The new Constitution of Japan guarantees the following rights to the citizens:

***(1) Right to Equality***

The people of Japan enjoy equality before law and there is no discrimination in political, economic or social spheres because of race, creed, sex, social status or family origin. Peerage has been abolished. Marriage is based only on the mutual consent of both partners. The Constitution guarantees the essential equality of the sexes.

***(2) Right to Freedom***

The Constitution guarantees the freedom of thought and conscience. No person shall be held in bondage of any kind. Involuntary servitude, except as punishment for crime is, prohibited. The people have the inalienable right to choose their public officials and to dismiss them. Universal adult suffrage is guaranteed. Secrecy of the ballot shall not be violated in all elections. Freedom of assembly and association as well as speech, press and all other forms of expression are guaranteed.

The Constitution guarantees the freedom of occupation or avocation and the freedom to choose his residence, to the extent that it does not interfere with the public welfare. There is also freedom to acquire foreign nationality and to move to foreign countries.

No person shall be deprived of life, liberty, nor shall any other criminal penalty be imposed, except according to the procedure established by law. No body shall be arrested without a warrant issued by a competent judicial officer, which specifies the crime which the person is charged with. In all cases of arrest, the person should be given the immediate privilege of counsel, nor shall be detained without adequate cause and on demand such cause shall be shown to the person in open in the presence of his counsel. The right of all persons to be secured in their homes has been guaranteed. Each search and seizure shall be made upon separate warrant issued by a competent judicial officer.

***(3) Economic Rights***

All people have the right and the obligation to work. Wages, hours of work, rest and leisure and other conditions of work are fixed by law. Exploitation of children is prohibited. The right to collective bargaining and organisation of Trade Unions is guaranteed. There is provision for guaranteeing the minimum standard of life. The State is required to take steps for the promotion and extension of social welfare and security of public health.

***(4) The Right to Property***

In Japan the property rights are defined by law in conformity with the public welfare. The citizens right to own or hold property is inviolable under the new Constitution. Just compensation should be paid if private property is acquired for public use.

***(5) The Right to Freedom of Religion***

Japan is a secular State and no religious organisation receives any privilege from the State. No person can be forced to take part in any religious act, celebration, rite or practice against his free will. No religious education shall be imparted in schools and colleges and no religious activity shall be performed by any state organ.

***(6) The Right to Education***

No discrimination shall be made in imparting equal education to all corresponding to their ability and as provided by law. There is provision for compulsory free education in Japan. It is obligatory on the part of people to send boys and girls under their protection to receive ordinary education.

***(7) Right to Constitutional Remedies***

If a person suffers due to the illegal act of any public official, he may sue for redress as provided by law from the state or the public entity. A person who is acquitted, after his arrest or detention, may sue the state for redress, as provided by law. Every person shall have the right to peaceful petition for redress of damage, for removal of public officials, for enactment, repeal or amendment of laws, ordinances or regulations.

**An Assessment**

The new Japanese Constitution is a remarkable achievement as it provides for and guarantees a large number of fundamental rights to the people which they never enjoyed before. The enjoyment of these civil and political rights has added to the dignity of the Japanese citizen and given him an honourable place in society. These fundamental rights lay the foundations of an egalitarian, liberal and democratic society based upon equality and justice and the abolitions of discrimination and special privileges of the feudal age. The elaborate provision of fundamental rights in the Japanese Constitution is more impressive and comprehensive than the American Bill of Rights. Rule of Law has been established in Japan and all are equal before the eyes of law. People have the equal right to seek the protection of the judiciary. There can be no arbitrary arrest or confinement. A citizen can move for a writ of Habeas Corpus, in case of wrongful confinement. No person can be tried or punished except as per the procedure of law. All kinds of exploitation is forbidden with special emphasis on children. Any discrimination on the basis of sex, birth, caste or race has been forbidden. Peerage has been abolished and women have been given equal rights.

Japan is declared as a secular state and the people have the right to freedom of religion and conscience. The state is forbidden to impart any religious education and no special favour is shown to any religion.

However, despite all the elaborate provisions and constitutional guarantees, Prof. Robert E. Ward holds the view that the fundamental rights guaranteed in part - III are so aspiring that for a long time they may be mere pious wishes and may not be realised as social or legal truths. As a result of the legacy of the long authoritarian tradition the Japanese people still betray a fear of officials and it is difficult on the part of the people to challenge illegal official or administrative actions which violate the fundamental rights. Prof. Berks writes that from the analysis of the cases sent to the civil liberties department of the Ministry of Justice it is evident that there is increase in the cases of misuse of official authority and physical violence. The idealism incorporated in the new Constitution is rarely executed in practice. Police atrocities against suspected offenders, violate all norms of civilized behaviour.

The actual realization of the fundamental rights guaranteed by the constitution has been stalled due to the conservative and pro-governmental approach followed by the Supreme Court of Japan. The Supreme Court is very often hesitant to declare the government laws or decrees as unconstitutional. The government imposes many restrictions on the rights of the people in the name of public welfare and the Supreme Court has remained silent, eventhough most of these acts violate specific fundamental rights. But despite all these restrictions, there has been no serious erosion of any Constitutionally guaranteed freedom through, legislation, executive or judicial action.

# 4

# The Japanese Executive

Till to-day there is great respect for the institution of monarchy in Japan. "The Emperor has been and still is the living symbol of the nation's history, heritage and achievements, of all that is glorious in the nation's past and present, of its continuity and durability". The Emperor symbolises the hopes, aspirations and promises of the nation and as a symbol he is enshrined in the hearts of the people who attribute everything good to his virture. The Meiji Constitution conferred sovereignty on the Emperor and he was the head of the empire and the source of all authority.

Before 1945 most of the elaborate powers of the Emperor were exercised by his Ministers or the Councillors of the Supreme War Council. The military leadership was supreme in Japan and the Emperor was a mere figure head. He was only the symbol of the state.

The new Constitution of 1947 inaugurated a democratic liberal constitution in Japan and the Emperor was made the constitutional ceremonial head of the state. The dualism was abolished and the makers of the constitution 'humanized' the person of the Emperor under the new Constitution, the sovereignty is no longer vested in the Emperor. It is vested in the people of Japan. The Emperor like his British counterpart, enjoys great dignity and prestige but no real powers. The real powers are conferred on the Diet and the cabinet is made responsible to it. The powers of the government are exercised by the cabinet.

Article 2 of the constitution provides that the Imperial throne shall be dynastic and be succeeded in accordance with the Imperial House Law enacted by the Diet.

### Powers of the Emperor

According to the 1947 Constitution, the Emperor is the symbol of the state and derives his power from the people. The Emperor is required to exercise all his powers on the advice and approval of the Cabinet. The Emperor shall perform the following acts as per the constitution

***(1) Executive Powers***

He appoints the Prime Minister as designated by the Diet. He approves the appointment and dismissal of Ministers and other officials as provided for by law. He receives the full powers and the credentials presented by the Ambassadors and Ministers of foreign countries. The Emperor is the fountain of honour and as such awards honours. He attests the instruments of ratification and other diplomatic documents as provided for by law.

***(2) Legislative Powers***

He promulgates the national laws, constitutional amendments, cabinet orders and treaties. The sessions of the Diet are called by him. He dissolves the House of Representatives, after the expiry of its term or on the recommendation of the Prime Minister. He orders for general elections to the Diet and issues a proclamation for that purpose.

***(3) Judicial Powers***

The Emperor attests general and special amnesty. He sanctions commutation of punishment, reprieve and restoration of rights.

## The Position of the Emperor

It is mentioned in the first chapter of the Constitution that the Emperor is the symbol of the State, of the unity of the people and derives his powers from the will of the people with whom is vested the sovereign power. The Emperor performs all his functions on the advice of the Cabinet. He does not possess any privileges. Thus his powers now are merely formal and he is the titular head of the nation. The absolute powers vested in him prior to 1947 have been abolished and he has been converted into a constitutional head. Even his ceremonial functions are exercised on the advice of the cabinet. Treaties are not concluded in his name; these are simply promulgated by him. His position has become so weak due to the new Constitution that he can neither give away any property nor receive it, nor can be receive any gift without the assent of the Diet.

The Emperor of Japan under the new Constitution is even weaker to his British counterpart. The British Monarch has the discretion in the appointment of the Prime Minister, when no party has got majority, but even this discretion is denied to the Emperor of Japan. The person nominated by the Diet is appointed as Prime Minister by the Emperor. He has no power to dissolve the House of Representatives. This power is vested with the Cabinet and the Emperor has to act on its advice. The Emperor has no power to veto the Bills, nor can he return them to the Diet. He only promulgates the laws passed by the Diet. The British Monarch possess three important rights, such as, the right to be consulted, the right to encourage and the right to warn and with the help of these rights very often he influences the decisions of the Cabinet. But the Japanese Emperor does not enjoy these rights. He is prohibited to take any interest in politics and should refrain from making any statement with a view to influence public opinion. He is not the Supreme Commander of the armed forces, because Japan has renounced war. Unlike the British Monarch he has no power to influence the foreign policy of the country. Thus to Japanese Emperor is even weaker to the British Monarch.

But despite the transformation of the Monarchy into a democratic and constitutional institution, the Japanese Emperor enjoys lots of importance and honour. In Japan it is the oldest royal family which is sanctified by history and traditions and the people adore their Emperor. He is regarded as sacred and the source of all inspiration. He enjoys the love and confidence of his subjects. He is the living symbol of the strength and unity of the nation. Before 1946, the Emperor was kept aloof from the people and even in his presence they were required to bow their heads and not look at his personage. Now he mixes with the people, shakes hands with them and receives their respects.

The 1947 Constitution has democratised and humanized the institution of Emperor. He is no longer considered divine or 'God on Earth'. His acts can now be criticised and he can be a topic for discussion. But despite the reduction in his powers, the reverence of the Japanese people towards their Emperor continues unhindered in the same manner as before.

### The Cabinet

The new Constitution of 1947 specifically recognize the Cabinet, system in Japan. This cabinet is like any parliamentary cabinet the chief executive authority of the country and it is markedly different from its predecessor. The powers of the cabinet are discussed in Chapter V and Articles 65-75 enumerate these powers. The executive powers are vested in the Cabinet as per Article 65. Articele 66 states: "The Cabinet shall consist of the Prime Minister who shall be its head and other ministers of state, as provided for by law". The cabinet is collectively responsible to the Diet. If a no-confidence motion is passed by the Diet, the Cabinet shall resign from office. It is the highest organ of the 'Executive power'. Thus all the required principles of parliamentary government are incorporated in the new Constitution of Japan.

## Organisation of the Cabinet

The Prime Minister is appointed first on the basis of his nomination by the Diet and then the other Ministers are appointed. Thus he is the key figure in the organisation of the Cabinet. Generally he is the leader of the majority party in the House of Representatives. The election of the Prime Minister is made soon after the election of the Diet, when it meets in its first session. In case of differences between the two Houses regarding the election of the Prime Minister, the matter is referred to a joint committee of both the Houses. If the joint committee fails to arrive at an agreement or the House of Councillors fails to make the designation within ten days after the House of Representatives has made the designation, the decision of the House of Representatives will be considered decisive and final. Thus the Prime Minister is not the choice of the majority party, he is elected by the whole House. He has to contest the election in the Diet, after every general election, irrespective of his party-majority in the Diet.

According to Article 66 the Prime Minister should be a member of the Diet and other Ministers shall be civilians. After the election of the Prime Minister by the Diet, he is formally appointed by the Emperor. The other Ministers are appointd by the Prime Minister and majority of them belong to the House of Representatives. He also allocates the portfolios to the Ministers. The appointment of the Ministers with their representative portfolios are presented for the attestation of the Emperor in a ceremony in the Imperial Palace.

## Functions of the Cabinet

The Prime Minister exercises control and supervision over various administrative departments and submits bills, reports on domestic and foreign policy of the Diet.

The Cabinet formulates important political decisions and decides the policies to be pursued by the government. It submits the budget before the Diet in each fiscal year. The Bills are also submitted by the Cabinet to the Diet. It negotiates and concludes treaties and manages the foreign relations of the country. The Cabinet controls and administers the civil service. When the House of Representatives is dissolved, emergency session of the House of Councillors can be convoked by the Cabinet. It submits reports to the Diet at regular intervals and at least once a year on the state of national finance. The meeting of the Diet is convened on its advice. The Cabinet issues orders for the execution of the provisions of the constitution. The House of Representatives is dissolved on the advice of the Cabinet. It is the duty of the Cabinet to administer the laws faithfully and conduct the affairs of the state.

The final account of expenditure and revenues alongwith the statement of Audit, prepared by the Board of Audit, is submitted to the Diet by the Cabinet. Matters relating to general amnesty, special amnesty, commutation of punishment, reprieve and restoration of rights are decided by the Cabinet.

It designates the Chief Judge of the Supreme Court and appoints all other judges. On the advice of the Cabinet proclamation is issued for general election of the members of the Diet.

According to Article 74, all laws and orders shall be signed by the competent Minister of State and countersigned by the Prime Minister. No legal action can be taken against the Ministers during the term of their office, without the consent of the Prime Minister.

These powers reveal that Japan has a Cabinet-system of Government in the British model. The Cabinet is responsible to the Diet for all its acts of omissioin and commission.

## An Assessment of the Japanese Cabinet System

In Japan there are two types of Cabinet Ministers–those who hold portfolios and those who do not hold any protfolio. The Ministers who do not hold any portfolio perform certain important administrative functions. Every Minister is assisted by three Vice-Ministers.

The Cabinet Secretariat is headed by a Director who looks after the routine affairs of the Cabinet. There are two Deputy Directors to assist the Director. The agenda for the Cabinet meetings is prepared by the Cabinet Secretariat. It also keeps the record of relevant papers and decisions.

The Prime Minister presides over the meetings of the Cabinet, which meets at his official residence, ordinarily twice a week in Camera.

No quorum is fixed and the decisions are taken by unanimous vote. The proceedings of the Cabinet are not formally recorded, but the Ministers have to sign, when a decision is taken on any particular matter. Any Minister who refuses to sign must resign or otherwise he would he removed from the Cabinet by the Prime Minister. The Ministers are supposed to maintain the secrecy of Cabinet proceedings.

The Cabinet is the central directing instrument of government in administration and legislation. The national executive is under its supreme control and it maintains co-ordination among the various departments of administration. It governs the country and determines the policy to be placed before the Diet. It runs the administration of the country and submits the legislative proposals before the Diet. It takes the important decisions regarding the national affairs like the British Cabinet. Thus there has been enormous increase in the powers of the Japanese Cabinet.

However, inspite of these similarities between the Japanese and the British Cabinet, there are two basic differences between the two systems. While in Japan all the Ministers are Cabinet Ministers and attend the meetings of the Cabinet in their own right, in Great Britain only those Ministers who hold important portfolios enjoy the Cabinet rank. They alone are entitled to attend the meetings of the Cabinet and not all the members of the Council of Ministers.

## The Prime Minister of Japan

### *Appointment*

Like the British Cabinet system, in Japan also the Cabinet must enjoy the support of the majority in the representative chamber of the legislature. The leader of the majority party is appointed as Prime Minister by the Head of the State and he is requested to form the Ministry. The Head of the State is bound to call the leader of the party which commands majority support to form the government and he has no choice in the matter.

The Prime Minister is elected by the Diet and in case of deadlock between the two houses, attempt is made to resolve it by constituting a Joint Committee. But the decision of the House of Representatives prevails after ten days, if during this period the Joint Committee fails to reach an agreement. The person who is elected through this procedure, is formally issued the letter of appointment as Prime Minister by the Emperor. Thus the Japanese practice of appointment of the Prime Ministers differs from that in Great Britain and India. While in

Britain and India, the leader of the majority party is directly appointed as Prime Minister by the head of the State, in Japan, the appointment is made after he is elected by the Diet.

## Functions of the Prime Minister

The Japanese Prime Minister, like any other country having the Cabinet system of government, enjoys a very vital position in the government and may be considered as the keystone of the administration. He enjoys enormous powers, though in comparison to the British and Indian Prime Ministers his powers may appear to be limited.

The important functions performed by the Japanese Prime Minister are as follows:

(i) The Prime Minister constitutes the government and submits the list of persons to the Emperor, who are to be appointed to the Council of Ministers with the appointment of the Prime Minister, in reality the functions of the Diet and the Emperor are over. After that every thing rests with the Prime Minister and his decisions regarding the formation of the government is final.

(ii) The Prime Minister is free to take anybody into the Council of Ministers and remove any body from the Ministry who does not enjoy his confidence in pursuance of Article 68 of the Constitution. He can reshuffle his Cabinet as and when he likes. He has complete control over his Cabinet.

(iii) He controls and coordinates the various activities of the Ministers and resolves the differences among them. He is the Chairman of the Cabinet and presides over all the meetings. All the Ministers have to carry out the wishes of the Prime Minister. He has got the power to reject or accept any proposal submitted by a particular Minister.

(iv) As the leader of the House of Representatives in particular and of the Diet in general, the Prime Minister makes announcements of important policies. At the time of debates in the Diet, the Prime Minister may intervene on behalf of any Minister and answer the questions.

(v) Appointments to all important officers are made by the Prime Minister in consultation with his Cabinet colleagues. But in case of difference of opinion on any such matter, the decision of the Prime Minister shall be final.

(vi) All the decrees and laws are countersigned by him on behalf of the Cabinet.

(vii) The dates for the sessions of the Diet and its elections are determined by the Prime Minister.

(viii) The international agreements of Japan with other countries are signed by the Prime Minister.

(ix) Till the final consideration by the Cabinet, any departmental order may be suspended by the Prime Minister.

(x) For any legal action against the Ministers, the approval of the Prime Minister is necessary.

**Position of the Prime Minister**

The Prime Minister occupies a very vital position in the Constitutional system of Japan. He is superior among equals and in fact he represents the executive authority of the State. The powers of the Japanese Prime Minister under the new Constitution have increased manyfold due to the abolition of the Privy Council and the Supreme War Council, the two organs which shared power with him prior to the adoption of the New Constitution. The Prime Minister enjoys very wide powers and has eclipsed the Emperor and other Ministers of the Council of Ministers. He exercises his powers independently and as far as his executive powers are considered he is not subordinate to any other executive authority.

The position of the Prime Minister can be analysed under the following heads:

***(i) Supreme Control over the Cabinet***

The supremacy of the Prime Minister over his Cabinet colleagues is beyond any doubt. He appoints the Ministers, distributes the portfolios among them, can reshuffle ther cabinet as and when he likes, can impose his will on the Minister, may accept or reject proposals made by a Minister, can submit the proposal submitted by a single Minister for the consideration of the whole Cabinet and finally can remove the Minister who do not enjoy his confidence. In all his decisions regarding the formation and functioning of the Cabinet the decision of the Prime Minister is final and approval of the Emperor is merely formal.

As Chairman of the Cabinet, the Prime Minister Presides over its functions, coordinates the activities of the various Ministries and decides the disputes among the Ministers. He supervises the activities of the Ministers and can suspend any order of a particular Minister.

The Cabinet proceedings are kept secret. He maintains strict control over the Cabinet as its chairman. No legal action can be taken against any Minister without his approval. He is supreme to the life and death of the Cabinet. The whole cabinet goes out of office when he tenders his resignation. As long as he continues, legally the Cabinet is in office although the other Ministers resign. As the sole representative of the Cabinet he announces the national and foreign policy of the country in the Diet.

***(ii) As Leader of the Diet***

The Prime Minister owes his office to the Diet as he is elected by it and he continues in office as long as he enjoys the confidence of the House of Representatives. Government decisions on national and foreign policy matters are announced by the Prime Minister in the Diet. Proceedings of the House of Representatives are guided by him and the House looks to him for the announcement of all important matters pertaining to national interest.

The Cabinet is responsible to the Diet and the Prime Minister as its leader is also accountable to the Diet. But in reality the Prime Minister is the leader of the Diet. If the House of Representatives becomes too refractory a critic, then the Prime Minister can the Emperor for its dissolution and order for fresh election. Thus the Diet can be compelled by the Prime Minister to act according to his wishes. The Prime Minister's position in the Diet is further strengthened as very often he enjoys the support of the majority in the House of Representatives.

***(iii) As Leader of the Nation***

The Prime Minister enjoys undisputed position as the leader of the nation. He plays a vital role in the administration of the country and to a great extent determines its future course of development. He is respected by the people and they expect him to solve all their problems and bring glory and prosperity to the country. He is the most important person in the Government and maintains the link between the Emperor and the people. After the abolition of the Privy council and the Supreme War Council, the Prime Minister does not share his executive power with any other authority or organ. He has the power to conclude treaties and represent Japan in international conferences. He is empowered to make any commitment on behalf of the nation. The wisdom and the personality of the Prime Minister determine to a great extent the social and economic progress of the country.

The Prime Minister is the "corner-stone of the Cabinet-arch" and wields the actual authority of the Emperor. Due to his wide powers, influence and patronage, he enjoys great prestige and honour and the whole nation looks to him as the saviour, when the country is confronted with any crisis or danger.

# 5
# The Diet

Diet is the name of the Japanese Parliament which has got two Houses viz. House of Councillors and the House of Representatives. It is the Central legislature and has come into existence through.

The Diet had very limited powers under the Meiji Constitution and all powers were vested in the Emperor. The Diet was a legislative body only in the name and the Emperor could accept or reject any Bill according to his discretion. The Diet was only required to affix the stamp of approval on the decisions already taken by the Executive. Subsequently before the War all powers were assumed by the Military leaders and though the Diet was allowed to continue, in reality it had not control over the government.

The new democratic constitution of Japan was adopted after the Second World War. By this constitution the powers of the Emperor were curtailed and the supremacy of the military leaders was abolished. The Diet was made the highest organ of state-power by the new Constitution and it was vested with the law-making power to the exclusion of other organs. Under the present Constitution the Diet exercises all powers to which the central legislature in a parliamentary country is entitled.

The composition and functions of the House of Representatives and House of Councillors are discussed below:

### House of Representatives

It is the popular chamber of Japan and has 467 members who are directly elected by the voters for a period of four years, unless sooner dissolved.

Originally its membership was 300 but it was in treased in 1902 due to liberalised franchise rules. In 1925 the membership was raised to 466 with the introduction of adult-franchise. The Prefectures are divided into electoral districts for the purpose of election and each prefecture may have one to five electoral districts. There are seven electoral districts in Tokyo. Each electoral district sends 3 to 5 representatives. Each voter has one vote and any Japanese citizen who has completed twenty years of age is entitled to vote, if he or she is not otherwise disqualified.

**Qualification of the Members**

The qualification for membership in the Diet is fixed by law and these are mentioned below:

(i) He must be a Japanese citizen.
(ii) He should not be less than 25 years and must have been the resident of the district continuously for three months.
(iii) He should not have been declared mentally unsound by competent authorities and should not be convicted for any serious crime.
(iv) He should not hold any office of profit under the government.
(v) He should not be an undischarged insolvent.
(vi) He must not have been deprived of the membership by an Act of the Diet.
(vii) No body can be a member of both the Houses of the Diet.

**Tenure of the House**

The House of Representatives is elected for a period of four years, unless sooner dissolved. If the House passes a vote of no-confidence against the Cabinet, either the Cabinet has to resign or the House is dissolved within ten days. Within 40 days time the new election must be held and the first session of the House must be called within 30 days of the election.

**Functions of the House of Representatives**

Like any other parliamentary democracy, the supremacy of the popularly elected House has been established by the Japanese Constitution. It has final say in law-making and the Cabinet is accountable to this House. The various functions of the House are discussed below:

***(i) Legislative Function***

The House enjoys unlimited supremacy in the sphere of law-making. If a Bill passed by the House of Representatives is rejected or amended by the House Councillors, it will become an Act, if it is repassed for a second time by the House of Representatives by a two-thirds majority of the members present. To resolve the differences between the two Houses, a joint Committee may be constituted, but if this Committee fails to resolve the problem, the aforesaid procedure is adopted. The House of Councillors can only delay a Bill for a period of two months and after this if the Bill passed by two-thirds majority of the members present by the House of Representatives, it shall become a law of the Diet. Bills rejected by the House of Representatives cannot be considered by the House of Councillors. Thus in the sphere of law-making the House of Representatives enjoys the final power.

***(ii) Executive Functions***

The Cabinet is accountable to the House of Representatives and can continue in office as long as it enjoys the confidence of this House. It has to resign if a vote of no-confidence is passed against it by the House of Representatives or its policies are rejected. Thus the House of Representatives controls the executive in Japan.

The National and foreign policy of Japan is announced by the Cabinet in the House. It also informs the State of national finances to the House in regular intervals and particularly at the time of placing the budget before the House. The House has the power to investigate into the activities of the executive through Committees of Investigation. No treaty can become effective without the approval of the Diet. The control of the House over the executive is also enforced by asking questions and supplementary questions. The House can ventilate the grievances of the people against the executive during the Question-Hour.

Though it is said that the Prime Minister is elected by the Diet, but in reality he is the choice of the House of Representatives. If there is a difference of opinion between the House of Representatives and the House of Councillors, regarding the election of the Prime Minister, the matter is referred to the Joint Committee of both the Houses, which tries to resolve the problem. But if the Joint Committee fails to resolve the problem or if the House of Councillors fails to make designation within ten days, after the choice has been made by the House of Representatives, the decision of the House of Representatives is accepted as final and this is considered as the decision of the whole Diet. In addition to the Prime Minister, majority of the Ministers of the Cabinet also belong to the House of Representatives.

*(iii) Financial Functions*

According to the constitution, the Budget is introduced in the House of Representatives and this House has got complete control over the purse of the nation. Levying of new taxes and the changing of the existing taxes are subject to the consent of the House of Representatives. After the Budget is passed by the House of Representatives and the House of Councillors takes no decision over it within thirty days or no solution is made through the Joint Committee, or the House of Councillors takes a different decision from the House of Representatives, then the Budget as approved by the House of Representatives becomes the Budget of the Diet and is deemed to have been approved by both the Houses.

*(iv) Judicial Functions*

Impeachment of the judges of the Supreme Court can be made by the House of Representatives alongwith the House of Councillors. The Court of Impeachment is constituted by taking seven members from each House. A President of the Court is elected by these fourteen members. There is also provision for an Indictment Committee consisting of an equal number of members from each House of the Diet, which initiates the impeachment proceedings. A member of the Diet cannot simultaneously become a member of both the Committees.

*(v) Electoral Function*

The electoral laws are required to be fair and impartial and there should be no discrimination on the grounds of race, creed, sex, social status, family origin, property, income or education. The House of Representatives can make or amend the electoral laws. Disputes related to qualification are determined by each House of the Diet. The Prime Minister of Japan is elected by the House of Representatives alongwith the House of Councillors. The speaker and Deputy Speaker are also elected by the House of Representatives in its meeting.

*(vi) The Constituent Functions*

Amendments to the Constitution can be initiated in either House of the Diet. It must be passed by a two-thirds majority of all members of each House. After that a referendum is held and the amendment as approved by the Diet is submitted to the people. It becomes a part of the constitution, if approved by a majority of all votes cast.

**House of Councillors**

The House of Councillors consists of 250 elected members and has replaced the House of Peers which was a hereditary House. This House is the upper chamber of the Japanese Diet. Out of 250 members, 150 are elected on a geographical basis. The whole country is divided into 46 Electoral districts for the purpose which correspond with the prefectures. Roughly 2 to 8 seats are allotted to each prefecture in proportion to its population. The remaining members are elected by the nation at large.

### Tenure

The House of councillors is a permanent House in the sense that the House as a whole can never be dissolved. The members are elected for six years of whom one half retire after every three years.

### Qualification for Membership

In order to be the member of the House a person must have completed thirty years of age and the other qualifications are same as those for the members of the House of Representatives. No person can simultaneously become the member of both the Houses of the Diet.

### Quorum

One-third of the total membership is required to be present to constitute the quorum of the House. In the absence of the required quorum, no business can be transacted in the House.

### President of the House

The House elects its President who is known as "Gicho", at the beginning of the session by means of secret ballot. His term is concurrent with the term of the House.

### Functions of the House of Councillors

Like the House of Representatives the House of Councillors also performs several functions, which are discussed below:

#### *(i) Legislataive Function*

In the Legislative field it enjoys identical powers with the House of Representatives. In order to become a law, a Bill has to be passed by both the Houses of the Diet, separately. The introduction of the Bill may be made in either House of the Diet. However, as per the Constitution, the supremacy of the House of Representatives has been established in the legislative matters. Thus the House of Councillors can only delay a Bill for a period of sixty days after its receipt from the House of Representatives. If the Bill is repassed for the second time by two-thirds majority of the Representatives, it becomes the law of the land by passing either the rejection or amendment of the House of Councillors.

***(ii) Executive Functions***

Although in general terms it is said that the cabinet is accountable to the Diet, in reality it is only accountable to the House of Representatives. Hence compared to the House of Representatives the House of Councillors has less control over the Executive of the country. Article 69 provides: "If the House of Representatives passes a no-confidence resolution or rejects a confidence motion, the cabinet shall resign enmasse, unless the House of Representatives is dissolved within 10 days". But despite this provision the House of Councillors can put questions, initiate debates on important issues of national and international importance and can force the government to follow a particular policy or to face unpopularity and public resentment. Investigation Committees can be appointed by the House of Councillors to investigate into any matter. But all said and done, it has no power to compel the Cabinet to resign.

***(iii) Financial Functions***

No Money Bill can originate in the House of Councillors, which is the Upper House of the Japanese Diet. In respect of Money Bills, the House of Councillors can delay a Bill only for 30 days. If it makes a decision different from the House of Representatives and when no agreement is reached through the Joint Committee of both the Houses and fails to take final action within 30 days after the receipt of the Budget, passed by the House of Representatives, then the decision of the House of Representatives shall be the decision of the Diet. Thus in financial matters the House of Councillors enjoys a secondary position.

***(iv) Constituent Functions***

In the sphere of the amendment of the Constitution the House of Councillors enjoys equal powers with the House of Representatives. An amendment has to be passed by two-thirds or more votes of all the members of each House and then it is submitted for the ratification of the people.

***(v) Electoral Functions***

The House of Councillors alongwith the House of Representatives takes part in the election of the Prime Minister. In this sphere also the House of Representatives enjoys supremacy over the House of Councillors. In case of difference of opinion regarding the election of the Prime Minister, between the two Houses, and if the Joint Committee fails to resolve the difference and the House of Councillors does not make its designation of the Prime Minister, within ten days of the designation of the House of Representatives, then the decision of the House of Representatives shall be deemed as the decision of the Diet. The House of Councillors can change the electoral law alongwith the House of Representatives and can enact laws regarding the formation of electoral districts, methods of a voting and other matters pertaining to the election of members to both the Houses of the Diet. Disputes relating to the qualification of its members are decided by the House of Councillors. By a resolution passed by the majority of two-thirds or more of the members present, the House can deny a seat to any member. The President, Vice-President and the Chairman of the Standing Committees are elected by the House of Councillors.

***(vi) Judicial Functions***

The judges of the Supreme Court can be impeached by the Court of Impeachment which is constituted by taking seven members from each House. There are also equal number of members from both the Houses in the Indictment Committee which initiates the impeachment proceedings. No member can be simultaneously the member of Court of Impeachment and the Indictment Committee.

## The Speaker of the House of Representatives

In Japan the Speaker of the House of Representatives is called as the 'Gicho'. The Speaker is elected by secret ballot at the beginning of the session. The Speaker's term coincides with the term of the House. A new Speaker is elected when the Speaker in office resigns, dies or accepts any office of profit. There are also other officers of the House like the Deputy Speaker, Chairman of the Standing Committee and Secretary General, who are also elected by the House.

The Japanese Speaker is more like the American Speaker rather than the British Speaker. He maintains his party affiliation even after his election as Speaker and takes all possible steps to further the interest of his party in the House. The Speaker has to contest the election and has to face stiff opposition as he takes active interest in the political affairs of the country. Thus the British practice of the speaker remaining politically neutral after his election, is not followed in Japan.

## Functions of the Speaker

The Japanese Speaker enjoys great dignity, honour and authority. His powers and functions are discussed below:

(i) The Speaker is the custodian of the rights of the House and its members.

(ii) The order of business in the House is determined by him and he is the spokesman of the House.

(iii) The rules of the House are interpreted by him.

(iv) He conducts the proceedings of the House and presides over its meetings.

(v) He has the power to recognize the members on the floor of the House.

(vi) He gives his ruling on all points of order and his decision is final in all such matters.

(vii) The Bills are put to vote and the results are announced by him.

(viii) He has the power to adjourn the House. He maintains discipline in the House and may suspend a member for disorderly behaviour. He can expel a member only when a resolution to that effect is passed by a two-thirds majority of the members present.

(ix) He has got the power to expunge unparliamentary observations from the proceedings of the House.

(x) The time limit for the debates and speeches are fixed by him.

(xi) Resignations of the members from the House are accepted by him.

(xii) He represents the collective will of the House. He can refer the Bills to the appropriate Committees.

## The Committees of the House

There are four types of Committees in the Diet viz. The Standing Committee, Sepcial Committees, Joint Conference Committee and Joint Committees play a vital role in the legislative process of Japan. The work of legislation is completed speedily and effectively by the various Committees.

### *(i) Standing Committees*

The role played by the Standing Committees in the process of law-making cannot be exaggerated. Bills passed in the Diet are referred to the various Standing Committees concerned, where the Bills are thoroughly examined. The Committee may hold public meetings and may invite people to give their opinions and arguments for and against the Bill. Memorandum may also be independently submitted by the people to the Committee. The Committees makes a report to the House after it has thoroughly discussed the Bill. The Chairman of the Committee submits the Bill to the House. If the Bill is unworthy of consideration, it may be pigeon-holed, and the Committee does not make any report of the House.

### *(ii) Special Committees*

A Special Committee may be appointed by each House of the Diet to investigate into any particular problem like a disaster, an administrative scandal, repatriation, trade and commercial transactions etc. After the particular work is completed the Special Committee comes to an end. But the Standing Committees are appointed for the duration of the session. The Chairman of the concerned House appoints the members of the Special Committee, but the Chairman of the Special Committee is elected by the members from among themselves. The Special Committee may be allowed to continue its work beyond the session of the House in which it was constituted. The decisions in the Committee are made by majority vote and the Chairman exercised a casting vote in case of a tie.

Like the Standing Committees the Special Committees can also summon people to give evidence and express their opinion before the Committee. Anybody who disobeys the orders of the Committee can be charged with contempt. The Committee presents its report to the concerned House. If there is no unanimity, the majority report is presented before the House.

### *(iii) Joint Conference Committee*

To resolve the dead-lock between the two Houses of the Diet, this Committee is constituted consisting of 20 members equally drawn from both the Houses. The members elected from each House elect their Chairman, and each Chairman alternately presides over meetings of a Joint Committee. Difference of opinion between the House of Representatives and the House of Councillors with regard to legislative Bills, Budget, treaties, designation of the Prime Minister and constitutional questions leads to the constitution of the Joint Committee. The decisions are taken by the Committee supported by a two-thirds majority of the members present and voting.

### (iv) Joint Legislative Committee

The Committee consists of ten members from the House of Representatives and eight members from the House of Councillors. The elected members of each House elect their own Chairman who preside over the meetings of the Committee alternately. The Committee takes its decision by two-thirds majority of the members present and voting. The Committee advises the Diet on matters of national policy which are likely to create problems, proposals for new legislation, cabinet orders in force and the revision of laws and rules pertaining to the Diet.

## The Legislative Procedure

As Japan is a unitary country, the Diet is the sole law-making organ. It can make laws on any subject and on any matter without any restriction. A Bill can be introduced in either House of the Diet and must be passed by both the Houses, before it becomes an Act.

The Bills may be classified into two kinds: the government Bills and Member's Bills. A Minister introduces a Government Bill in the Diet on behalf of the government. A Member's Bill is introduced by a member, who is not a Minister, in the House to which he belongs. From the point of view of the content there is no difference between a Government Bill and a Member's Bill as both may relate to public or private matters.

The various stages through which a Bill has to go before it finally becomes an Act, are discussed below:

### *(i) Preparation of the Bill*

The Cabinet frames policy and after the policy is so framed, the appropriate administrative departments take up the responsibility of translating the policy into the form of a Bill. A Department may also draft a Bill, if it feels the necessity for a Bill incorporating the required provisions. The drafting section of the Department drafts the Bill, and sends it to the Departments' Document's Section Chief in the Secretariat. From there it goes to the concerned Minister through the Parliamentary Vice-Minister. After the Minister approves the Bill, he submits it to the Prime Minister, who may place it in the agenda of the Cabinet for its consideration. A Department may also seek the assistance of the Bureau of Legislation in drafting a Bill. When called by the Cabinet the concerned Minister or the director of the Bureau of Legislation shall explain the details of the Bill before the Cabinet.

### *(ii) Introduction of the Bill*

The Government introduces the Bill in the House of its choice, after the Bill is approved by the Cabinet. Introduction of the Money Bills can be done only in the House of Representatives, in the name of the Prime Minister. A copy of the Bill is sent to the other House within five days of the introduction of the Bill. The Bill is circulated among the members of the House by the Speaker and then on the recommendation of the Committee of Ways and Means, it is submitted by him to the appropriate Committee. The Bill may be directly discussed in the House without referring it to the Committee, if it relates to a very urgent matter.

### *(iii) Committee Stage*

The Bill may be referred to a Standing Committee or a Special Committee according to the nature of the Bill. The Committee stage is extremely important in the career of a Bill as in this stage it is discussed threadbare and care is taken to see that the Bill is in confirmity with the existing law and constitution. The Committees may ask for any date or information from any department and may ask any Minister or member of the House to appear before the Committee and give his opinion.

It may even ask the Prime Minister to appear before it. The Committee may take all necessary steps to collect information from home and aborad. It may hold public meetings and people may be invited to express their feelings about the proposed Bill as the issue under consideration. It may also seek the opinion of the Director of the Bureau of Legislation.

The officers of the Diet are required to assist the Committee in its work. The Committee makes the report to the concerned House after thorough examination and investigation. The report may be unanimous or a majority report is submitted. The majority also has the right to submit its own report to the House. The Committee is also free not to make any report on the Bill, in which can it will be deemed to have been rejected by the Committee and the House will not proceed with its consideration. This amounts to pigeon-holding the Bill by the Committee.

### *(iv) Consideration by the House*

The House takes up the Bill for consideration after the report of the Committee is received. The report is presented by the Chairman of the Committee, who presents the majority report together with the minority report, if any. The members are free to discuss the suggest amendments, but all amendments must be supported by at least twenty members in case of the House of Representatives and ten members in case of the House of Councillors. Proposals for amendments to Money Bills must be supported by at least 50 members and 20 members respectively. The time limit for discussions over the Bill alongwith the porposed amendments is fixed by the Speaker and every Article is passed by voting. The Bill as a whole is deemed to have been passed after all the Articles are passed by the House. Voting is done by open ballot, but secret ballot may also be taken on the demand made by one-fifth of the members present. In case of a tie the Speaker casts the deciding vote.

***(v) Bill in the other House***

When a Bill is passed by one House, it is sent to the other House, where it has to again go through the stages mentioned above. The Bill is sent to the Emperor for promulgation, if approved by the other House. In case of difference of opinion between the two Houses, the Bill is referred to a Joint Committee of both the Houses, for resolving the differences. In case the Joint Committee fails to resolve the differences, the House of Representatives can override the House of Councillors by two-thirds, vote.

***(vi) Emperor's Approval***

The Speaker submits a Bill approved by the Diet to the Emperor through the Cabinet. The Cabinet submits the Bill to the Emperor for promulgation with the signature of the concerned Minister, after the date of promulgation is decided by the Cabinet. The Bill becomes an Act after it is signed by the Emperor. The promulgation of the Act is published in the 'official gazette'. The Act must be published within 30 days of the Speaker's Report.

**The Budget**

A more or less same procedure is followed to pass the Budget. However, there are some differences between the passing of the ordinary Bill and the Budget. The differences are discussed below:

(i) The Budget is discussed first in the Cabinet in the month of January every year, where the demands are submitted by the various departments. After necessary cuts in the demands the proposals are returned to the departments for resubmission. The revised demands are sent by the departments to the Minister of Finance, who prepares the draft and submits it to the Cabinet. Then the Cabinet considers it for the second time. After the Budget is thoroughly discussed by the Cabinet, it is ready for submission before the Diet. The Ministry of Finance does the entire work and the Bureau of Legislation has no role to play in the formulation of the Budget.

(ii) The introduction of the Budget is made in the House of Representatives and it is followed by speeches of the Prime Minister. Finance Minister and the Economic Policy Board. The next day the Budget is sent to the House of Councillors for discussion.

(iii) The Budget Bill Committee is a very important Commitee which consists of 51 members. The Prime Minister and other important Cabinet Ministers appear before the Committee to justify the estimates submitted by the various departments.

(iv) In matters pertaining to the passing of the Budget, the House of Representatives has got the power to override the decision of the House of Councillors in case of disagreement between the two Houses and in case of the failure of the Joint Conference Committee to resolve the differences. The House of Councillors can only delay the budget for a period of 30 days after it is passed by the House of Representatives.

# 6

# The Judiciary

The judicial system was set up in Japan, after it came in contact with China. There was no judicial system in Japan before the 7th Century. The legal system which was greatly influenced by the Chinese system did not meet the requirements of the Japanese people. The introduction of feudalism in Japan replaced the Chinese legal system. A new feudal legal system was introduced to meet the needs of a feudal society.

The establishment of the Meiji Government in 1868 brought the end of feudalism in Japan and the need for a new legal system was felt in the German and French model a new legal system was introduced.

Japan followed the continental legal system before the World War. The Anglo-saxon Jurisprudence did not influence the Japanese legal system. During the Meiji period the judiciary was subordinated to the executive. The Ministry of Justice directly controlled the courts which had very limited powers. The Courts did not have the power to declare any law as unconstitutional. Disputes between the government and citizens were beyond the jurisdiction of the Courts.

The Courts were divided into the following three categories:

(i) Ordinary, Civil and Criminal Courts.
(ii) Court of Administrative Litigation.
(iii) Military Court.

The Supreme Court was at the top of the judicial structure. The court consisted of one Chief Justice and 45 Justices and had nine divisions composed of five Judges each. Appeal from the High Courts were taken to the Supreme Court and all cases of treason and serious offences could be directly taken to this Court.

There were seven High Courts one each in the seven districts into which the Empire was divided and these Courts functioned under the Supreme Court. There were 50 district Courts below the High Courts, at least one being located in each prefecture. The High Court had both civil and criminal jurisdiction. There were nearly 300 local courts which functioned under the district courts.

The Court of Administrative Litigation and the Military Court functioned in addition to these ordinary courts.

## Judicial System after the Second World War

The judicial procedure and the structure of the Courts have undergone radical and revolutionary changes under the 1947 Constitution. The Anglo-Saxon judicial system was introduced in the place of the Continental system.

The "Common law" principles were accepted for the first time in Japan. The independence of the Judiciary both from the executive and the legislature was emphasised. The Supreme Court instead of the Ministry of Justicve has acquired the controlling power over the courts. All the legal disputes are now referred to the ordinary law courts and the Administrative Courts have been abolished. The Courts can now declare a law as unconstitutional if it violates the Constitution. Thus the prestige of the judiciary has been enhanced in addition to the assertion of its independence. The spirit of the new system is incorporated in Article 76 of the Constitution which reads: "The whole judicial power is vested in a Supreme Court and in such inferior Courts as are established by law. No extraordinary tribunals shall be established, nor shall any organ or agency of the Executive be given final judicial power. All judges shall be independent in the exercise of their conscience and shall be bound only by this Constitution and the laws".

The main features of the post-war judicial system are discussed below:

(i) The Courts are independent and they are not under the control of the Ministry of Law. They are free from the control of the executive. The salaries and allowances of the judges cannot be reduced during their tenure of service. The judges of the Supreme Court can be removed by impeachment only or on grounds of physical and mental incapacity. At present the judicial system is controlled by the Supreme Court. Recruitment, training and work of the judges and the preparation of the Budget of the Department of Justice are all done by the Supreme Court.

(ii) The work of investigation is the responsibility of the Ministry of Law. This has resulted in the separation of judicial administration from criminal investigation.

(iii) There has been the abolition of the extraordinary courts. No tribunal can be appointed by the Executive and the entire work of justice is under the control of the Supreme Court.

(iv) At present Japan follows the Rule of Law and the Administrative Tribunals have been abolished. All types of cases including the administrative disputes are now referred to the ordinary courts.

(v) Previously warrants of arrest were issued by the police officers and procurators. Under the new Constitution this is prevented. Now only the judges can issue the warrants of arrest or detention.

(vi) Before the promulgation of the new Constitution, the police used to extract forced confessions and this has been abolished now. At present questions can be put by the accused to the witnesses. No person can be held guilty merely on the ground of his confession that he has committed the crime.

(vii) Under the present constitution the Supreme Court can determine the constitutionality of any law and can declare an Act as unconstitutional, if it violates the Constitution. Thus these powers have greatly enhanced the prestige of the Supreme Court. The judiciary has been made the guardian of the constitution and the rights of the Japanese citizens. The reorganisation of the Judiciary and the induction of the new philosophy, has completed the democratic process in Japan.

## Organisation of the Judiciary

### *The Supreme Court*

The Supreme Court is the apex court of Japan and it is located at Tokyo. The Court consists of one Chief Justice and 14 other Judges. The minimum age qualification of a judge is 40 years. Only the judges are required to be legal experts of not less than twenty years professional standing and the rest of the judges are learned persons of experience.

## Appointment of Judges

The Emperor appoints the Chief Justice on the advice of the Cabinet and the other Judges are appointed by the Cabinet and attested by the Emperor.

The appointment of the Judges is reviewed by the people at the first general election of the House of Representatives following their appointment. It is further reviewed after a lapse of ten years at the time of election to the House of Representatives. If the people give unfavourable verdict then the Judges would be removed from the office. But no Judges has ever been removed by this method. The

Judges may also be removed by impeachment. If a Judge is physically and mentally incompetent to perform his duties, he may be removed from office. The executive has no power to take any disciplinary action against the Judges.

The salaries and allowances of the Judges cannot be reduced during the term of their office.

## Jurisdiction of the Supreme Court

The Supreme Court has got only appellate jurisdiction and entertains those appeals wherein the question of the constitutionality of any law, order, regulation or official act is involved. It is the final court of appeal. The decisions may be unanimous or majority decisions may be taken. A Judge is free to give his dissenting opinion in writing. Rules of procedure and disciplinary matters are decided by the Court itself. The rule-making powers of the Supreme Court can be delegated by it to the lower courts. The judges of the lower courts are nominated by the Supreme Court and the names so proposed are approved by the cabinet.

## The Lower Courts

Below the Supreme Court of Japan there are several lower courts, which take active part in the administration of justice. These are discussed below:

## High Courts

In Japan there are eight High Courts below the Supreme Court, which have both the original and the appellate jurisdiction. In its original jurisdiction it deals with serious crimes like high treason and attempts to overthrough the government through illegal and violent methods. It has very wide appellate jurisdiction and in all such cases its decision is final. The number of judges varies from one High Court to another, according to the pressure of work in the region. While there are 64 Judges in the High Court of Tokyo, the Sapporo High Court consists of only 7 Judges.

## District Courts

The District Courts also have both original and appellate jurisdiction. There are 49 District Courts. These Courts deal with criminal cases of very serious nature and civil cases involving huge amounts, in their original jurisdiction. Cases from the Summary Courts come in appeal to the District Courts.

### Summary Courts

There are about 570 Summary Courts in Japan, which function at the lowest level of the judicial system. These courts are located in major cities and villages. All ordinary criminal cases subject to imprisonment for less than a month and civil cases involving an amount of not more than 5,000 yens, come within the jurisdiction of the summary Courts.

### Courts of Domestic Relations

The Domestic Relations Courts are half-arbitral and half-judicial in nature, and consist of both Judges and laymen. These Courts may be compared with the Panchayats in India. Mattes pertaining to division of property, inheritance, adoption, divorce etc., come within the jurisdiction of these courts. These courts of Domestic Relations are meant to promote unity and harmony within the family and among the relations by the amicable settlement of various disputes.

### Evaluation of the Judicial Systems

The influence of the Anglo-saxon Jurisprudence can be easily noticed on the Japanese judicial system established by the new Constitution. This has led to a complete transformation of the Japanese judicial system. The Courts now function without any interference from anybody and they have been made independent from the control of the executive. The judges can now administer justice more effectively and impartially without any consideration of fear or favour.

The Rule of Law has been established in Japan and the Administrative Tribunals have been abolished. The rights of the accused are protected by the amendment of the criminal law and the Criminal Procedure Code. An integrated judicial system has been established with the Supreme Court at the top of the structure. The decision of the Supreme Court is final and it makes rules for the inferior courts and supervises their work. The judicial administration is directed by the Supreme Court which also determines the recruitment and training of the judicial officers.

The constitutionality of the law and executive orders is determined by the Supreme Court. This power was not enjoyed by the court under the Meiji Constitution. The Supreme Court's power of Judicial Review has made it the guardian of the Constitution and the rights of the people.

The Japanese Supreme Court does not exercise its power of

Judicial Review like its American counterpart. It has expressed its unwillingness to declare executive orders or directives as unconstitutional and exercises this power only under exceptional circumstances. The laws passed by the Diet are also very rarely delcared as unconstitutional by the Supreme Court. In the opinion of the Court, the constitutionality or otherwise of a law is a political matter and the sovereign people should decide the matter through the Ballot.

The Courts do not enjoy very great respect in Japan as the people want to decide most of their disputes out of Court. The Courts are seen as places frequented by wrong-doers and the lawyers are considered as friends and defenders of evil man. According to Robert E. Ward, "The Japanese are a rather remarkably monlitigious people. They are traditionally suspicious of the Courts and of formal legal processes and have a pronounced preference for settling disputes by informal methods of conciliation and mediation". In the words of Dr. Yanaga, "No serious efforts have been made as yet to bring the Courts closer to the people and to win their confidence and support".

❑❑❑